Peter H. W. Lau
Identity and Ethics in the Book of Ruth

Beihefte zur Zeitschrift für die
alttestamentliche Wissenschaft

Herausgegeben von
John Barton · Reinhard G. Kratz
Choon-Leong Seow · Markus Witte

Band 416

De Gruyter

Peter H. W. Lau

Identity and Ethics in the Book of Ruth

A Social Identity Approach

De Gruyter

ISBN 978-3-11-024760-2
e-ISBN 978-3-11-024761-9
ISSN 0934-2575

Library of Congress Cataloging-in-Publication Data

Lau, Peter H. W.
　　Identity and ethics in the book of Ruth : a social identity approach / Peter H.W. Lau.
　　　　p. cm. – (Beihefte zur Zeitschrift für die alttestamentliche Wissenschaft, ISSN 0934-2575 ; Bd. 416)
　　Includes bibliographical references and index.
　　ISBN 978-3-11-024760-2 (hardcover : alk. paper)
　　1. Ethics in the Bible.　2. Sociology, Biblical.　3. Bible. O.T. Ruth – Criticism, Narrative.　4. Bible. O.T. Ruth – Social scientific criticism. I. Title.
　　BS1315.6.E8L39　2010
　　222'.3506–dc22
　　　　　　　　　　　　　　　　　　　　　　　　　　　2010034691

Bibliographic information published by the Deutsche Nationalbibliothek

The Deutsche Nationalbibliothek lists this publication in the Deutsche Nationalbibliografie; detailed bibliographic data are available in the Internet at http://dnb.d-nb.de.

© 2011 Walter de Gruyter GmbH & Co. KG, Berlin/New York

Printing: Hubert & Co. GmbH & Co. KG, Göttingen
∞ Printed on acid-free paper
Printed in Germany
www.degruyter.com

Foreword

This book is a revision of my doctoral dissertation accepted by the University of Sydney in January 2009. I would like to express my gratitude to the following people and organisations:

My supervisor, Shani Berrin Tzoref, whose guidance, generosity, and insightful feedback have been invaluable. I appreciated your continued direction even after you departed for Jerusalem. My thanks also to Mark Leuchter, who supervised after Shani left. You extended my thinking in many areas and helped me understand the subtleties of HB studies.

The staff at Tyndale House, Cambridge, for their warm welcome and making our stay so enjoyable and productive. I would also like to thank Ronald Clements for commenting on earlier drafts of this study, the stimulating discussions, and encouragement. Thanks also to James Aitken and Cambridge University for a grant that enabled me to experience the land of Israel. My heartfelt thanks to the Divine Grace Foundation for financial assistance while we were in Cambridge.

John Davies for getting the dissertation ball rolling, Ian Young for assisting with the section on the Dating of Ruth, Zeba Crook for feedback on social-scientific matters, and Daniel Hawk for his responses to the overview on Ruth studies. Thank you to those who commented on the sections of this study I shared at the SBL International Meeting, Auckland 2008, and at the Sydney chapter of the Fellowship of Biblical Studies, 2009. My thanks also to my grandmother, Alma Goon, and Chang Tsyh Yong for their careful proofreading and to Darren Yong for helping prepare the Scripture index. Of course, any remaining errors are my responsibility.

To my parents, for life-long support and encouragement in all my endeavours, including my academic pursuits.

Finally, my loving family, who have shared this wonderful adventure with me: my wife Kathryn and our children who were all born during the gestation of this book. Zachary was born as I started my dissertation, Jeremy in the middle, and Sophie a year ago. To my family I dedicate this book.

Peter H. W. Lau
University of Sydney and Malaysian Theological Seminary
October 2010

Table of Contents

Foreword v

Abbreviations ix

Introduction
   I. Approaches to Hebrew Bible Ethics 1
   II. A Social-Scientific Approach 6
   III. Survey of Interpretive Approaches to the Book of Ruth 12
   IV. Conclusion 18
   V. Outline of Study 18

Ancient Israelite Identity
   I. Towards an Ancient Israelite Social Understanding of the Self 20
   II. The Social Identity Approach 25
   III. The Self in the Social Identity Approach 29
   IV. The Social Identity Approach and Ancient Israelite Identity 32
   V. Narrative, Identity, and Ethics 39
   VI. The Implied Reader 42
   VII. The Dating of the Book of Ruth 44
   VIII. Summary and Conclusion 53

Boaz: Identity and Ethics
   I. The Identity of Boaz 55
   II. The Actions of Boaz 60
   III. The Identity and Actions of Mr. So-and-So 74
   IV. The Identity and Actions of Boaz 79
   V. The Identity and Inaction of Boaz 83
   VI. An Assessment of Boaz's Actions from a Social Identity
       Perspective 85
   VII. Summary and Conclusions 87

Ruth: Identity and Ethics
   I. The Transformation of Ruth's Identity 90

    II. The Personal Component of Ruth's Identity 101
    III. The Impact on the Identity of an Implied Reader 110
    IV. Summary and Conclusions 118

Naomi: Identity and Ethics
    I. The Loss of Naomi's Identity 120
    II. The Regaining of Naomi's Identity 126
    III. The Impact on the Identity of an Implied Reader 135
    IV. Summary and Conclusions 143

A Provenance for the Book of Ruth
    I. The Monarchic Period 145
    II. The Persian Period 159
    III. Summary and Conclusion 188

Summary and Conclusions
    Summary 191
    Conclusions 193

Bibliography 197

Scripture Index 225

Abbreviations

AB	Anchor Bible
ABD	*Anchor Bible Dictionary.* Edited by David N. Freedman. 6 vols. New York: Doubleday, 1992
AcT	*Acta theologica*
AJT	*American Journal of Theology*
ANET	*Ancient Near Eastern Texts Relating to the Old Testament.* Edited by James B. Pritchard. 3d ed. Princeton: Princeton University Press, 1969
AOS	American Oriental Series
BA	*Biblical Archaeologist*
BAR	*Biblical Archaeology Review*
BASOR	*Bulletin of the American Schools of Oriental Research*
BDB	Brown, Francis, S. R. Driver, and Charles A. Briggs. *A Hebrew and English Lexicon of the Old Testament.* Oxford: Clarendon Press, 1907
BHQ	*Biblia Hebraica Quinta*
BHS	*Biblia Hebraica Stuttgartensia*
Bib	*Biblica*
BibInt	*Biblical Interpretation: A Journal of Contemporary Approaches*
BSac	*Bibliotheca Sacra*
BT	*The Bible Translator*
BTB	*Biblical Theology Bulletin*
BWANT	Beiträge zur Wissenschaft vom Alten und Neuen Testament
BZAW	Beihefte zur ZAW
CBQ	*The Catholic Biblical Quarterly*
CC	Continental Commentaries
CurBS	*Currents in Research: Biblical Studies*
DCH	*Dictionary of Classical Hebrew.* Edited by David J. A. Clines. Sheffield: Sheffield Academic Press, 1993–

ExpTim	*Expository Times*
FRLANT	Forschungen zur Religion und Literatur des Alten und Neuen Testaments
GBH	Joüon, Paul. *A Grammar of Biblical Hebrew.* Translated and revised by Takamitsu Muraoka. 2 vols. Subsidia biblica 14/1–2. Rome: Pontificial Biblical Institute, 1991
GKC	*Gesenius' Hebrew Grammar.* Edited by E. Kautzsch. Translated by A. E. Cowley. 2d. ed. Oxford: Clarendon Press 1910
HALOT	Koehler, Ludwig, Walter Baumgartner, and Johann J. Stamm. *The Hebrew and Aramaic Lexicon of the Old Testament.* Translated and edited under the supervision of M. E. J. Richardson. 4 vols. Leiden, 1994–1999
HAT	Handbuch zum Alten Testament
HS	*Hebrew Studies*
HSM	Harvard Semitic Monographs
HTKAT	Herder Theologischer Kommentar zum Alten Testament
HTR	*Harvard Theological Review*
HUCA	*Hebrew Union College Annual*
IBHS	*An Introduction to Biblical Hebrew Syntax.* Bruce K. Waltke and M. O'Connor. Winona Lake: Eisenbrauns, 1990
ICC	International Critical Commentary
IDB	*The Interpreter's Dictionary of the Bible.* Edited by George A. Buttrick. 4 vols. Nashville: Abingdon, 1962
IEJ	*Israel Exploration Journal*
Int	*Interpretation*
ITC	International Theological Commentary
JAAR	*Journal of the American Academy of Religion*
JANES	*Journal of the Ancient Near Eastern Society*
JAOS	*Journal of the American Oriental Society*
JBL	*Journal of Biblical Literature*
JETS	*Journal of the Evangelical Theological Society*
JJS	*Journal of Jewish Studies*
JNES	*Journal of Near Eastern Studies*

JNSL	*Journal of Northwest Semitic Languages*
JPS	Jewish Publication Society
JSNT	*Journal for the Study of the New Testament*
JSOT	*Journal for the Study of the Old Testament*
JSOTSup	*Journal for the Study of the Old Testament*, Supplement Series
JSS	*Journal of Semitic Studies*
JTS	*Journal of Theological Studies*
KAT	Kommentar zum Alten Testament
LCL	Loeb Classical Library
LXX	Septuagint
MAL	Middle Assyrian Laws
Midr. Ruth Rab.	*Midrash Rabbah: Ruth*. Translated by Louis I. Rabinowitz. London: Sonsino, 1939
NAC	New American Commentary
NASB	New American Standard Bible
NCBC	New Century Bible Commentary
NIBCOT	New International Biblical Commentary on the Old Testament
NICOT	New International Commentary on the Old Testament
NIDOTTE	*New International Dictionary of Old Testament Theology and Exegesis*. Edited by Willem A. VanGemeren. 5 vols. Grand Rapids: Zondervan, 1997.
NET	New English Translation
NIV	New International Version
NJPS	Tanakh: The Holy Scriptures: The New JPS Translation according to the Traditional Hebrew Text
NRSV	New Revised Standard Version
OTG	Old Testament Guides
OTL	Old Testament Library
OTS	Old Testament Studies
OtSt	*Oudtestamentische Studiën*
RB	*Revue Biblique*
REB	Revised English Bible
RTR	*Reformed Theological Review*
SBL	Society of Biblical Literature

SBLDS	SBL Dissertation Series
SBS	Stuttgarter Bibelstudien
SBT	Studies in Biblical Theology
SJOT	*Scandinavian Journal of the Old Testament*
SNTSMS	Society for New Testament Studies Monograph Series
TDOT	*Theological Dictionary of the Old Testament.* Edited by G. Johannes Botterweck, Helmer Ringgren, and Heinz-Josef Fabry. Translated by John T. Willis, Geoffrey W. Bromiley, David E. Green, and Douglas W. Stott. 15 vols. Grand Rapids: Eerdmans, 1974–2006
TS	*Theological Studies*
TOTC	Tyndale Old Testament Commentaries
TZ	*Theologische Zeitschrift*
UBS	United Bible Societies
VT	*Vetus Testamentum*
VTSup	Supplements to Vetus Testamentum
WBC	Word Bible Commentary
ZAW	*Zeitschrift für die Alttestamentliche Wissenschaft*
ZBK	Zürcher Bibelkommentare
ZTK	*Zeitschrift für Theologie und Kirche*

Introduction

I. Approaches to Hebrew Bible Ethics

A central concern of this study is to show that narrative inherently contains ethical principles. Although "descriptive" texts differ from "prescriptive" texts, this study applies the social-scientific method to the Ruth narrative (henceforth RN) in order to demonstrate that narrative is also useful for deriving ethics.[1] That is, narrative also has normative value.

Within the field of Hebrew Bible (henceforth HB) ethics,[2] there has been a conspicuous neglect of narrative. At times, interest in the area appears to be inversely proportional to the amount of space devoted to the genre in the HB. Indeed, narratives are frequently excluded altogether in discussions of HB ethics. Works of two influential scholars will suffice as examples.[3] In his treatment of HB ethics, Eckart Otto limits his discussion to two main blocks of teaching: the law and wisdom.[4] In a recent review, he reiterated his scepticism towards deriving ethics from biblical narrative, based on his view that if narrative is historical, it is by nature descriptive instead of prescriptive.[5] Similarly, Walter Kaiser excludes narrative from his organisation of the biblical ethical material around the central idea of God's holiness, and his demands as revealed in the Decalogue, the Book of the

---

1   It is questionable whether one can make a sharp demarcation between "descriptive" and "prescriptive" texts since, in a normative universe, even "descriptive" texts have prescriptive or normative cash value. See Robert N. Cover, "Foreword: *Nomos* and Narrative," *Harvard Law Review* 97 (1986): 4-5.
2   "Ethics" in this study will be taken to denote not only rules and principles for right conduct, but also a vision for a good life. Cf. Paul Ricoeur, "Reply to Peter Kemp," in *The Philosophy of Paul Ricoeur* (ed. Lewis Edwin Hahn; Chicago: Open Court, 1995), 395-98. This definition incorporates elements of deontological and consequentialist ethical theories, as well as virtue ethics.
3   See also Hetty Lalleman, *Celebrating Law? Rethinking Old Testament Ethics* (Carlisle: Paternoster, 2004), who acknowledges the importance of biblical stories for conveying ethical principles, but focuses on the laws found in the Torah. For my review, see Peter H. W. Lau, "Review of Hetty Lalleman, Celebrating Law? Rethinking Old Testament Ethics," *RTR* 65 (2006): 177-178.
4   Eckart Otto, *Theologische Ethik des Alten Testaments* (Theologische Wissenschaft 3/2; Stuttgart: Kohlhammer, 1994).
5   Eckart Otto, "Review of John Barton, *Understanding Old Testament Ethics: Approaches and Explorations,*" *Review of Biblical Literature* [http://www.bookreviews.org] (2003).

Covenant, the Holiness Code, and Deuteronomy.[6] Although he recognises the moral content of other biblical genres,[7] he identifies the "heart of Old Testament ethics" in the explicit commands mainly found in the Pentateuch.[8] Consequently, this is used as a "lodestone" from which to view the ethical teaching of the whole HB.

This type of approach has the advantage of clarity, due to its focus on the explicit moral teaching of the HB. A focus on legal texts more readily produces clear moral principles that can set boundaries for proper behaviour and guide conduct.[9] Conversely, as scholars have noted, it is relatively more difficult to derive ethical teaching from narratives. Problems include determining the moral standpoint of the writer,[10] or which moral world is being promoted.[11] Yet an approach that neglects narrative omits a vast proportion of the HB, which in the Hebrew canon includes sections of the Torah, the Former Prophets, and a substantial proportion of the Writings. Indeed, the Torah (law) contains a large proportion of narrative. At least from the point of view of sheer weight of texts, a balanced and complete understanding of HB ethics requires a consideration of the narrative texts in the HB.[12]

Moreover, an approach to HB ethics that focuses solely on rules does not truly reflect the human situation. A moral theory that draws on the Enlightenment ideal of objective, scientific knowledge cannot do justice to the existential aspect of ethics, the mediated character of agents, and the historical nature of ethical norms.[13] By contrast, a theory of ethics based on narrative is particularly effective in highlighting these features. For instance, by focusing on the particular situations found in narrative, Martha Nussbaum stresses the importance of narrative in refining perceptions of

---

6   Walter C. Kaiser, *Toward Old Testament Ethics* (Grand Rapids: Academic, 1983).
7   Kaiser's attitude towards finding moral instruction in narrative can be found in his writings concerning teaching and preaching from OT narrative. See, e.g., Walter C. Kaiser, *Toward an Exegetical Theology* (Grand Rapids: Baker Book House, 1981), 197-210, and most recently, Walter C. Kaiser, *Preaching and Teaching From the Old Testament: A Guide for the Church* (Grand Rapids: Baker Academic, 2003), esp. 63-82.
8   Kaiser, *Toward Old Testament Ethics*, 42.
9   Cf. Stanley Hauerwas, *Truthfulness and Tragedy: Further Investigations in Christian Ethics* (Notre Dame: University of Notre Dame Press, 1977), 26.
10 Gordon J. Wenham, *Story as Torah: Reading the Old Testament Ethically* (Edinburgh: T&T Clark, 2000), 1-2.
11 John Barton, *Understanding Old Testament Ethics: Approaches and Explanations* (Louisville: Westminster John Knox, 2003), 2-4.
12 Cf. Barton, *Understanding Old Testament Ethics*, 2.
13 William A. Barbieri, "Ethics and the Narrated Life," *The Journal of Religion* 78 (1998): 361-86(65).

the complex material in life.¹⁴ And John Barton writes of the "existential force" narrative can impart to moral truths that is not found in ethical injunctions.¹⁵

What is required, then, is an approach to HB ethics that takes into consideration the interdependence between explicit moral principles and narrative. As Stanley Hauerwas argues:

> Even though moral principles are not sufficient in themselves for our moral existence, neither are stories sufficient if they do not generate principles that are morally significant. Principles without stories are subject to perverse interpretation …, but stories without principles will have no way of concretely specifying the actions and practices consistent with the general orientation expressed by the story.¹⁶

Thus, general moral principles are necessary for moral formation. They are not, however, sufficient in themselves. Indeed, there is a reciprocal relationship: moral principles require a narrative context for correct interpretation, while narrative requires moral principles to guide and set boundaries for conduct.¹⁷

This essential interrelationship between explicit moral principles and narrative can be seen in the HB: there is a reciprocal relationship between law and narrative. On the one hand, the narrative embedding of the law¹⁸ influences both its interpretation and its motivational framing. For instance, the historical prologue in Deuteronomy (Deut 1-4) is foundational for the interpretation of the whole law that follows,¹⁹ and the prior and future narrative contexts of the law are used to provide motivational framing.²⁰ On the other hand, the law influences the

---

14 Martha C. Nussbaum, *Love's Knowledge: Essays on Philosophy and Literature* (New York: Oxford University Press, 1990). For the appropriation of Nussbaum's work on narrative and ethics to biblical studies, see, e.g., John Barton, *Ethics and the Old Testament* (2d ed.; London: SCM, 1998).
15 Barton, *Ethics and the Old Testament*, 32.
16 Stanley Hauerwas, "Vision, Stories, and Character," in *The Hauerwas Reader* (ed. John Berkman and Michael Cartwright; Durham: Duke University Press, 2001), 170.
17 Cf. Immanuel Kant, who is said to have asserted: "Experience without theory is blind, but theory without experience is mere intellectual play," as quoted in Stephen L. Darwall, *Philosophical Ethics* (Boulder: Westview, 1998), 23.
18 E.g., the laws in Deut 4-30 are given within the narrative context of chapters 1-3 and 31-34. The laws in Exod 19-24 are given within the narrative context of chapters 1-18. The Decalogue also has a narrative introduction (Deut 5:1-6; cf. Exod 20:1-2).
19 See Paul A. Barker, *The Triumph of Grace in Deuteronomy: Faithless Israel, Faithful Yahweh in Deuteronomy* (Carlisle: Paternoster, 2004), 51. Cf. Waldemar Janzen, *Old Testament Ethics: A Paradigmatic Approach* (Louisville: Westminster John Knox, 1994), 67.
20 For instance, the Sabbath commandment in Deut 5:15 not only casts a retrospective glance at the Exodus, but also a prospective glance at a time when Israel would be in the

surrounding narrative. For instance, both Thomas Mann and Gary Millar observe the importance of narrative in reinforcing the call of the law for an ethical response in Deuteronomy in line with the covenant established between YHWH and his people.[21] There is, then, an inextricable bond between law and narrative in the HB.

A. Recent Studies Deriving Ethics from HB Narrative

Mary Mills uses narrative criticism to explore a range of biblical characters and stories for the contribution these make to the "broader picture of moral vision" of the HB.[22] While Mills intentionally diverts her attention away from HB legal concerns, Gordon Wenham argues that narrative and law present different ethical expectations, in his monograph *Story as Torah*.[23] Employing literary, historical, and rhetorical criticism, Wenham concentrates on two narrative books—Genesis and Judges—in order to elucidate the ethical ideals an implied author is trying to instil in his implied readers. Of especial relevance to the present discussion is Wenham's observation that there is a "gap between law and ethics" in the HB.[24] The picture in the HB is that "much more is expected of the righteous than merely keeping the letter of the law."[25] While the law outlines the baseline ethical requirement, narratives describe the ideal of

---

Promised Land. The continued enjoyment of the land is presented in the law as a motivation to obey God (esp. Deut 6:3; see also 4:40; 5:16, 33; 6:18, 24; 7:13; 8:1; 25:15). In contrast, no ANE laws are motivated by a historical event; see Rifat Sonsino, *Motive Clauses in Hebrew Law: Biblical Forms and Near Eastern Parallels* (SBLDS 45; Chico, Calif.: Scholars Press, 1980).

21 Thomas W. Mann, *The Book of the Torah: The Narrative Integrity of the Pentateuch* (Atlanta: John Knox Press, 1988), 146-56; J. Gary Millar, *Now Choose Life: Theology and Ethics in Deuteronomy* (New Studies in Biblical Theology 6; Leicester: Apollos, 1999).

22 Mary E. Mills, *Biblical Morality: Moral Perspectives in Old Testament Narratives* (Aldershot: Ashgate, 2001), 2. She specifically examines the characters Abraham, David, and Esther, and the stories of Ruth, Joseph, and Jonah.

23 Wenham, *Story*, esp. 73-107. An interest in the relationship between law and narrative is also seen in Daniel Friedmann, *To Kill and Take Possession: Law, Morality, and Society in Biblical Stories* (Peabody: Hendrickson, 2002), who seeks to determine the legal and moral concepts underlying the biblical stories. In contrast to Wenham, however, he finds "an obvious discrepancy" between the narratives and the Pentateuchal laws.

24 Cf. Gordon J. Wenham, "The Gap between Law and Ethics in the Bible," *JJS* 48 (1997): 17-29.

25 Wenham, *Story*, 4.

godly behaviour.²⁶ Wenham's observation will be considered in this study, since it will analyse the behaviour of the protagonists in the RN, including how their actions compare with the requirements of the law pertaining to their situation.

The most comprehensive recent presentation of a hermeneutical system for a Christian ethical appropriation of narratives is presented by Robin Parry. He examines the Dinah story (Gen 34) right from a close textual level to its wider contexts (literary, canonical, historical Christian and Jewish interpretations), and within the philosophical and theological concerns underlying narrative ethics.²⁷ More recently, Athena Gorospe examines the ethical significance of Moses' reverse migration (Exod 4:18-26). Applying Paul Ricoeur's theory of narrative and identity, she draws out some ethical implications for a Filipino migrant, viz. herself.²⁸ Following Ricoeur, Gorospe eschews any attempt to seek authorial intention from the text. The outcome of this crucial move is that there is a shift in emphasis from deriving meaning from the text, and textual constructs, to the experience of real readers as they interact with the text.

Although Gorospe discusses the significance of the episode for the identity of Moses, and derives a comprehensive application for Filipino migrants, there is no mention of its importance for a reader implied by the text. The lack of this intermediate step can lead to jarring modern-day appropriation, as evidenced in this excerpt:

> I have proposed ... that the narrative of Moses' return to Egypt provides an alternative to the story of the American dream, with its global capitalistic and consumerist underpinnings, that orients many Filipino migrants and their families and shapes their identity. Rather than a journey of achievement measured primarily by economic success, Moses' story shows the return of a migrant with a sense of God's call and desire to respond to the needs of his people.²⁹

I am not suggesting that this may not be a valid application for this specific group. Rather, without the intermediate step of producing a meaning for

---

26 Wenham restricts "the law" to refer to "the regulations and legal enactments contained in ... the so-called law codes" (e.g., Exod 21-23; Lev 18-20; Deut 12-25); Wenham, "Gap," 17, fn. 2. Cf. Wenham, *Story*, 79: "Law is expressed in rules, which prescribe how people should act in certain circumstances and what will happen if they do not."

27 Robin A. Parry, *Old Testament Story and Christian Ethics: The Rape of Dinah as a Case Study* (Paternoster Biblical Monographs; Bletchley: Paternoster, 2004). Narrative texts have also been incorporated into recent systematic formulations of HB ethics. One recent example is Christopher J. H. Wright, *Old Testament Ethics for the People of God* (Leicester: IVP, 2004).

28 Athena E. Gorospe, *Narrative and Identity: An Ethical Reading of Exodus 4* (Biblical Interpretation Series 86; Leiden: Brill, 2007), 104-05.

29 Gorospe, *Narrative and Identity*, 319.

an implied historical reader, this is one of an almost limitless number of possibilities thrown up by a text. Moreover, it is very difficult to substantiate the chosen application.

Gorospe is particularly critical of overly text-centred approaches to narrative ethics that ignore the social situations of modern-day readers.[30] Yet a shift too far in the direction of real readers can lead to ethical application that is in danger of breaking its moorings to the social situations implied by the text. The employment of a social-scientific approach derives meaning from a narrative while still maintaining contact with the social background of a historical reader.

II. A Social-Scientific Approach

Although its lineage can be traced back to the nineteenth century, the recent surge in the use of social-scientific approaches to the Bible began around thirty years ago.[31] It has been applied widely to New Testament texts, yet there has only been limited application to the HB by a handful of scholars. Apropos the HB, social-scientific approaches have drawn from sub-disciplines including sociology,[32] political science,[33] and anthropology.[34] The collection of essays in *Ancient Israel: The Old Testament in Its Social Context* provides a diverse sample of recent explorations using social-scientific methods.[35] Shane Kirkpatrick's study of Daniel 1–6 demonstrates the value of an extensive anthropological reading.[36] In this case, Kirkpatrick applies a cultural model of honour developed from the circum-Mediterranean region already applied by numerous NT scholars.[37]

---

30   Gorospe, *Narrative and Identity*, 2-6.
31   A survey of literature can be found in Charles E. Carter, "A Discipline in Transition: The Contributions of the Social Sciences to the Study of the Hebrew Bible," in *Community, Identity, and Ideology: Social Science Approaches to the Hebrew Bible* (ed. Charles E. Carter and Carol L. Meyers; Winona Lake: Eisenbrauns, 1996), 13-23; John H. Elliott, *Social-Scientific Criticism of the New Testament* (London: SPCK, 1993), 17-35; Philip F. Esler and Anselm C. Hagedorn, "Social-Scientific Analysis of the Old Testament," in *Ancient Israel: The Old Testament in Its Social Context* (ed. Philip F. Esler; London: SCM, 2005), 15-32.
32   E.g., Norman K. Gottwald, *The Tribes of Yahweh: A Sociology of the Religion of Liberated Israel, 1250-1050 BCE* (Maryknoll: Orbis, 1979).
33   See, e.g., the five essays in the second half of Douglas A. Knight and Carol L. Meyers, eds., *Ethics and Politics in the Hebrew Bible* (Semeia 66; Atlanta: Scholars Press, 1994).
34   In particular, shame and honour have been used as a lens through which to view HB texts. See, e.g., Lyn M. Bechtel, "Shame as a Sanction of Social Control in Biblical Israel: Judicial, Political, and Social Shaming," *JSOT* 49 (1991): 47-76; Saul M. Olyan, "Honor, Shame, and Covenant Relations in Ancient Israel and Its Environment," *JBL* 115 (1996):

There are different streams of social-scientific criticism. Although there is some overlap, Elliott makes a general distinction between descriptive and explanatory approaches.[38] While the former involves "social description," the latter employs social-scientific theory and models for the purpose of explanation or interpretation. Studies concerned with "social" matters can be broken down further into five groups: (1) social description; (2) social history; (3) social organisation with the deliberate use of social theory and models; (4) social and cultural environment concentrating on social and cultural scripts; and (5) analysis of biblical texts.[39] This study contains both descriptive and explanatory elements, with a specific focus on an analysis and interpretation of the Ruth narrative.

The central and abiding arguments against the social-scientific enterprise can be grouped under the umbrellas of reductionism and determinism. Since the arguments have been dealt with extensively elsewhere, I will only sketch them briefly here, and indicate how this study will attempt to avoid some of the pitfalls.[40]

First, the charge of reductionism is that social-scientific approaches explain complex social processes in terms of the narrow confines of the defined hypothesis. One particular concern is that by viewing the biblical text through a social-scientific lens, other aspects of the text, such as literary or theological, are removed. This forms part of John Collins' critique of Kirkpatrick's social-scientific approach to Daniel 1–6:

> There can be no doubt that honor is indeed a fundamental issue in Dan 1–6, and this point may not have received due emphasis from previous com-

---

201-18. See also the first three essays in Victor H. Matthews and Don C. Benjamin, eds., *Honor and Shame in the World of the Bible* (Semeia 68; Atlanta: Scholars Press, 1994).

35 Philip F. Esler, *Ancient Israel: The Old Testament in Its Social Context* (London: SCM, 2005).

36 Shane Kirkpatrick, *Competing for Honor: A Social-Scientific Reading of Daniel 1–6* (Biblical Interpretation Series 74; Leiden: Brill, 2005).

37 E.g., Bruce J. Malina and Jerome H. Neyrey, "Honor and Shame in Luke-Acts: Pivotal Values of the Mediterranean World," in *The Social World of Luke-Acts: Models for Interpretation* (ed. Jerome H. Neyrey; Peabody: Hendrickson, 1991), 25-65; Jerome H. Neyrey, *Honor and Shame in the Gospel of Matthew* (Louisville: Westminster John Knox, 1998).

38 Elliott, *Social-Scientific Criticism*, 20.

39 Philip F. Esler, *The First Christians in Their Social Worlds: Social-Scientific Approaches to New Testament Interpretation* (London: Routledge, 1994), 18-20.

40 For a discussion and refutation of these and other arguments, see, e.g., Carter, "Transition," 23-28; Elliott, *Social-Scientific Criticism*, 87-100; Philip F. Esler, "Social-Scientific Models in Biblical Interpretation," in *Ancient Israel: The Old Testament in Its Social Context* (ed. Philip F. Esler; London: SCM, 2005), 3-14; Bruce J. Malina, "The Social Sciences and Biblical Interpretation," in *The Bible and Liberation: Political and Social Hermeneutics* (ed. Norman K. Gottwald; Maryknoll: Orbis, 1983), 19-20.

mentators.... At the same time, the near-exclusive concern with issues of honor seems one-sided. It is one thing to say that previous scholarship was been [sic] overly concerned with the eschatology of Nebuchadnezzar's dream in Dan 2 but quite another to pay no attention to it at all.[41]

The risk is producing a reading that flattens the inherent contours of a text. Every analytical method, however, can have this effect, because each approach concentrates attention to specific aspects of a text.[42]

The pitfall to be avoided is the identification of all phenomena as purely social. The key is to adopt an approach that is cognisant of the multi-dimensional character of a biblical text.[43] Hence, the use of social-scientific approaches in this study will be to supplement other methods of critical interpretation in order to elucidate the rhetorical effect of the RN on an implied reader. This is predicated upon the understanding that the Ruth text is a vehicle of communication shaped by cultural and social factors. It is thus produced within a particular historical period in which it also constitutes a specific response; a biblical text not only yields historical or theological information, it can also provide social information. A concern of this study is to determine how the RN functions as a vehicle for the construction of identity.[44] As such, social-scientific criticism will be used alongside other modes of critical analysis, especially narrative, but also historical, textual, and literary criticism. Although mainly applying a social-scientific method, this study will be multi-disciplinary, which is the approach taken by the majority of current social-scientific practitioners.[45]

Second, the charge of determinism is that social-scientific approaches interpret biblical phenomena predictively, according to models or "social laws". As such, it leads the interpreter to view the biblical evidence in a certain way, or assume that a particular pattern of conduct must be present. This is evidenced in David Horrell's critique of Esler's approach in his Galatians commentary. Horrell asserts that Esler interprets Paul's actions on the basis of a "challenge-response model": "Here the model not only

---

41 John J. Collins, "Review of Shane Kirkpatrick, *Competing for Honor: A Social-Scientific Reading of Daniel 1-6*," *Review of Biblical Literature* [http://www.bookreviews.org] (2008).

42 Elliott, *Social-Scientific Criticism*, 90. For instance, historical criticism concentrates on events.

43 Cf. Carter, "Transition," 26.

44 Cf. Esler, *The First Christians*, 18.

45 For instance, Anselm C. Hagedorn, "Nahum—Ethnicity and Stereotypes: Anthropological Insights into Nahum's Literary History," in *Ancient Israel: The Old Testament in Its Social Context* (ed. Philip F. Esler; London: SCM, 2005), 223-39, fuses a historical-critical approach with anthropology, and while Philip F. Esler, *Conflict and Identity in Romans: The Social Setting of Paul's Letter* (Minneapolis: Fortress, 2003), employs social identity theory, he also addresses historical and theological issues.

supplies the understanding of Paul's methods and motives—such evidence being lacking in the text—but also 'trumps' without exegetical argument any other interpretations of this verse, since Esler's interpretation is based on what Mediterranean man would clearly do."[46] Although the divergence of social-scientific approach between Horrell and Esler derives from their fundamental understanding of human social behaviour,[47] Horrell's critique does still raise questions about the appropriate employment of models.

Central to the avoidance of determinism is the use of models as heuristic tools. Bruce Malina defines a model as "an abstract simplified representation of some real world object, event, or interaction, constructed for the purpose of understanding, control, or prediction."[48] Yet Malina's understanding of the predictive power of models may be too strong; rather, they function heuristically by prompting the search for patterns, correlations, and coherency among masses of material.[49] Within this understanding, models are used to view and understand the data found within biblical texts; it is a comparative process. For instance, with a model of stereotypes in mind, an interpreter will be more sensitive to the nuances of the interactions between Israelite characters and Ruth as a Moabite, and has a framework from which to interrogate the text.

The use of models involves a process that is neither exclusively deductive nor inductive, but inclusive of both in what Charles S. Peirce first described as "abduction."[50] This involves a back-and-forth movement between deduction and induction, model and data, from evidence to hypothesis. It is what "fleshes out the scenario to allow for intelligible, historically sensitive reading."[51] In this study, models of identity, kinship, ethnicity, and immigration will be brought to bear on the RN. A benefit of

---

46   David G. Horrell, "Models and Methods in Social-Scientific Interpretation: A Response to Philip Esler," *JSNT* 78 (2000): 92.

47   Bengt Holmberg, "The Methods of Historical Reconstruction in the Scholarly 'Recovery' of Corinthian Christianity," in *Christianity at Corinth: The Quest for the Pauline Church* (ed. Edward Adams and David G. Horrell; Louisville: Westminster John Knox, 2004), 268-69. While Esler holds that humans generally reproduce the values and institutions of the social system of which they are a part, Horrell holds the "structuration" perspective of Anthony Giddens, which emphasises the participation of the human actor in the transformation of, as well as participation in, social structures.

48   Malina, "The Social Sciences," 14.

49   Elliott, *Social-Scientific Criticism*, 44.

50   For further description see Elliott, *Social-Scientific Criticism*, 48-49.

51   Bruce J. Malina, "Interpretation: Reading, Abduction, Metaphor," in *The Bible and the Politics of Exegesis: Essays in Honor of Norman K. Gottwald on His Sixty-Fifth Birthday* (ed. David Jobling, Peggy L. Day, and Gerald T. Shepherd; Cleveland: Pilgrim Press, 1991), 260.

using such models is that they place testable controls on meanings, as well as provide a framework for future study.[52]

Indeed, the choice is not whether to use models, but whether or not they are used consciously. As Elliott notes, "Every imagining or reconstructing of 'how it actually was back then' necessarily involves the use of some conceptual model."[53] Without explicit models, an interpreter will still reconstruct social and conceptual models, but the danger is that they will be influenced by unexamined prejudgements and presuppositions that may reflect "an ethnocentric embedding in our culture."[54] The onus, then, is on finding suitable models to apply to the biblical text. Appropriate and adequate models are those that have been constructed on the basis of empirical evidence, and must fit well with the text under examination.[55] What is required is a critical use of models, with modification to the HB context.

With these caveats regarding the use of models in mind, the aim is to use models heuristically, rather than strictly predictively, so that some room is left for human agency and freedom within the models. Moreover, common to the charges of reductionism and determinism is that the model takes precedence over the text; in interpretation the accent falls on the model instead of the text. So this study will aim to keep the models as servants of the interpretive process.

Since ancient Near Eastern identity is generally held to be predominantly collectivist or social in orientation, in this study I will primarily employ social-scientific models from the discipline of social psychology, viz. social identity theory (SIT) and self-categorisation theory (SCT). Philip Esler first introduced the social identity approach to New Testament studies,[56] and has applied it in a limited way to some HB narratives.[57] Following Esler, Anselm Hagedorn uses a social identity framework for his comparative analysis of ancient Greek law and the

---

52 Malina, "The Social Sciences," 21.
53 Elliott, *Social-Scientific Criticism*, 44-45.
54 Esler, "Social-Scientific Models in Biblical Interpretation," 4.
55 Malina, "The Social Sciences," 22.
56 Esler, *Conflict and Identity*; Philip F. Esler, *Galatians* (London: Routledge, 1998); Philip F. Esler, "Jesus and the Reduction of Intergroup Conflict: The Parable of the Good Samaritan in the Light of Social Identity Theory," *BibInt* 8 (2000): 325-57.
57 Philip F. Esler, "2 Samuel–David and the Ammonite War: A Narrative and Social-Scientific Interpretation of 2 Samuel 10-12," in *Ancient Israel: The Old Testament in Its Social Context* (ed. Philip F. Esler; London: SCM, 2005), 191-207; Philip F. Esler, "Ezra-Nehemiah as a Narrative of (Re-Invented) Israelite Identity," *BibInt* 11 (2003): 413-26.

ancient Israelite legal system.⁵⁸ Most recently, Jan Bosman applied social psychology to the oracles concerning the nations in Nahum,⁵⁹ and following Bosman, Louis Jonker utilised the approach in his determination of identity in the book of Chronicles.⁶⁰ Both Bosman and Jonker focus on the function of the biblical text in identity formation at the national level or as a pointer to underlying identity processes. This will be one concern of this study, but it will also examine the actions of the characters at the story level through the lens of social identity.

Social identity approaches are useful for studying both intergroup and intragroup relations. In scholarly circles, the two main dates for the composition/redaction of the RN are both periods of potential group conflict. A hypothesis dating the composition of the RN to the mid- to late-Monarchic period is associated with intergroup conflict arising from external military threat. The subsequent development of the monarchy and urbanisation lead to intragroup tensions primarily at the smaller social group level. A hypothesis dating the composition of the RN to the Persian period is associated with intergroup conflicts at the larger social group level, the ethnic/national group vis-à-vis outsiders.

This study attempts to understand the ethics promoted in the RN by viewing them in a particular historical and social context. It will address historical-critical and literary issues relating to the text, but will be supplemented by questions and answers deriving from a social identity approach. Although one particular approach will be primarily brought to bear on the RN, the aim is not to test the validity of the approach *per se*, but to highlight the social presuppositions within the society, utilise it to provide insights into the role of literary narratives in promoting social norms in ancient Israel, and the social provenance of the text. The specific interest in social theory does not explain all the features of the text; the author no doubt also had theological and political concerns. Nonetheless, it remains a contention of this study that an appreciation of the ethics of the RN must also take into consideration the social situation in which the text first arose.

---

58   Anselm C. Hagedorn, *Between Moses and Plato: Individual and Society in Deuteronomy and Ancient Greek Law* (FRLANT 204; Göttingen: Vandenhoeck & Ruprecht, 2004).
59   Jan P. Bosman, "Social Identity in Nahum: A Theological-Ethical Enquiry" (D.Th. diss., University of Stellenbosch, 2005).
60   Louis Jonker, "Reforming History: The Hermeneutical Significance of the Books of Chronicles," *VT* 57 (2007): 21-44; Louis Jonker, "Who Constitutes Society? Yehud's Self-understanding in the Late Persian Era as Reflected in the Books of Chronicles," *JBL* 127 (2008).

III. Survey of Interpretive Approaches to the Book of Ruth

A. Introduction

This survey aims to situate the approach of this study within the trends of scholarship on the book of Ruth. Reading strategies for the book of Ruth have generally shadowed wider biblical trends. The following survey of interpretive approaches to the book of Ruth will be according to historical-critical and literary categories, highlighting issues specific to the study of Ruth. The survey will conclude by situating this study within the social-scientific approach, and its relation to the other approaches.

B. Historical-Critical

This approach underlies numerous studies of the book of Ruth. For instance, Jacob Myers and George Glanzman applied a redaction-critical method.[61] More recently, Athalya Brenner posited that the book of Ruth is composed of two strands, a Naomi story and a Ruth story.[62] Owing to its different locations in the LXX and MT, the canonical-critical perspective has proved an especially productive approach to the book of Ruth.[63] Both Robert Boling and Edward Campbell noted the correspondences between the end of Judges (esp. 19-21) and the book of Ruth.[64] Conversely, applying a canonical-historical method, Michael Moore posits that the placement of the book of Ruth after Judges in LXX is for contrastive purposes.[65] Since the period of the Judges (Ruth 1:1) and David (4:17, 22)

---

61   Jacob M. Myers, *The Linguistic and Literary Form of the Book of Ruth* (Leiden: Brill, 1955); George S. Glanzman, "The Origin and Date of the Book of Ruth," *CBQ* 21 (1959): 201-07.

62   Athalya Brenner, "Naomi and Ruth," *VT* 33 (1983): 385-97.

63   In this discussion, canonical criticism refers to the method whereby the position a particular book holds in a canon will guide its interpretation. It is categorised within historical-critical approaches because it rests on the assumption that the order of books within the canons have undergone deliberate redaction. As such, it focuses on a later moment in the history of a text. See Brevard S. Childs, *Introduction to the Old Testament as Scripture* (Philadelphia: Fortress, 1979).

64   Robert G. Boling, *Judges* (AB 6A; Garden City: Doubleday, 1975), 276; Edward F. Campbell, *Ruth* (AB 7; Garden City: Doubleday, 1975), 35-36. Cf. Tod Linafelt and Timothy K. Beal, *Ruth & Esther* (Berit Olam; Collegeville: Liturgical Press, 1999), xvii-xxv.

65   Michael S. Moore, "To King or Not to King: A Canonical-Historical Approach to Ruth," *BBR* 11 (2001): 27-41.

are explicitly mentioned in the RN, the canonical-historical method opens up fruitful lines of enquiry.

Historical criticism remains influential in scholarship on the book of Ruth. For instance, tracing a lineage to form-critical ideas, a discussion of genre is mandatory in almost all commentaries on Ruth, typically beginning with Hermann Gunkel's classic description of the book as a novella, and then presenting the commentator's preferred genre.[66] Furthermore, articles continue to be based on form-critical ideas, such as Johanna Bos' study of the "counter betrothal type-scenes" (Gen 38; Judg 4:17-22; Ruth 3),[67] and James Black's study of the "bride-in-the-dark" narratives (Gen 19, 29, 38; Ruth).[68]

C. Literary

D. F. Rauber's 1970 JBL article represents one of the earliest forays into applying literary theory to the RN.[69] Surprised by the "literary naïveté" he found pervading the field of biblical studies, he presented an analysis of the book of Ruth as a narrative, and called for an approach to the text viewing it as a unity against the prevailing tendency in biblical studies towards fragmentation. Since the time of his article, there has been a proliferation of studies that can be classified under the "literary" umbrella, and a unanimous understanding of the RN as a unity.

Structuralism is one method that has been applied to Ruth studies.[70] Jack Sasson analysed the RN according to the dramatis personae, and the function they play in furthering the plot.[71] Since, according to Sasson, the

---

66 E.g., Frederic W. Bush, *Ruth, Esther* (WBC 9; Dallas: Word Books, 1996), 30-47 (between tale and novella); Campbell, *Ruth*, 3-10 (historical short story); Robert L. Hubbard, *The Book of Ruth* (NICOT; Grand Rapids: Eerdmans, 1988), 47-48 (short story); André LaCocque, *Ruth* (trans. K. C. Hanson, CC; Minneapolis: Fortress, 2004), 8-18 (biblical novella). In fact, a discussion of genre necessitates the convergence of historical and literary perspectives.

67 Johanna W. H. Bos, "Out of the Shadows: Genesis 38; Judges 4:17-22; Ruth 3," *Semeia* 42 (1988): 37-67.

68 James Black, "Ruth in the Dark: Folktale, Law and Creative Ambiguity in the Old Testament," *Literature and Theology* 5 (1991): 20-36.

69 D. F. Rauber, "Literary Values in the Bible: The Book of Ruth," *JBL* 89 (1970): 27-37.

70 The wide-ranging nature of structuralism renders it more a philosophical system, whose interpretive theory has been applied to literary criticism; Carl R. Holladay, "Contemporary Methods of Reading the Bible," in *NIB* (Nashville: Abingdon, 1994), 140-41.

71 Jack M. Sasson, *Ruth: A New Translation with a Philological Commentary and a Formalist-Folklorist Interpretation* (2d ed.; Sheffield: JSOT Press, 1989), 196-218.

RN follows a pattern common to folktales,[72] it cannot be a reliable source for legal or historical information.[73] By contrast, Harold Fisch had utilised structuralist notions in his VT article, "Ruth and the Structure of Covenant History."[74] As can be gleaned from the title, he rightly argued that a structuralist application does not necessarily have to be ahistorical, by referring back to other stories in the pattern of *Heilsgeschichte*. In this way, Fisch was also drawing on elements of intertextuality.

Intertextuality has also been appropriated to Ruth studies. One obvious reason is that the RN makes explicit references to other texts, presuming readerly knowledge of stories such as the accounts of Rachel and Leah, and Tamar and Judah. Although the concept of a text being understood in light of other texts was already a central idea of form criticism, recent intertextual approaches move beyond a focus on genre to thematic resemblances and similar situations. Since this could present a limitless number of texts, some scholars limit the potential texts to those likely to have been available to the author of the text. Kirsten Nielsen's Ruth commentary is one example of this methodology, drawing upon the patriarchal narratives, and "women's stories that deal with infertility and triumph over it."[75] Since this study focuses on an implied reader, Nielsen's notion of intertextuality will be adopted.[76]

Rhetorical criticism also finds a voice within Ruth studies. Following the concerns of James Muilenberg's programmatic 1969 JBL article, Murray Gow outlines the aims of his rhetorical approach in his Ruth monograph as: (1) to delimit the literary unit; and (2) to observe the literary features of a composition.[77] In his study, Gow intentionally focuses on the literary structure of the RN and the themes this elucidates, with a view to discovering the theology and historical intention of the book. Consequently, it is a limited literary analysis of the RN.

By contrast, narrative criticism is primarily concerned with the literary features of a narrative. This method has now become a mainstay in Ruth

---

72 Although Sasson observes that Ruth is in the form of a folktale, he is also careful to avoid strictly labelling it as such, since there is a lack of evidence to confirm that Ruth circulated orally, a prerequisite for folktales; Sasson, *Ruth*, 214.

73 Jack M. Sasson, "Ruth," in *The Literary Guide to the Bible* (ed. R. Alter and F. Kermode; London: Fontana, 1987), 320.

74 Harold Fisch, "Ruth and the Structure of Covenant History," *VT* 32 (1982): 425-37.

75 Kirsten Nielsen, *Ruth: A Commentary* (trans. Edward Broadbridge, OTL; Louisville: Westminster John Knox, 1997), 13. See also Ellen van Wolde, "Texts in Dialogue with Texts: Intertextuality in the Ruth and Tamar Narratives," *BibInt* 5 (1997): 1-28.

76 Nielsen's approach has a diachronic aspect, as well as seeking specific connections between a limited number of texts; hence, it is better defined as "inner-biblical allusion."

77 Murray D. Gow, *The Book of Ruth: Its Structure, Theme and Purpose* (Leicester: Apollos, 1992), 21-25.

studies. Although it was published in 1975, Edward Campbell's commentary remains one of the most perceptive applications of narratology to the RN.[78] Similarly, Robert Hubbard's commentary also applies narratology to the RN, without sacrificing theological and historical concerns.[79] Both of these commentaries are sensitive to the effects of the narrative upon a reader but would have benefited from further cultural and sociological considerations.

A concern for the reader is also reflected in the latest form of rhetorical criticism, which is primarily interested in the message of a text and its persuasive effect for either an implied or real reader.[80] It has been chiefly applied to the Prophets, due to the nature of prophetic communication.[81] However, the underlying method can also be applied to other forms of biblical literature, including narrative. Indeed, as mentioned previously, Gordon Wenham has applied this form of rhetorical criticism to two HB narrative texts.[82] It is this most recent development of rhetorical criticism that will especially inform this study.

The focus on the reader in the latest form of rhetorical criticism overlaps with the reader-response method. Danna Fewell and David Gunn applied the reader-response method to the RN.[83] As a branch of literary theory with an accent on the reader, Fewell and Gunn provided a reading based on the understanding that the RN is a complex composition.[84] Since the RN contains gaps, the reader is essential in constructing the story. Fewell and Gunn are upfront about their personal involvement as readers, including the feminist values they bring to the text.[85] Their study helpfully draws attention to the possibility of multiple interpretations stemming from the different presuppositions readers bring to the reading of the RN. Their predilection to read against the grain of the text, however, renders

---

78 Campbell, *Ruth*.
79 Hubbard, *Ruth*.
80 See, in particular, Dale Patrick and Allen Scult, *Rhetoric and Biblical Interpretation* (JSOTSup 82; Sheffield: Almond, 1990).
81 See, e.g., J. G. McConville, *Exploring the Old Testament: The Prophets* (vol. 4; London: SPCK, 2002); Thomas Renz, *The Rhetorical Function of the Book of Ezekiel* (Leiden: Brill, 1999).
82 Wenham, *Story*.
83 Danna N. Fewell and David M. Gunn, "Boaz, Pillar of Society: Measures of Worth in the Book of Ruth," *JSOT* 45 (1989): 45-59; Danna N. Fewell and David M. Gunn, *Compromising Redemption: Relating Characters in the Book of Ruth* (Louisville: Westminster John Knox, 1990); Danna N. Fewell and David M. Gunn, "'A Son is Born to Naomi!': Literary Allusions and Interpretation in the Book of Ruth," *JSOT* 40 (1988): 99-108.
84 Fewell and Gunn, *Compromising*, 16.
85 Fewell and Gunn, *Compromising*, 17.

some of their interpretations of the characters' motivations unconvincing. A preferable method would be to constrain interpretations by textual and historical factors.

Not unexpectedly, feminist or womanist scholars, as a general description of readers approaching the text with a specific perspective or agenda, comprise the largest group of reader-response critics in Ruth studies. The female perspective is explored in essays found in two *Feminist Companions* to Ruth,[86] and the woman's experience is explored by thirty Jewish women in *Reading Ruth*.[87] Most monographs with a gender approach to the HB contain a chapter on Ruth and/or Naomi,[88] and sensitivity to feminist concerns is found in many recent commentaries.[89] As can be seen in the foregoing discussion, their method is not uniform, drawing from the whole breadth of interpretive strategies.[90] Since the RN contains two female protagonists, the insights from this perspective will be taken into account during this study. A reading from the perspective of an implied reader, however, means that these will be tempered by the cultural and historical situation of an ancient Israelite.

D. Social-Scientific

While Carl Holladay categorises social-scientific approaches under the historical-critical rubric,[91] it is best to view it as a stand-alone approach.[92] It

---

86 Athalya Brenner, ed., *A Feminist Companion to Ruth* (Sheffield: Sheffield Academic Press, 1993), with the second volume also containing essays on the book of Esther: Athalya Brenner, ed., *Ruth and Esther: A Feminist Companion to the Bible* (Sheffield: Sheffield Academic Press, 1999).

87 Judith A. Kates and Gail T. Reimer, eds., *Reading Ruth: Contemporary Women Reclaim a Sacred Story* (New York: Ballantine, 1994).

88 E.g., Nehama Aschkenasy, *Woman at the Window: Biblical Tales of Oppression and Escape* (Detroit: Wayne State University Press, 1998), 145–56; Jacqueline E. Lapsley, *Whispering the Word: Hearing Women's Stories in the Old Testament* (Louisville: Westminster John Knox, 2005), 89-108; Katharine D. Sakenfeld, *Just Wives?: Stories of Power and Survival in the Old Testament and Today* (Louisville: Westminster John Knox, 2003), 27-48.

89 E.g., Irmtraud Fischer, *Rut* (HTKAT; Freiburg: Herder, 2001); LaCocque, *Ruth* ; Katharine D. Sakenfeld, *Ruth* (Interpretation; Louisville: John Knox Press, 1999).

90 See, e.g., the post-colonial womanist reading of the book of Ruth using a divination perspective, by Musa W. Dube, "Divining Ruth for International Relations," in *Other Ways of Reading: African Women and the Bible* (ed. Musa W. Dube; Atlanta: Society of Biblical Literature, 2001), 179-98.

91 Holladay, "Contemporary Methods," 1:135-36.

92 Cf. Norman K. Gottwald, *The Hebrew Bible: A Socio-Literary Introduction* (Philadelphia: Fortress, 1985), 26-29.

has affinities with the historical-critical method, especially in its interest in understanding the text within its original social context. It goes beyond the historical paradigm, however, in its appropriation of social-scientific methods and models in understanding the social dynamics from which the texts arose. It also has affinities with literary approaches, in that it also focuses on the text as a vehicle of communication between an author and a reader or audience. Within literary approaches, then, it is most similar to the latest rhetorical methods. Indeed, scholars have noted the overlap between the social-scientific and rhetorical paradigms: both methods elucidate how a text works to communicate.[93]

Although there has always been an interest in the social background of the RN, studies utilising an explicit social-scientific approach have only recently appeared in Ruth studies. In his 1993 article, John Berquist applies the sociological process of role dedifferentiation to the book of Ruth, and finds that the gender roles of Ruth, Naomi, and Boaz all dedifferentiate to some extent.[94] However, difficulties with his sociological analysis arise because it lacks historical-cultural controls. For instance, his conclusion that the book of Ruth deconstructs gender might have been modified if the implication of the "patriarchal framework" for an implied reader was given full weight. Nonetheless, Berquist's early study pointed to the fruitfulness of a sociological approach in understanding social behaviour in and subsequently, exegesis of a biblical text.

Victor Matthews' 2004 commentary draws on known social customs such as hospitality codes, marriage customs, and inheritance laws in order to understand the text within its original context.[95] But the brevity of the commentary, at thirty-six pages, limits the degree to which he is able to engage in detailed sociological discussion. The outcome is that there are only brief and non-sustained applications of social models.[96] His introductory comments on personal identity in an ancient rural setting are further developed in his 2006 BTB article.[97] Chiefly drawing on Positioning Theory but also other social theories, Matthews outlines the

---

93   John H. Elliott, *What is Social-Scientific Criticism?* (Minneapolis: Fortress, 1993), 100; Vernon K. Robbins, "Social-Scientific Criticism and Literary Studies: Prospects for Cooperation in Biblical Interpretation," in *Modelling Early Christianity: Social-Scientific Studies of the New Testament in Its Context* (ed. Philip F. Esler; London: Routledge, 1995), 274-89.

94   Jon L. Berquist, "Role Differentiation in the Book of Ruth," *JSOT* 57 (1993): 23-37.

95   Victor H. Matthews, *Judges/Ruth* (NCBC; Cambridge: Cambridge University Press, 2004).

96   This may partly be a result of the target readership of the commentary series (NCBC), which is described as "a wide range of intellectually curious individuals."

97   Victor H. Matthews, "The Determination of Social Identity in the Story of Ruth," *BTB* 36 (2006): 49-54.

process by which Naomi and Ruth become "social exiles" as they leave Moab, how they remain liminal and marginalised within the community in Bethlehem, and the resolution of the social dilemma through Ruth's marriage to Boaz. Ultimately, they also "transform the society and economy" of Bethlehem.[98]

Matthews' work is a stimulating introduction to the appropriation of social-scientific theories, highlighting the potential of this approach. This study will develop his work further, by applying social models more extensively. In particular, his use of identity in interpreting texts will be extended further. For instance, this study will delineate the components of ancient Israelite identity, the different kinship groups inherent in ancient Israelite social identity, and the tensions that can arise from simultaneous membership of these groups. Furthermore, the influence of the RN on identity and subsequent action for a reader in its original historical and cultural setting will also be explored.

IV. Conclusion

This study, then, is an attempt to examine and tease out some of these intertwined social issues as found in the RN from the point of view of identity. Relying primarily on the social-scientific method, it will seek not only to determine the original social context of the RN, but also the intended rhetorical impact or persuasive intent for an implied reader. As such, it straddles the historical-critical and literary categories.

V. Outline of Study

Chapter One outlines the methodological assumptions undergirding this study of the RN. A discussion of ancient Israelite identity is followed by an outline of the social identity approach, then an application of the social identity approach to ancient Israelite identity. The relation between narrative, identity, and ethics is then examined. Since the historical context of an implied reader is an important component in the reception of the text, the first chapter concludes with an evaluation of the dating of the RN.

Chapters Two to Four view the identity and actions of the protagonists in the RN through the lens of social identity theory. Boaz, Ruth, and Naomi are examined in turn using the model for ancient Israelite identity developed in Chapter One. This is followed in each chapter by a discussion

---

98 Matthews, "Social Identity," 54.

of the possible impact the protagonists would have on the identity and actions of an implied reader.

The discussion in Chapter Five pinpoints a more specific historical provenance for the book of Ruth, based on the emphases arising from viewing the text from a social identity perspective. Although a placement in the Monarchic Period is possible, a provenance in the Persian Period is found to best fit the social emphases of the RN.

Ancient Israelite Identity

I. Towards an Ancient Israelite Social Understanding of the Self

In contrast to the ancient Israelite conception of the self, the modern Western conception is predominantly individualistic.[1] This autonomous notion of the self is in contrast to the HB conception of selfhood. Wheeler Robinson contrasted modern notions of the self with the concept in the HB. His understanding of so-called "primitive" psychology is encapsulated in his well-known concept "corporate personality": "the treatment of the family, the clan, or the nation, as the unit in place of the individual."[2] John Rogerson helpfully summarises the two aspects of Robinson's corporate personality as: (1) corporate responsibility; and (2) "a psychical unity between members of the same social group, in which the limits of an individual's personality are not clearly defined."[3]

Echoes of these sentiments can be found in the work of more recent scholars, especially the second aspect.[4] For instance, Carol Meyers (1997) avers: "In the merging of the self and family, one can observe a collective, group-oriented mind-set, with the welfare of the individual inseparable from that of the living group."[5] Further on, she elaborates:

> In premodern agrarian settings such as early Israel ... individualistic elements of human existence, including a person's range of psychological processes and feeling states, were characteristically subordinate to the person's role in the family unit.... A person was not an autonomous entity but someone's *father, mother, daughter, son, grandparent*, and so forth.[6]

---

1   See Charles Taylor, *Sources of the Self: The Making of the Modern Identity* (Cambridge: Cambridge University Press, 1989), x and Part 2.
2   H. Wheeler Robinson, "Hebrew Psychology," in *The People and the Book: Essays on the Old Testament* (ed. Arthur S. Peake; Oxford: Clarendon, 1925), 376.
3   John W. Rogerson, "The Hebrew Conception of Corporate Personality: A Re-Examination," *JTS* 21 (1970): 6.
4   For an examination of the former aspect, see Joel S. Kaminsky, *Corporate Responsibility in the Hebrew Bible* (JSOTSup 196; Sheffield: Sheffield Academic Press, 1995).
5   Carol L. Meyers, "The Family in Early Israel," in *Families in Ancient Israel* (ed. Leo G. Perdue, et al.; Louisville: Westminster John Knox, 1997), 21.
6   Meyers, "Family," 22 (emphasis original).

Meyers is correct to highlight the group orientation of individuals in ancient Israelite society. Nonetheless, it is also possible to overstate the case, ending up with an understanding of the self which is completely merged with significant others. Certainly, an ancient Israelite would not have understood his/her individual identity in the same way as the current Western conception; it would be flawed methodology to impose a strict post-Enlightenment understanding of selfhood onto the HB Scriptures. Nonetheless, there are at least five ways in which individuality surfaces in the HB.

First, the HB presentation of the concept of "self" is conveyed through three main words: לב, נפש, and רוח. While these have overlapping semantic domains, each adds a different nuance to the underlying Israelite conception of personhood.[7] Second, Saul Olyan finds evidence of distinct individual voices behind the Prophetic texts of Jeremiah, Second Isaiah, and Ezekiel.[8] Although the personas may be authorial constructions, they nonetheless point to aspects of "the individuality, subjectivity, and uniqueness of the particular persons behind the voices."[9] Third, the use of the autobiographical genre points to the presence of individuality in thought. The most fully developed autobiographical text in the HB is Ecclesiastes, and other examples of this genre can be found in ancient Near Eastern texts.[10] Fourth, is evidence of self-reflection from HB narratives.[11] In the RN, narratorial expressions of autonomous thought in Boaz are found in Ruth 3:14[12] and 4:3.[13] Fifth, is HB retribution theology, which is

---

7   For לב see BDB, 524-25; Fabry, H.-J., "לב; לבב," *TDOT* VII:412-13. For נפש see BDB, 659-661; H. Seebass, "נפש," *TDOT* IX:505-512. In the HB רוח refers to a person's character (Eccl 7:8) or will (e.g., Isa 29:24). The volitional aspect is reinforced by the fact that רוח and לב are often used in parallel (e.g., Ezek 11:19-20). Cf. Tengström, S., "רוח," *TDOT* XIII:376-77.

8   Saul M. Olyan, "The Search for the Elusive Self in Texts of the Hebrew Bible," in *Religion and the Self in Antiquity* (ed. David Brakke, Michael L. Satlow, and Steven Weitzman; Bloomington: Indiana University Press, 2005), 40-50.

9   Olyan, "The Search for the Elusive Self," 41.

10 Tremper Longman, *The Book of Ecclesiastes* (NICOT; Grand Rapids: Eerdmans, 1998), 18, mentions the following ancient Near Eastern texts: Sinuhe, Wen-Amon, the Sargon Birth Legend, and many first-person royal inscriptions. For a definition of "autobiography" see Tremper Longman, *Fictional Akkadian Autobiography: A Generic and Comparative Study* (Winona Lake: Eisenbrauns, 1991), 40-41.

11 Cf. Maren Niehoff, "Do Biblical Characters Talk to Themselves? Narrative Modes of Representing Inner Speech in Early Biblical Fiction," *JBL* 111 (1992): 577-95.

12 This involves translating ויאמר with "and he thought," as in: "And he thought (ויאמר), 'Let it not be known that the woman (האשה) came to the threshing floor.'" Although the majority of English translations and a significant number of commentators translate this "and he said," within the context of this verse, the alternative translation is preferable, as accepted by, e.g., Bush, *Ruth*, 177-78; Wilhelm Rudolph, *Das Buch Ruth, das Hohe*

found not only at the corporate level, but also at the individual level. It is often argued that an individualistic ethic is a late development, with the key evidence being the exilic text Ezek 18:1-32 (cf. the parallel text Jer 31:29-30).[14] Yet individual responsibility is also found in many texts that are ostensibly set in the pre-settlement period, such as Gen 3:14-19; Lev 20:9, 11-12, 16, 27 (cf. Josh 2:19; Ezek 33:4); Num 13:1–14:38; Deut 24:16.[15] Individual responsibility is predicated upon autonomous thought and action.

This evidence suggests that there was a degree of demarcation of the self, along with the presence of individual agency. Therefore, it would be overstating the case to describe the HB conception of an ancient Israelite as one who is completely subsumed within their corporate identities. Walther Eichrodt attempts to capture how this individuality functions within Israelite society through his concept of "solidarity":

> In interplay with this solidarity thinking we find a living individuality which, as distinct from individualism, is to be understood as the capacity for personal responsibility and for shaping one's own life. This does not stand in mutually exclusive opposition to, but in fruitful tension with, the duty of solidarity, and as such affects the individual and motivates his conduct.[16]

This study will show how the personal autonomy and initiative of individuals can nonetheless function to further the goals of a collectivistic society.

Yet the picture that is emerging is more complex than this. Cultural psychologists have observed that not only is individuality present, but that individualistic behaviour is also found within collectivistic societies. This is because a particular member of a given culture will vary in their collectivist

---

Lied, die Klagelieder (KAT 17; Gütersloh: Mohn, 1962), 55-57; Erich Zenger, *Das Buch Ruth* (ZBK 8; Zürich: Theologischer Verlag, 1986), 69.

13 "So I, I thought I would inform you (ואני אמרתי אגלה אזנך לאמר): 'Buy it in the presence of those sitting here.'" This reading is favoured by, inter alios, Campbell, *Ruth*, 144; Rudolph, *Ruth*, 158; Ernst Würthwein, *Die fünf Megilloth: Ruth, Das Hohelied, Esther* (HAT 18; Tübingen: Mohr, 1969), 19; Yair Zakovitch, *Das Buch Rut: Ein jüdischer Kommentar* (trans. Andreas Lehnardt, SBS 177; Stuttgart: Katholisches Bibelwerk, 1999), 155.

14 E.g., Gerhard von Rad, *Old Testament Theology* (trans. D. M. G. Stalker; Edinburgh: Oliver and Boyd, 1965), 266; Helmer Ringgren, *Israelite Religion* (trans. David Green; London: SPCK, 1966), 286.

15 Regardless of the composition dates of these texts, to some extent they still have to be plausible reconstructions of the historical period to be accepted by their implied readers. That is, the idea of individual responsibility must have formed part of the worldview of an Israelite living in the period prior to the monarchy to be acceptable to readers at a later date.

16 Walther Eichrodt, *Theology of the Old Testament* (trans. John A. Baker, 2 vols.; Philadelphia: Westminster, 1966), 2:232 (orig. publ. 1961).

or individualist tendencies.[17] Moreover, Harry Triandis argues that individualism and collectivism can coexist and are "simply emphasized more or less in each culture, depending on the situation."[18] As Zeba Crook notes, while individualism and collectivism are overarching ideologies that "shape expectations of what constitutes proper individual behaviour" within a society, they do not rule out other types of behaviour.[19] So although cultures can be plotted along a linear plane, with individualism and collectivism at either end, there is no real-life society on either end.[20] Hence, these cultural categories function as heuristic tendencies, indicating which orientation people within these societies value most.[21]

Triandis describes the four attributes of a collectivistic culture: the definition of the self as interdependent; the primacy of ingroup goals; the primary emphasis on group norms as the determinant of behaviour; and the importance of communal relationships.[22] The mentality characteristics of this group can be termed "dyadic" or "collectivist." The psychological orientation is dyadic as opposed to monadic, meaning that the basic unit of social analysis is not the individual but the dyad, a person in relation with and connected to at least one other social unit, especially the family.[23] In short, each individual is in constant need of another person to delineate his/her own identity. Such a person also understands his/her distinct social position both horizontally (with others sharing the same status) and vertically (with others above and below in social rank). The psychological orientation is also collectivist in the sense that priority is not given to the self, but to the larger group to which the self belongs. The welfare of the individual becomes inseparable from that of the living group.[24] Indeed in

---

17 Peter B. Smith and Michael H. Bond, *Social Psychology Across Cultures: Analysis and Perspectives* (New York: Harvester Wheatsheaf, 1993), 41-42.
18 Harry C. Triandis, "Collectivism and Individualism as Cultural Syndromes," *Cross-Cultural Research* 27 (1993): 162.
19 Zeba A. Crook, "Structure versus Agency in Studies of the Biblical Social World: Engaging with Louise Lawrence," *JSNT* 29 (2007): 269-70.
20 Crook, "Structure versus Agency," 269-71.
21 Defining the corresponding personality patterns of individualism and collectivism as idiocentrism and allocentrism respectively, Harry C. Triandis and David Trafimow, "Cross-National Prevalence of Collectivism," in *Individual Self, Relational Self, Collective Self* (ed. Marilynn B. Brewer and Constantine Sedikides; Philadelphia: Psychology Press, 2001), 262, note that there are approximately 60% allocentrics in collectivist cultures, and 60% idiocentrics in individualist cultures.
22 Harry C. Triandis, "Individualism and Collectivism," in *The Handbook of Culture and Psychology* (ed. David R. Matsumoto; Oxford: Oxford University Press, 2001), 36.
23 Bruce J. Malina and Jerome H. Neyrey, "First-Century Personality," in *The Social World of Luke-Acts: Models for Interpretation* (ed. Jerome H. Neyrey; Peabody: Hendrickson, 1991), 73.
24 Meyers, "Family," 21.

relation to the family, even a person's psychological processes and feeling states are characteristically subordinate to the person's role in the family unit.[25]

Recently, researchers have proposed two different forms of collectivism: category-based and relationship-based. While people in Western cultures emphasise the categorical distinctions between ingroups and outgroups, those in East Asia have a tendency to think about groups as relationship-based.[26] In group contexts East Asians understand themselves as embedded within a network of shared relationships, e.g., family members, friends, and acquaintances. This distinction has been corroborated by findings in other non-Western cultures, with the relationship-based social identity also being prevalent in China and Africa.[27]

This dual categorisation of social identity may be explained by differences in individual mobility and the relative importance placed on values of independence verses interdependence in relationships between self and others in a society.[28] Other antecedents to collectivism include resource scarcity, the presence of large families, and the need for co-operation in agricultural activities. External threats to existence, such as military attack, also encourage this cultural pattern,[29] more specifically category-based collectivism.[30] Since these underlying factors can be used to differentiate all societies, the general division into category-based and relationship-based societies is applicable to all cultures at all times. Thus, empirically speaking, it would be reasonable to infer that the former predominates in individualistic societies, including modern Western cultures, while the latter predominates in non-Western cultures and pre-modern societies, including ancient Israel.

---

25 Meyers, "Family," 22.
26 Masaki Yuki, "Intergroup Comparison versus Intragroup Relationships: A Cross-Cultural Examination of Social Identity Theory in North American and East Asian Cultural Contexts," *Social Psychology Quarterly* 66 (2003): 166-83. See also Marilynn B. Brewer and Ya-Ru Chen, "Where (Who) Are Collectives in Collectivism? Toward Conceptual Clarification of Individualism and Collectivism," *Psychological Review* 114 (2007): 133-51.
27 Marilynn B. Brewer and Masaki Yuki, "Culture and Social Identity," in *Handbook of Cultural Psychology* (ed. Shinobu Kitayama and Dov Cohen; New York: Guilford Press, 2007), 310-11; see references therein.
28 Brewer and Yuki, "Culture and Social Identity," 311-12.
29 Harry C. Triandis et al., "An Etic-Emic Analysis of Individualism and Collectivism," *Journal of Cross-Cultural Psychology* 24 (1993): 368. In contrast, the antecedents to individualism are affluence, social mobility, geographical mobility, cultural complexity, urbanism, exposure to the mass media, and vocations that require individual pursuits.
30 My thanks to Masaki Yuki for pointing this out (personal communication, 12/5/08).

The predominantly collectivist orientation of ancient Israelite society fits well with the emphasis on the social self in social psychology; hence, this theory will be employed in order to glean insights into Israelite identity.

II. The Social Identity Approach

The social identity approach encompasses two theories based on the same assumptions: social identity theory (SIT) and self-categorisation theory (SCT).[31] These theories have been subjected to extensive empirical testing and broadly applied to disparate fields.[32] Since it is a complex and wide-ranging approach, I will focus on the elements that are pertinent to this study of the RN.

Henri Tajfel published his seminal essay on SIT in 1972. His theory derives from a debate surrounding the relationship between the individual and the group. On the one hand, the Floyd Allport school of thought considers the group simply as the sum of its parts: "There is no psychology of groups which is not essentially and entirely a psychology of individuals. Social psychology ... is part of the psychology of the individual."[33] That is, the status of the group is only as a collection of individuals, and so social psychology does not study the group *per se*, but the psychology of the individuals concerned. Hence, groups are viewed as an irrelevance.

On the other hand, Tajfel and his cohorts investigate how a group installs itself in the mind of individuals to affect their behaviour.[34] He proposes that social identity is established through comparison to and distinctiveness from other groups: "[S]ocial identity [is] understood as deriving in a comparative and 'relational' manner from an individual's

---

31 The latter theory is a development and continuation of social identity theory.
32 Since the mid-1970s, it has been applied to prejudice, stereotyping, language use, and organisational psychology. It has also been utilised in the areas of clinical health psychology, linguistics, and political science.
33 Floyd H. Allport, *Social Psychology* (Boston: Houghton Mifflin, 1924), 4. Similarly, he states on page 9: "If we take care of the individuals, psychologically speaking, the groups will be found to take care of themselves."
34 Michael A. Hogg and Dominic Abrams, *Social Identifications: A Social Psychology of Intergroup Relations and Group Processes* (London: Routledge, 1988), 12-19.

group membership."³⁵ In this way a group provides its members with a positive social identity,³⁶ and belonging to a group has three dimensions:
1. "the cognitive dimension," which covers the simple recognition of belonging to a group;
2. "the evaluative dimension," which covers the positive or negative connotations of belonging;
3. "the emotional dimension," which refers to the attitudes that members hold toward insiders and outsiders.³⁷

These dimensions shape the social identity of a person, which is defined as: "[T]he individual's knowledge that he belongs to certain social groups together with some emotional and value significance to him of group membership,"³⁸ where "social group" is "two or more individuals who share a common social identification of themselves or ... perceive themselves to be members of the same social category."³⁹ From these definitions it can be seen that social identity is a psychological phenomenon: identity is largely based upon self-descriptions in terms of the defining characteristics of social groups to which one belongs.⁴⁰

A. Norms

Within this understanding of social identity, the group promotes norms for its members. These are the attitudes, beliefs, and values that define acceptable and unacceptable behaviour for group members.⁴¹ They help group members construe the world and determine appropriate behaviour in new and ambiguous situations by bringing order and predictability to

---

35 Henri Tajfel, *Differentiation between Social Groups: Studies in the Social Psychology of Intergroup Relations* (London: Academic, 1978), 87.
36 Or positive "collective self-esteem." See Jennifer Crocker and Riia Luthanen, "Collective Self-Esteem and Ingroup Bias," *Journal of Personality and Social Psychology* 58 (1990): 60-67.
37 Tajfel, *Differentiation between Social Groups*, 28.
38 English translation of Henri Tajfel, "La catégorisation sociale," in *Introduction à la Psychologie Sociale* (ed. Serge Moscovici; Paris: Larousse, 1972), 31, as quoted in Hogg and Abrams, *Social Identifications*, 7.
39 John C. Turner and Howard Giles, *Intergroup Behaviour* (Oxford: Basil Blackwell, 1981), 15.
40 Cf. Hogg and Abrams, *Social Identifications*, 19: "People derive their identity ... in great part from the social categories to which they belong. The group is thus in the individual, and the psychological processes responsible for this are also responsible for the form that group behaviour takes."
41 Hogg and Abrams, *Social Identifications*, 159.

their environment.[42] In this way, they simplify and regulate social interaction, and in the process also function to maintain and enhance ingroup identity. Hence, norms can also be understood as "identity descriptors."[43]

Within a social identity approach, norms are an alternative to "ethics." Esler notes two main problems with the use of the term "ethics."[44] First, since the Enlightenment the study of ethics primarily focuses on the solution to moral dilemmas.[45] This emphasis has only been partially diminished by the recent interest in Aristotelian virtue ethics, with its central concern for character rather than rules or consequences.[46] Second, the contemporary field of ethics is preoccupied with the actions of individuals, which does not suit a collectivist society, such as that found in the HB. SIT overcomes both problems by viewing norms as a vital aspect of group identity.

The law and narratives now found in the HB contribute to Israelite identity by outlining group norms. Scholars have observed that the book of Deuteronomy can be viewed as a constitution document for Israel as a nation.[47] From a social identity perspective, the law contained therein circumscribes appropriate attitudes and behaviours for the nation, marking out their privileged status and unique identity (e.g., Deut 4:6-8). The RN then demonstrates a particular way of applying the law that is expected of members of the Israelite ingroup. It not only prescribes a minimal adherence to the law, it encourages an expansive application.

B. Stereotyping

SIT also sheds light on stereotyping. This is the grouping of complex information and the development of schematic mental images of certain categories of person.[48] Within SIT, stereotypes are

---

42 Rupert Brown, *Group Processes: Dynamics within and between Groups* (Oxford: Basil Blackwell, 1988), 42-48.
43 Esler, *Conflict and Identity*, 20-21.
44 Esler, *Conflict and Identity*, 21.
45 Cf. Barbieri, "Narrated Life," 363-65.
46 For a Christian appropriation, see, e.g., Stanley Hauerwas, *The Peaceable Kingdom: A Primer in Christian Ethics* (Notre Dame: University of Notre Dame, 1984); Stanley Hauerwas, *Vision and Virtue* (Notre Dame: University of Notre Dame, 1974).
47 See, programmatically, S. Dean McBride, "Polity of the Covenant People: The Book of Deuteronomy," *Int* 41 (1987): 229-44.
48 Henri Tajfel, "Social Stereotypes and Social Groups," in *Intergroup Behaviour* (ed. John C. Turner and Howard Giles; Oxford: Basil Blackwell, 1981), 272-302.

generalizations about people based on category membership. They are beliefs that all members of a particular group have the same qualities, which circumscribe the group and differentiate it from other groups. A specific group member is assumed to be, or is treated as, essentially identical to other members of the group.[49]

This is often the case with nations, which are associated with geographical stereotypes.[50] In the HB the Israelites are often differentiated from other nations, e.g., YHWH commands the Israelites in Lev 18:24: "Do not make yourselves unclean by any of these things, for by all these the nations I am driving out before you have become unclean."

Moreover, stereotypes are associated with evaluation, and have consequences for subsequent behaviour. In general, a person's ingroup is usually evaluated positively, while outgroups are evaluated negatively.[51] Positive self-stereotyping in areas such as personality traits, behaviour, behavioural norms, attitudes and beliefs strengthen the sense of belonging to the group.[52] An example of negative stereotyping in the HB is found in Deut 23:3-4, where all Ammonites and Edomites are excluded from the assembly on the basis of actions attributed to their forebears. The stereotyping of Ruth as a Moabitess will be discussed in Chapter Three.[53]

The extent to which stereotyping is used to amplify ingroup/outgroup differentiation will depend on the local context of intergroup interaction. Tajfel and Turner identify three variables that make an important contribution to the emergence of ingroup favouritism:

1. the extent to which individuals identify with an ingroup and internalise that group membership as an aspect of self-concept;

---

49 Hogg and Abrams, *Social Identifications*, 65.
50 Cf. Bruce J. Malina and Jermone H. Neyrey, *Portraits of Paul: An Archaeology of Ancient Personality* (Louisville: Westminster John Knox, 1996), 117-20.
51 But see also Kathleen Ethier and Kay Deaux, "Negotiating Social Identity When Contexts Change: Maintaining Identification and Responding to Threat," *Journal of Personality and Social Psychology* 67 (1994): 243-51; Steve Hinkle and Rupert Brown, "Intergroup Comparisons and Social Identity: Some Links and Lacunae," in *Social Identity Theory: Constructive and Critical Advances* (ed. Dominic Abrams and Michael A. Hogg; London: Harvester Wheatsheaf, 1990), 48-70.
52 Hogg and Abrams, *Social Identifications*, 66-74. Individuals have a vested interest in being associated with positive categories, since these can confer positive self-evaluation and create feelings of self-worth.
53 Although the foregoing discussion is predicated upon category-based collectivism, stereotypes also hold for relationship-based collectivism. This is because people from any culture have multiple self-components, including relational and collective self-schema.

2. the extent to which the prevailing context provides ground for comparison between groups; and
3. the perceived relevance of the comparison outgroup.[54]

The last two factors are significant in the production of ethnocentrism, which flourishes under conditions in which intergroup distinctiveness is perceived to be under erosion or under threat.[55] Another situation in which there is not only increased ethnocentrism, but also outgroup hostility is when there is competition over physical resources or political power, either real or imagined.[56] One historical context in which ethnocentrism, or own-group enhancing stereotypical differences, is particularly marked is the Persian Period. At certain times during the Monarchic Period, there were also perceived threats, particularly of a military nature and due to the influx of northerners. The social processes of these eras will be examined in Chapter Five.

III. The Self in the Social Identity Approach

Within SIT the self has two separate components: personal identity (the personal self) and social identity (the collective self). But what is the relationship between an individual and the community of which he/she is a part? How is a person's psychology transformed by his/her group ties? And what are the factors influencing whether a person acts according to collective expectations? These are the types of questions that SCT attempts to address, as developed by Turner and his associates in the 1980s.[57]

---

54 Henri Tajfel and John C. Turner, "An Integrative Theory of Intergroup Conflict," in *The Social Psychology of Intergroup Relations* (ed. William G. Austin and Stephen Worchel; Monterey: Brooks/Cole, 1979), 41. An individual is more likely to display favouritism when an ingroup is central to their self-definition and a given comparison is meaningful or the outcome is contestable. Indeed, an individual may display outgroup favouritism if the outgroup's relative superiority is not contested or the task is irrelevant to the ingroup; see, e.g., Katherine J. Reynolds, John C. Turner, and S. Alexander Haslam, "When are We Better than Them and They Worse than Us? A Closer Look at Social Discrimination and Positive and Negative Domains," *Journal of Personality and Social Psychology* 78 (2000): 64-80.
55 Hogg and Abrams, *Social Identifications*, 77.
56 Robert A. LeVine and Donald T. Campbell, *Ethnocentrism: Theories of Conflict, Ethnic Attitudes, and Group Behavior* (New York: Wiley, 1971); Muzafer Sherif and Carolyn W. Sherif, *Groups in Harmony and Tension: An Integration of Studies on Intergroup Relations* (New York: Harper, 1953).
57 John C. Turner, "Social Categorization and the Self-Concept: A Social Cognitive Theory of Group Behaviour," in *Advances in Group Processes* (ed. Edward J. Lawler; Greenwich: JAI Press, 1985), 77-122; John C. Turner, "Towards a Cognitive

If SIT is primarily interested in intergroup relations, then SCT is concerned with intragroup relations. It focuses on the cognitive processes involved in producing group behaviour. Fundamental to this theory is self-categorisation, which leads to self-stereotyping and the depersonalisation of self-perception. When social identity becomes more salient than personal identity, people view themselves less as individuals and more as prototypical representatives of their ingroup category.[58] Hence, there is a depersonalisation of the self, from unique individual differences to "shared social category membership and associated stereotypes."[59]

This process transforms individual behaviour into collective behaviour as people understand and act in terms of a collective sense of self. It leads people to think, feel, and behave in terms of the relevant ingroup prototype. In other words, self-categorisation renders normative certain attitudes and associated behaviours, and causes people to behave in line with such group norms.[60] Hence, social identities influence behaviour through the mediating role of group norms. Furthermore, when a person's social identity becomes salient, there are increased perceptions of interchangeability between oneself and ingroup members. This provides the basis for cooperation and coordinated action in achieving shared goals and interests. In short, when social identity is made salient, group identification both influences individuals' reactions to the group as a whole and impacts individuals' interactions with other ingroup members.

Redefinition of the Social Group," in *Social Identity and Intergroup Relations* (ed. Henri Tajfel; Cambridge: Cambridge University Press, 1982), 15-40.

58 Within SCT, personal and social identity initially represented the poles of a bipolar continuum. Subsequently, this conception was replaced by the notion that they represented different levels of self-categorisation. In some situations both categories of self-definition may be present; the relative salience of different levels determines the degree to which behaviour expresses individual differences or collective similarities. See John C. Turner, *Rediscovering the Social Group: A Self-Categorization Theory* (Oxford: Basil Blackwell, 1987); Turner, "Social Categorization," 77-122.

59 John C. Turner, "Social Identification and Psychological Group Formation," in *The Social Dimension: European Developments in Social Psychology* (ed. Henri Tajfel; Cambridge: Cambridge University Press, 1984), 528. Depersonalisation is "the basic process underlying group phenomena"; Turner, "Social Categorization," 99.

60 E.g., Deborah J. Terry and Michael A. Hogg, "Group Norms and the Attitude-Behavior Relationship: A Role for Group Identification," *Personality and Social Psychology Bulletin* 22 (1996): 776-93. Cf. Michael A. Hogg and Joanne R. Smith, "Attitudes in Social Context: A Social Identity Perspective," *European Review of Social Psychology* 18 (2007): 89-131.

According to SCT, the salience of a category is a function of its relative accessibility and fit.[61] There are a number of factors affecting accessibility ("perceiver readiness"). These include a person's past experience, present expectations and current motives, values, needs, and goals.[62] The level of ingroup identification, the degree to which it is central, valued, and ego-involving is another important factor.[63] Accessibility is also influenced by a reduction in uncertainty about self-conception, social interaction, and people's behaviour, as well as self-enhancement.[64] People use accessible categories to make sense of their social context. Categories are used to investigate how well the categorisation accounts for the similarities and differences between people (comparative fit) and how well the stereotypical properties of the categorisation account for the behaviour of people (normative fit). The principle of relative fit implies that self-conception is dynamic and responsive to changes in the specific context. Consequently, in a given situation, if a category is relatively accessible and there is a close match between the category and reality, it will become salient and produce associated attitudinal and behavioural changes.

SCT's focus on intragroup processes can assist in the interpretation of the RN. The book of Ruth presents situations in which the social identities of two of the protagonists (Boaz and Ruth) are more salient than their personal identities, in contrast to their foils ("Mr. So-and-So" and Orpah), issuing in group-centred behaviour. The positive outcome for the protagonists promotes the benefits of identifying with the kinship group, and subsequently thinking and acting for collective goals. This suggests that there may have been some tension or disagreement within the community to which the RN was written, and may therefore point to certain historical periods in which the value of social identity needed to be emphasised.

Within the social identity approach, both personal and social components contain a number of identifications. Social identifications are derived from belonging to groups, such as nationality, sex, ethnicity, or

---

61 For further discussion concerning salience, see Penelope J. Oakes, "The Salience of Social Categories," in *Rediscovering the Social Group: A Self-Categorization Theory* (ed. John C. Turner, et al.; Oxford: Basil Blackwell, 1987), 117-41.
62 See Penelope J. Oakes, S. Alexander Haslam, and John C. Turner, *Stereotyping and Social Reality* (Oxford: Basil Blackwell, 1994), ch. 8.
63 See, e.g., Bertjan Doosje and Naomi Ellemers, "Stereotyping under Threat: The Role of Group Identification," in *The Social Psychology of Stereotyping and Group Life* (ed. Russell Spears, et al.; Oxford: Blackwell, 1997), 257-72.
64 Michael A. Hogg, "Subjective Uncertainty Reduction through Self-Categorization: A Motivational Theory of Social Identity Processes," *European Review of Social Psychology* 11 (2000): 223-55; Michael A. Hogg et al., "Uncertainty, Entitativity, and Group Identification," *Journal of Experimental Social Psychology* 43 (2007): 135-42.

occupation. Personal identifications usually denote specific individual attributes, which are grounded in relationships with specific individuals or objects.[65] This is represented in the following figure:

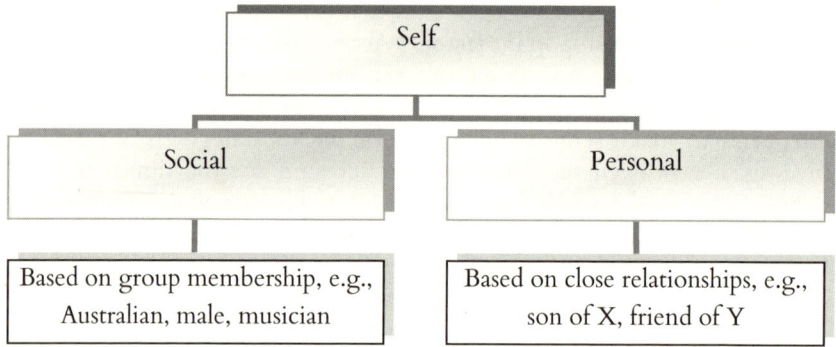

Figure 1: The self in social identity theory[66]

Brewer and Gardner propose a useful refinement to this model. Although both components of identity are to some extent socially derived, personal identity can be reserved for the component not derived from relationships with specific individuals (or objects).[67] They suggest a tripartite division of the self:
1. the individual self (defined by personal traits that differentiate one person from others);
2. the relational self (defined by dyadic relationships between the self and significant others); and
3. the collective self (defined by group membership that differentiates between "us" and "them").

The individual self corresponds to the personal self in the social identity approach, while the relational and collective selves can be classified as

---

65 Cf. Charles Stangor et al., "Categorization of Individuals on the Basis of Multiple Social Features," *Journal of Personality & Social Psychology* 62 (1992): 207-18. Within SCT, personal identity or individuality is viewed in the same way as social identity, viz. dynamic, variable, and context-dependent; see John C. Turner and Rina S. Onorato, "Social Identity, Personality, and the Self-Concept: A Self-Categorization Perspective," in *The Psychology of the Social Self* (ed. Tom R. Tyler, Roderick Moreland Kramer, and Oliver P. John; Mahwah, N.J.: Lawrence Erlbaum Associates, 1999), 11-46.
66 Adapted from Hogg and Abrams, *Social Identifications*, 24.
67 Marilynn B. Brewer and Wendi Gardner, "Who Is This 'We'? Levels of Collective Identity and Self Representations," *Journal of Personality & Social Psychology* 71 (1996): 83-93.

subsets of the social self. The advantage of this further division has been mentioned previously: it has heuristic value in explaining the different forms of collectivism. Members of individualist societies tend to manifest category-based collectivism in group situations. This is consistent with the self-categorisation model, in which collective selves involve depersonalised connections with others by virtue of common membership in a symbolic group. By contrast, members of collectivist societies generally manifest relationship-based collectivism in group situations, in which relational selves are personalised through close dyadic relationships, and the extension of these relationships through networks of interpersonal relationships.

IV. The Social Identity Approach and Ancient Israelite Identity

In the HB personal and social identity is indicated by the data used in identifying biblical characters. These are: the tribe, the clan, the father's house, and the individual (cf. Josh 7:16-18; Judg 6:15; 1 Sam 10:20-21).[68] In the HB, there is also the presence of a pan-tribal collective described as the עם or גוי of "all Israel" (esp. Josh 3-4).[69] Although a dominant view in the humanities is that nationalism is a modern phenomenon,[70] it seems undeniable that "Israel" as constructed from HB data is analogous to the modern understanding of a "nation," or something very similar to it.[71] According to Steven Grosby, the prerequisites for the definition of a "nation" are the belief in the existence of a "people," a specific territory

---

68 For further discussion regarding these kinship groups in the pre-exilic period, see especially Shunya Bendor, *The Social Structure of Ancient Israel: The Institution of the Family (beit 'ab) from the Settlement to the End of the Monarchy* (Jerusalem Biblical Studies 7; Jerusalem: Simor, 1996); Baruch Halpern, "Jerusalem and the Lineages in the Seventh Century BCE: Kinship and the Rise of Individual Moral Liability," in *Law and Ideology in Monarchic Israel* (ed. Baruch Halpern and Deborah W. Hobson; Sheffield: JSOT Press, 1991), 49-59, and classically, Gottwald, *Tribes*, 237-337.

69 See Steven E. Grosby, *Biblical Ideas of Nationality: Ancient and Modern* (Winona Lake: Eisenbrauns, 2002), 15-16.

70 E.g., Benedict R. O'G Anderson, *Imagined Communities: Reflections on the Origin and Spread of Nationalism* (London: Verso, 1983); Ernest Gellner, *Nations and Nationalism* (Ithaca: Cornell University Press, 1983).

71 Cf. Mark G. Brett, "Nationalism and the Hebrew Bible," in *The Bible in Ethics* (ed. John W. Rogerson, Margaret Davies, and M. Daniel Carroll; Sheffield: Sheffield Academic, 1995), 136-63; David M. Goodblatt, *Elements of Ancient Jewish Nationalism* (Cambridge: Cambridge University Press, 2006); Doron Mendels, *The Rise and Fall of Jewish Nationalism: Jewish and Christian Ethnicity in Ancient Palestine* (Grand Rapids: Eerdmans, 1997); Stuart D. E. Weeks, "Biblical Literature and the Emergence of Ancient Jewish Nationalism," *BibInt* 10 (2002): 144-57.

belonging only to that people, and as a result of that co-residence an attribution of kinship.[72] Thomas Eriksen suggests that sovereignty within the land is a prerequisite, providing the best mark of differentiation between an ethnic group and a nation.[73] Hence, a nation is often constituted from different ethnic groups.

Based on this understanding, Israel during the United Monarchy was a nation, and the same was true of Israel and Judah within their own territories after the division. Since Israel ceased to exist in 722 B.C.E., the term "Israel" was eventually transferred to an entity predominantly held together by a common belief in YHWH.[74] Yet according to the description of "Israel" found in Ezra-Nehemiah (henceforth EN), it is difficult to define it as a nation. Rather, the self-definition of the "reconstituted Israel" was primarily along genealogical lines, as well as adherence to the law of YHWH. Although they held political and territorial aspirations, in reality they were under Persian rule, and lived amongst "the peoples of the land," those who were incumbent in the land. Hence, in the Persian context "Israel" is best classified as an ethnic group with nationalistic aspirations.

The basic kinship structure seems to have persisted throughout the pre-exilic period. Even the establishment of the monarchy did not alter the basic social structure significantly; Israelite society continued to be based on family and clan units even beyond the Monarchic Period.[75] Evidence

---

72 Grosby, *Nationality*, 13-27.
73 Thomas H. Eriksen, *Ethnicity and Nationalism: Anthropological Perspectives* (London: Pluto Press, 1993), 6. The main features of an ethnic group as outlined in John Hutchinson and Anthony D. Smith, "Introduction," in *Ethnicity* (ed. John Hutchinson and Anthony D. Smith; Oxford: Oxford University Press, 1996), 6-7, are: (1) a common proper name; (2) a myth of common ancestry; (3) shared historical memories; (4) one or more elements of common culture; (5) a link with a homeland without its physical occupation; and (6) a sense of solidarity. Since these features may also apply to other collectivities, James C. Miller, "Ethnicity and the Hebrew Bible: Problems and Prospects," *CurBS* 6 (2008): 175, argues that the crucial factor for ethnic identity is the myth of a common ancestry.
74 Cf. Reinhard G. Kratz, "Israel als Staat und als Volk," *ZTK* 97 (2000): 1-17.
75 Bendor, *The Social Structure of Ancient Israel*, 216-28; Halpern, "Jerusalem," 214-15; Paula M. McNutt, *Reconstructing the Society of Ancient Israel* (Louisville: Westminster John Knox, 1999), 75-98; Hayim Tadmor, "'The People' and the Kingship in Ancient Israel: The Role of the Political Institutions in the Biblical Period," *Journal of World History* 11 (1968): 48. Cf. Yigal Levin, "Who Was the Chronicler's Audience? A Hint from His Genealogies," *JBL* 122 (2003): 229-45. Øystein LaBianca, "Salient Features of Iron Age Tribal Kingdoms," in *Ancient Ammon* (ed. Burton MacDonald and Randall W. Younker; Studies in the History and Culture of the Ancient Near East 42; Leiden: Brill, 1999), 19-23, argues that this was similarly the case with other Iron Age "kingdoms" (Ammon, Moab, Edom) of the Southern Levant.

for this can be found in the HB. For instance, the presence of Rechabites 3indicates the ongoing clan solidarity common in tribal societies (Jer 35:6-10), and the story of Jeremiah's redemption of his cousin's property (Jer 32:6-15) also assumes the presence of kinship responsibilities. Although both the father's house and clan group underwent minor change in the Persian Period,[76] the basic kinship structure remained for an implied reader.

The boundaries between these kinship groups were fluid.[77] A number of reasons are suggested.[78] First, the HB was written and compiled over a long time span, including tumultuous periods of detribalisation and retribalisation.[79] This would have led to fluidity in social organisation, primarily at the larger kinship group level; the father's house would not have been affected to a great degree. Second, instability means that the criteria for distinguishing between a large clan and a tribe would have been ambiguous. For instance, Judah might have originally been a clan that subsequently became a tribe and then a kingdom. Third, and most significantly, the fluidity in categorisation of kinship groups is because of the attribution of being related by blood to kinship groups where factually this might not be the case.[80] The fact that collectivities also came to be constituted by territorial reference adds to this imprecision in terminology.[81] However, as Steven Grosby rightly comments, the fluidity of the boundaries resulting in variations of classification "does not invalidate the argument that various units were sorted out into a hierarchy of

---

76 See Chapter Five.
77 This is noted by a number of scholars, including Niels P. Lemche, *Early Israel: Anthropological and Historical Studies on the Israelite Society before the Monarchy* (Leiden: Brill, 1985), 268; Martin Noth, *The History of Israel* (trans. Peter R. Ackroyd; 2d ed.; London: A. & C. Black, 1960), 106-07; Johannes Pedersen, *Israël: Its Life and Culture* (vol. I-II; London: Oxford University Press, 1926), 46-48; C. Umhau Wolf, "Terminology of Israel's Tribal Organization," *JBL* 65 (1946): 45-49.
78 After Grosby, *Nationality*, 18-20.
79 Grosby, *Nationality*, 18-19, fn. 11, mentions the apparent dispersion of the tribes of Simeon and Rueben as an instance of detribalisation, and the description of Benjamin's birth in Canaan (Gen 35:18) as an example of retribalisation. Cf. M. B. Rowton, "Dimorphic Structure and the Parasocial Element," *JNES* 36 (1977): 185-87.
80 This is particularly the case for kinship groups larger than the בית אב. Cf. Francis I. Andersen, "Israelite Kinship Terminology and Social Structure," *BT* 20 (1969): 31, who states that the "availability of adoption ... meant that legal and political relationships could be dressed up as family connections, social relationships and obligations as real as biological connection." See also Gottwald, *Tribes*, 287-90.
81 Kinship groups that were constituted by territorial reference might have included the clan and the tribe. See C. H. J. de Geus, *The Tribes of Israel: An Investigation into Some of the Presuppositions of Martin Noth's Amphictyony Hypothesis* (Studia Semitica Neerlandica 18; Assen: Van Gorcum, 1976), 138-39; Gottwald, *Tribes*, 257, 316; Niels P. Lemche, *Early Israel*, 269.

categories at any particular time."[82] The pertinent point in relation to this study is that individuals were members of various kinship groups, and that each member had various roles and responsibilities relating to membership in these groups.

Since a name supplied important information about a person's place in society, membership of kinship groups may be reflected in a person's name. The example of Saul particularly displays the full complement of social groups (1 Sam 9:1; 10:20-21):

Aspect of Identity	Designation	Name
People/Nation of Israel	עם	Israel
Tribe	שבט/מטה	Benjamin
Clan	משפחה	Matrite
Father's House	בית אב	Abiel
Individual	גבר/איש	Saul the son of Kish

These four main components of Saul's name (Saul the son of Kish, of the tribe of Benjamin, of the Matrite clan, from the father's house of Abiel) embody the most pertinent facts about his sociological relationships, and consequently, obligations. It lists the main kinship groups to which he belongs within the socio-political structure of ancient Israel.

Another way of understanding the identity of an individual Israelite is that they are placed in the centre of a series of concentric circles, indicating widening kinship relations, and the relative social influence on behaviour:

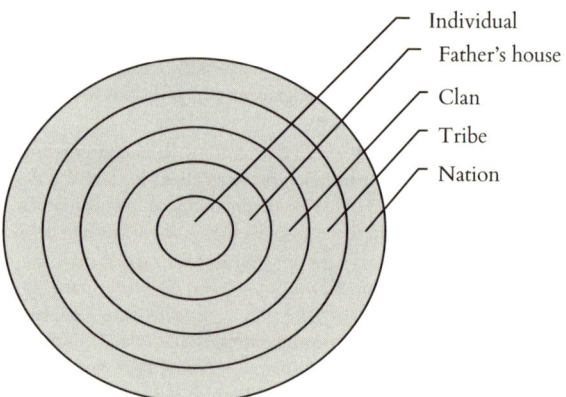

Figure 2: Concentric Israelite kinship group relations

---

82 Grosby, *Nationality*, 19.

The discussion of the social identity of the protagonists will be further divided into non-kinship groups and kinship groups. This division is not a strict demarcation of groups since they often overlap. The social groups discussed will focus on those that pertain to the main characters in the RN. Thus, the non-kinship groups discussed will cover generational and gender groups. The kinship groups will cover the father's house, the clan, the tribe, and the nation of Israel. Based on this division each Israelite would have membership in multiple groups. For instance, a person could be a male, a father, a head of a father's house, and a member of a certain clan and tribe within the nation of Israel. Nevertheless, this study will use the classification of non-kinship and kinship groups with their associated roles for the sake of clarity in discussion. Each of these identities is constructed from narratives derived both from society and the HB.

Gender roles are an integral aspect of ancient Israelite identity, with both social and physical factors influencing the roles held by men and women. These are roles by which people of each sex are expected to have psychological characteristics that equip them for the tasks that their sex typically performs.[83] Gender role casting begins in childhood, with children learning gender stereotypes before they reach preschool age.[84] This stereotype knowledge becomes increasingly refined across childhood.[85] From a social role perspective, sex-related attitudinal differences emerge both from the direct effects of sex-typed family and occupational roles on individual occupants of these roles and from culturally shared expectations that apply to women and men in general.[86] The roles that are typically occupied substantially more by one sex than the other produce these gender roles, because the characteristics that are required to carry out sex-typical tasks become stereotypical of women and men.

---

83 In this study the term "sexes" denotes the grouping of people into female and male categories. The term "gender" refers to the meanings that societies and individuals ascribe to female and male categories.

84 By the age of two, most children are aware of their own gender; Anne Campbell, Louisa Shirley, and Lisa Caygill, "Sex-Typed Preferences in Three Domains: Do Two-Year-Olds Need Cognitive Variables?," *British Journal of Psychology* 93 (2002): 203-17. By the age of three or four, children have a notion of their expected sex role; see, e.g., Judy Dunn and Claire Hughes, "'I Got Some Swords and You're Dead!': Violent Fantasy, Antisocial Behavior, Friendship, and Moral Sensibility in Young Children," *Child Development* 72 (2001): 491-505; Eleanor E. Maccoby, *The Two Sexes: Growing Up Apart, Coming Together* (Cambridge, Mass.: Belknap Press, 1998).

85 Diane N. Ruble and Carol L. Martin, "Gender Development," in *Handbook of Child Psychology* (ed. William Damon; New York: J. Wiley, 1998), 933-1016.

86 See Alice H. Eagly, *Sex Differences in Social Behavior: A Social-Role Interpretation* (Hillsdale, N. J.: Lawrence Erlbaum Associates, 1987); Wendy Wood and Alice H. Eagly, "A Cross-Cultural Analysis of the Behavior of Women and Men: Implications for the Origins of Sex Differences," *Psychological Bulletin* 128 (2002): 699-727.

Gender roles are also influenced by physical factors. The most important physical determinants of gender roles within a society are the essential sex differences represented by each sex's physical attributes and related behaviours, especially women's childbearing and nursing of infants and men's greater size, speed, and strength. Physical sex differences influence the roles held by men and women because certain activities are more efficiently accomplished by one sex.[87] It is thus easier for one sex than the other to perform certain activities of daily life under given conditions. The benefits of this greater efficiency emerge because women and men form complementary relationships in societies and engage in a division of labour. Most human activities in ancient Israel took place within the household, and a person's gender was a major factor in determining the various economic (production and consumption of goods), sexual-reproductive, educational, protective, and judicial responsibilities.[88]

The following figure presents the main components of ancient Israelite identity, taking into account the predominant kinship focus:

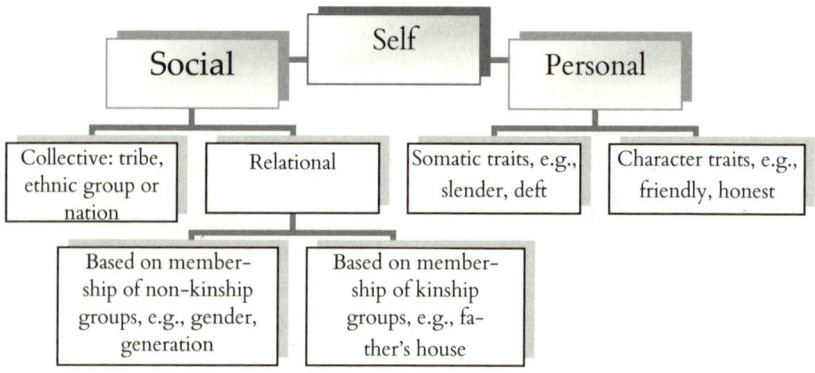

Figure 3: Modified theory of self for ancient Israelite identity

---

[87] See, classically, George P. Murdock and Caterina Provost, "Factors in the Division of Labor by Sex: A Cross-Cultural Analysis," *Ethnology* 12 (1973): 203-25. Contextual factors such as social, economic, technological, and ecological forces determine the concrete expression of gender roles in a particular society.

[88] For further discussion see especially McNutt, *Reconstructing*; Carol L. Meyers, *Discovering Eve: Ancient Israelite Women in Context* (Oxford: Oxford University Press, 1988).

A. Summary and Conclusion

In this study personal and social self-components will comprise the basic categories of ancient Israelite identity. Although personal identity would have been integral to ancient Israelite self-conception, it was not the dominant component; rather, as a member of a collectivist society, an Israelite understood himself/herself as an individual embedded within society. SIT fits well with the ancient Israelite understanding because a central tenet of this theory is that under certain circumstances "social identity is more salient than personal identity in self-conception, and that when this is the case behaviour is qualitatively different: it is group behaviour."[89] This would be the *modus operandi* for the majority of Israelites most of the time. The RN, however, presents situations in which personal and social identities of the protagonists are in tension. An examination of the response of the protagonists in these situations will yield information regarding the norms promoted in the RN, and consequently provide clues concerning the social milieu of the time.

V. Narrative, Identity, and Ethics

A. The Narrative Shaping of Identity

For more than thirty years, narrative has been recognised as intrinsic to our perception of experience. This has been recognised in fields as diverse as: the philosophy of history, where narrative is thought to be basic to historical understanding;[90] medicine, where patients use narrative to express and understand the aetiology of their illnesses;[91] and sociology,

---

89 Hogg and Abrams, *Social Identifications*, 22-23. Recently, Michael A. Hogg, "Social Identity and the Sovereignty of the Group," in *Individual Self, Relational Self, Collective Self* (ed. Marilynn B. Brewer and Constantine Sedikides; Philadelphia: Psychology Press, 2001), 125, has more forcefully asserted regarding self-conception: "The collective self ... reigns supreme, and the group is sovereign."

90 As Hayden V. White, *The Content of the Form: Narrative Discourse and Historical Representation* (Baltimore: Johns Hopkins University Press, 1987), 24, explains, when "historiography was transformed into an 'objective' discipline, it was the narrativity of the historical discourse that was celebrated as one of the signs of its maturation as a fully 'objective' discipline—a science of a special sort."

91 E.g., Lars-Christer Hydén, "Illness and Narrative," *Sociology of Health and Illness* 19 (1997): 48-69; Arthur Kleinman, *The Illness Narratives: Suffering, Healing, and the Human Condition* (New York: Basic Books, 1988); Gareth Williams, "The Genesis of Chronic Illness: Narrative Re-Construction," *Sociology of Health and Illness* 6 (1984): 175-200.

where narrative is viewed as the appropriate mode for recounting experience.[92] There are two general claims of the narrative view of life:
1. A descriptive claim: all human beings experience their lives as a narrative.[93]
2. A normative claim: to be a full person requires understanding our lives as a narrative.[94]

A distinction must be made, however, between life and narrative. Peter Lamarque correctly points out that it is wrong to elide the concepts of life and narrative.[95] Our life narrative is distinct from life itself because it is formed retrospectively. It may be true that we are characters within this narrative, but it is essentially a construct from our present perspective. As a construct, it has the potential for selecting the significant features of our life—both personal characteristics and events. The basic conditions for all narratives are continuity and causality.[96] Yet life narratives require another element: significance. Of all the raw data in our lives, only certain features are important and formative for our sense of self. From these we craft a meaningful narrative structure.[97] Furthermore, only narrative can order events into a plot so that the whole narrative is eventually imbued with significance from the way its parts are related to the whole. Hence, as an interpretation of life events, narrative gives the ability to select, arrange, and give significance and closure to events in a life. In this way, only narrative can contribute to identity.

---

92   E.g., Hannah Arendt, *The Human Condition* (Chicago: University of Chicago Press, 1958), esp. 175-92; Peter L. Berger, *Invitation to Sociology: A Humanistic Perspective* (Harmondsworth: Penguin, 1963), esp. 64-80; Erik H. Erikson, *Childhood and Society* (London: Imago, 1950), esp. 219-34.

93   See, e.g., Jerome Bruner, "Life as Narrative," *Social Research* 54 (1987): 11-32; Stephen Crites, "The Narrative Quality of Experience," *JAAR* 39 (1971): 291-311; Daniel Dennett, "The Self as a Center of Narrative Gravity," in *Self and Consciousness: Multiple Perspectives* (ed. Frank S. Kessel, Pamela M. Cole, and Dale L. Johnson; Hillsdale: Erlbaum, 1992); Alasdair MacIntyre, *After Virtue: A Study in Moral Theory* (2d ed.; Notre Dame: University of Notre Dame Press, 1984), 212.

94   See, e.g., MacIntyre, *After Virtue*, 218; Donald Polkinghorne, *Narrative Knowing and the Human Sciences* (Albany: State University of New York Press, 1988), 150; Taylor, *Sources of the Self*, 47.

95   Peter Lamarque, "On Not Expecting Too Much from Narrative," *Mind & Language* 19 (2004): 394-95.

96   Cf. Noël Carroll, *Beyond Aesthetics: Philosophical Essays* (Cambridge: Cambridge University Press, 2001), 126.

97   In contrast to temporal sequences, such as annals, chronicles, or even photographs, it is only narrative that can perspicuously describe causality and lend prominence to particular events or facts; cf. Carroll, *Aesthetics*, 121-28; David Novitz, *The Boundaries of Art* (Philadelphia: Temple University Press, 1992), 90.

B. Narratives and Identity Construction

This selection and arrangement of significant events takes place at a more deliberate level with written narratives. Modern literary approaches to biblical narrative highlight the literary devices encoded in a text, which link and configure the selected events of the story into a coherent whole. Since these narratives are written from a particular point of view, they express the attitudes and values of an author. Yet they also shape the identity of a reader.

Ricoeur's work is particularly helpful in drawing the link between narrative and identity. He describes how a written text projects a "world" through which a reader can be transformed, or ethically refigured.[98] According to Ricoeur, this ethical refiguration takes place in the act of interpretation, a process that encompasses explanation and understanding. Explanation deals with explicating or unfolding "the range of propositions and meanings."[99] Similar to the facts, laws, hypotheses, verifications, and deductions of the natural sciences, explanation of a text involves examining the structure of a text, or its internal relations. This is the work of narrative theory, as it examines the components of a narrative such as plot, character, and setting.

Understanding deals with comprehending or grasping "as a whole the chain of partial meanings in one act of synthesis."[100] It involves following the movement of a text from "sense to reference: from what it says to what it talks about."[101] That is, understanding is not found in the initial situation of the discourse, but the possible world to which it points. "It is by an understanding of the worlds, actual and possible, opened by the language that we may arrive at a better understanding of ourselves."[102] In short, the reading of a text involves a subjective, existential appropriation, which is based on objective structural analysis.[103]

It is through this process that narratives can influence the personal identity of a reader. Since both somatic and character traits are associated

---

98 Paul Ricoeur, "The Model of the Text: Meaningful Action Considered as a Text," in *Hermeneutics and the Human Sciences: Essays on Language, Action, and Interpretation* (ed. John B. Thompson; Cambridge: Cambridge University Press, 1981), 201-02.
99 Paul Ricoeur, *Interpretation Theory: Discourse and the Surplus of Meaning* (Fort Worth: Texas Christian University Press, 1976), 72.
100 Ricoeur, *Interpretation*, 72.
101 Ricoeur, *Interpretation*, 87-88.
102 Paul Ricoeur, "Myth as the Bearer of Possible Worlds," in *A Ricoeur Reader: Reflection and Imagination* (ed. Mario J. Valdés; New York: Harvester Wheatsheaf, 1991), 490.
103 For a fuller discussion of this process see Paul Ricoeur, *Time and Narrative* (trans. Kathleen Blamey and David Pellauer, 3 vols.; Chicago: Chicago University Press, 1984-1988).

with personal narratives, these can be modified through reading (or hearing) other narratives. In this way, narratives influence the personal identity of a reader, along with his/her attitudes, values, and actions.

Similarly, communities construct identity within a narrative framework. Ricoeur writes about:

> [T]hose events that a historical community holds to be significant because it sees in them an origin, a return to its beginnings. These events, which are said to be "epoch-making," draw their specific meanings from their capacity to found or reinforce the community's consciousness of its identity, its narrative identity, as well as the identity of its members.[104]

By defining or strengthening social identity, communal narratives provide coherence and significance to a group's existence, and consequently coherence and significance to each group member.

Yet if, according to social identity theory, identity contains personal and social self-components that are both essential, then there should be an intimate connection between personal and social narratives. Alasdair MacIntyre suggests that this is indeed the case:

> [T]he story of my life is always embedded in the story of those communities from which I derive my identity. I am born with a past; and to try to cut myself off from that past, in the individualist mode, is to deform my present relationships. The possession of an historical reality and the possession of a social identity coincide.[105]

Moreover, Ricoeur adds that these communal narratives have ethical import for each individual bound by these narratives: "These [communal] events generate feelings of considerable ethical intensity, whether this be fervent commemoration or some manifestation of loathing, or indignation, or of regret or compassion, or even the call for forgiveness."[106] To summarise, narratives are able to shape not only an individual's personal self-component, but also his/her social identity.

The HB contains ancient Israel's communal narratives. These narratives reflect and construct identity at the social level, and consequently have effects on the attitudes and actions of individuals within ancient Israel. These narratives also can also influence personal identity directly. This study will examine the RN with an especial interest in its effect on the identity (personal and social) and actions of an implied reader.

---

104 Ricoeur, *Time and Narrative*, 3:187.
105 MacIntyre, *After Virtue*, 221.
106 Ricoeur, *Time and Narrative*, 3:187.

VI. The Implied Reader

This study examines the ethics or norms promoted by the RN for an implied reader. Within literary theory, an implied reader is a textual construct, a reader or audience presupposed or implied by the text itself. An implied reader is embedded in the text, not derived extrinsic to it.[107] He/she is the "mirror-image" of the implied author derived from the text.[108] This is in contrast to the "real author" and the "real reader" who are the living, flesh-and-blood people who actually produced the text and read it.[109]

Nonetheless, the text implies that the reader is situated in a historical period. In the RN, this historical period is not clear. In broad terms, it could be any time after the birth of David, since that is the latest time mentioned in the discourse (4:17, 22). The implied reader is not situated at the same time as the story setting, as the narrator points out with his explanatory comment in Act 4: "Now this was the custom *formerly* in Israel" (לפנים; 4:7). This indicates that a reasonable amount of time had passed from the story setting (time of the Judges) to the discourse setting (initially taken as the late Monarchic to post-exilic period).[110] Thus, the historical situation of the implied reader also needs to be taken into consideration, but this is also constrained by the text. In this study, the interpretation of the RN will be constrained not only by textual and intertextual factors, but also by historical factors.

One way an implied author can influence identity and ethics is through point of view. In literary criticism, point of view is the position or perspective from which a story is told.[111] Following Seymour Chatman, Adele Berlin outlines three types of point of view: (1) perceptual—the perspective through which the events of the narrative are perceived; (2) conceptual—the perspective of attitudes and world view; and (3) interest—the perspective of someone's benefit or disadvantage.[112] Although this categorisation has been criticised,[113] Berlin notes that it is helpful in the

---

107 See Wayne C. Booth, *The Rhetoric of Fiction* (Chicago: University of Chicago Press, 1961), 138; Wolfgang Iser, *The Act of Reading: A Theory of Aesthetic Response* (Baltimore: John Hopkins University Press, 1978), 34.
108 The term "implied author" was coined by Booth, *The Rhetoric of Fiction*, 67, 70-71.
109 Cf. Wayne C. Booth, *The Company We Keep: An Ethics of Fiction* (Los Angeles: University of California Press, 1988), 125-26.
110 See the following section "The Dating of the Book of Ruth."
111 Cf. Adele Berlin, *Poetics and Interpretation of Biblical Narrative* (Sheffield: Almond Press, 1983), 46.
112 Berlin, *Poetics*, 47-48; after Seymour Chatman, *Story and Discourse: Narrative Structure in Fiction and Film* (Ithaca: Cornell University Press, 1978), 151-53.
113 For a recent critique, see Gary Yamasaki, *Watching a Biblical Narrative: Point of View in Biblical Exegesis* (New York: T&T Clark, 2008), 36-38.

context of biblical narrative, since the interest point of view is not always the same as the perceptual point of view, as we will find in the RN.[114] Perceptual point of view is also useful to ascertain because it can influence reader identification, empathy, and sympathy.[115] In turn, this can be used by an implied author to lead an implied reader towards a certain conceptual point of view. In other words, the determination of perceptual and interest points of view may provide an indication of the norms being promoted by an implied author.

To summarise, the aim of this study is to determine the effect that the RN is expected to have on its implied readers. To this end this study will attempt to interpret the text with the same background knowledge as the implied reader.

VII. The Dating of the Book of Ruth

The dating of the majority of the books of the HB is debated, and the book of Ruth is no exception. Since the historical context of the implied reader is an important component in the reception of the text, the following overview of proposed historical contexts is an important prerequisite for a discussion of the ethics of the book for an implied reader. Although it is possible that the RN could have been composed in the pre-monarchic and exilic periods, these periods have, rightly, only gained a few proponents.[116] The following discussion will therefore focus on the monarchic and post-exilic periods.[117]

A. A Post-Exilic Date

For most of the twentieth century, critical scholarship held a post-exilic dating for the RN. The main reasons for this late date include:
    1.   The alleged Aramaisms and late biblical Hebrew (LBH) forms.

---

114 For a fuller discussion and more comprehensive methodology for analysing point of view in biblical narratives, see Yamasaki, *Watching*, esp. 152-87.

115 Cf. Booth, *The Rhetoric of Fiction*, 281-82, as quoted in Berlin, *Poetics*, 49-50: "If granting to the hero the right to reflect his own story can insure the reader's sympathy, withholding it from him and giving it to another character can prevent too much identification."

116 For references see Hubbard, *Ruth*, 23-24.

117 Some also suggest stages of development, from the pre-exilic period to the post-exilic. These include Glanzman, "The Origin and Date of the Book of Ruth," 210-07; Myers, *Linguistic and Literary Form*.

2. The legal customs reflecting a time when the customs were obsolete or required explanation. For example, the explanation of the sandal custom (4:7) presupposes a time when the custom was no longer understood, and the difference in application of the levirate custom reflects either a reinterpretation or misunderstanding of the original custom.[118]
3. The similarity between the genealogy (4:18-22) and the "priestly" genealogies of the Pentateuch and Chronicles (e.g., 1 Chr 2:3-15).
4. The favourable portrayal of the Moabitess Ruth, which is thought to balance the ethno-centrism of post-exilic texts such as Ezra and Nehemiah.[119]
5. The allusion to a post-exilic "Deuteronomic" edition of the book of Judges (1:1).[120]
6. The canonical placement of Ruth among the Writings, based on the assumption that these were collected after the prophetic collection had been completed.[121]
7. The suitability of the theme of outward/homeward journey with the experience of the exile.[122]

Most recently, Ziony Zevit tentatively suggests a post-exilic date (525-500 B.C.E.) based on a combination of social, legal, and linguistic factors.[123]

Even within the post-exilic period of dating, however, there are differences of opinion. Although most argue for an early post-exilic date (fifth to fourth century B.C.E.) for the aforementioned reasons, others argue for a later post-exilic date. For example, Robert Gordis argues that the peaceful, idyllic tone presumes a period of relative tranquillity, and proposes a period between the "strife-ridden reforms" of Ezra/Nehemiah

---

118 E.g., LaCocque, *Ruth*, 18-21; Jean-Luc Vesco, "La date du livre de Ruth," *RB* 74 (1967): 242-43.
119 So, inter alios, Marjo C. A. Korpel, *The Structure of the Book of Ruth* (Pericope 2; Assen: Van Gorcum, 2001), 230-33; Zakovitch, *Rut*, 38-41, 62-64.
120 Cf. Robert H. Pfeiffer, *Introduction to the Old Testament* (London: Adam and Charles Black, 1948), 718.
121 Cf. Peter T. Nash, "Ruth: An Exercise in Israelite Political Correctness or a Call to Proper Conversion?," in *The Pitcher is Broken: Memorial Essays for Gösta W. Ahlström* (ed. Steven W. Holloway and Lowell K. Handy; JSOTSup 190; Sheffield: Sheffield Academic Press, 1995), 350-51.
122 Christian Frevel, *Das Buch Ruth* (Neuer Stuttgarter Kommentar: Altes Testament 6; Stuttgart: Theologischer Verlag, 1992), 34.
123 Ziony Zevit, "Dating Ruth: Legal, Linguistic and Historical Observations," *ZAW* 117 (2005): 576-94.

and the campaign of Alexander the Great.[124] The latest dating belongs to Erich Zenger, who views the final version of the book as belonging in the second century B.C.E. due to its alleged messianic aspect. He then proposes that the book promotes the Hasmoneans' political and religious ambitions.[125]

B. A Monarchic Date

A monarchic date has been the most popular view since the end of the twentieth century. Influential in this shift was Edward Campbell, who in 1975 proposed a date from about 950 to 700 B.C.E.[126] His grounds for an earlier dating included similarities in genre and theological perspective to earlier stories such as the Joseph story in Genesis, the Court History of David (2 Samuel), Judges, and 1 Kgs 22:1-36. Campbell proposes that it was produced orally in the time of Solomon and written down in the ninth century B.C.E., perhaps during the reign of Jehoshaphat.

Yet, similar to the post-exilic dating, there has been a wide range of proposals even within the Monarchic Period. The earliest is a Davidic dating, based on the view that the book is a dynastic "apology" supporting David.[127] Robert Hubbard leans towards a Solomonic dating,[128] while Moshe Weinfeld suggests a Northern provenance during the time of Elisha.[129] Daniel Block accepts Weinfeld's Northern provenance, but asserts a Josianic dating.[130] Jack Sasson, in looking for an appropriate setting for the glorification of David, also suggests a setting during the reign of Josiah.[131]

---

124 Robert Gordis, "Love, Marriage, and Business in the Book of Ruth: A Chapter in Hebrew Customary Law," in *A Light unto My Path* (ed. Howard N. Bream, Ralph D. Heim, and Carey A. Moore; Philadelphia: Temple University Press, 1974), 245-46.
125 Zenger, *Ruth*, 28.
126 Campbell, *Ruth*, 24.
127 E.g., Gow, *Ruth*, 205-06. A defence of Davidic rule, however, does not necessarily have to be written during his reign; see Nielsen, *Ruth*, 28.
128 Hubbard, *Ruth*, 34.
129 Moshe Weinfeld, "Ruth, Book of," in *Encyclopaedia Judaica* (Jerusalem: Keter Publishing House, 1996), 14:521-22.
130 Daniel I. Block, *Judges, Ruth* (NAC 6; Nashville: Broadman & Holman, 1999), 594-98.
131 Sasson, *Ruth*, 251.

C. Arguments for Various Dates

Despite the shift in scholarly opinion towards a monarchic date, there is still no consensus. Of nine commentaries, monographs, and articles on Ruth that have emerged so far in the twenty-first century, one argues for a date during the united monarchy,[132] two prefer either a late monarchic or early post-exilic date,[133] four a post-exilic date,[134] and two leave the dating question open.[135] This lack of consensus is related to the subjectivity of the arguments upon which dating is generally determined. Within the context of Biblical Criticism, four main sets of arguments are usually adduced: (1) historical-chronological; (2) theological-ideological; (3) literary-stylistic; and (4) linguistic-philological. In the following discussion some of the data that appeared above in the discussion of specific proposals will be repackaged within the context of methodology. This will demonstrate the malleability of the data.

1. Historical-Chronological

There are a few historical/chronological hints found in the RN, but these can be interpreted differently. For example, the narrative is set "in the days when the Judges judged" (Ruth 1:1), and ends with a genealogy terminating with King David (Ruth 4:18-22). There is even debate surrounding whether the concluding genealogy can provide a *terminus ad quem* for the composition of the work, depending on whether it is viewed as original or a later gloss. Even among those who accept the genealogy as original, there is disagreement about which exact period it might point to.[136] For it points to a time at least from the Davidic dynasty onwards, but how far into the future? Murray Gow argues for a date during David's reign, while Marjo Korpel uses the setting in the time of the Judges to argue for a post-exilic date. Or as Eric Rust argues, does the reference to

---

132 John R. Wilch, *Ruth: A Theological Exposition of Sacred Scripture* (Concordia Commentary; St. Louis: Concordia Publishing House, 2006), 15-16, places the composition of the RN in the latter half of David's reign.

133 Carolyn Pressler, *Joshua, Judges, Ruth* (Westminster Bible Companion; Louisville: Westminster John Knox, 2002); K. Lawson Younger, *Judges and Ruth* (NIV Application Commentary; Grand Rapids: Zondervan, 2002).

134 Fischer, *Rut*; Korpel, *Structure*; LaCocque, *Ruth*; Zevit, "Dating Ruth," 574-600.

135 J. Gordon Harris, Cheryl A. Brown, and Michael S. Moore, *Joshua, Judges, Ruth* (NIBCOT 5; Peabody: Hendrickson, 2000); Eugene F. Roop, *Ruth, Jonah, Esther* (Believers Church Bible Commentary; Scottsdale: Herald, 2002).

136 For a discussion regarding the originality of the genealogy, see, inter alios, LaCocque, *Ruth*, 8-14; Nielsen, *Ruth*, 21-28. Even if the genealogy is not original the narrative would still end by mentioning King David (Ruth 4:17).

Judges mean that the author was familiar with the book of Judges in its final form?[137]

2. Theological-Ideological

It is also frequently argued that the ideology of the RN is a strong pointer to its dating. In particular, its alleged universalist agenda points to a late date: although Ruth is a foreigner, she is nonetheless accepted into Israelite society and subsequently marries Boaz, an Israelite. This is most commonly viewed as propaganda against the EN reforms banning exogamy.[138] At the same time, however, this openness towards outsiders is used by Arndt Meinhold to argue for a pre-exilic date,[139] and M. David for an exilic date.[140] Ronald Hals considers the theology of God's "hidden all-causality" as an outgrowth of the "Solomonic enlightenment."[141] At this time there was a new humanism, and God appears more in the background of events. Yet this theology is also often attributed to the book of Esther, so this motif could support a Persian date.[142]

3. Literary-Stylistic

The third methodological criterion, the literary characteristics of the RN, is also open to interpretation. The peaceful, almost idyllic tone of the story prompts Leon Morris to assign an early monarchic date.[143] Yet this same feature prompts C. Goslinga to assign a Solomonic date,[144] and Robert Gordis a post-exilic date.[145] Dating has also been based on the similarities between Ruth and other HB "novellas" or "short stories." Edward

---

137 Eric C. Rust, *Judges, Ruth, 1 & 2 Samuel* (The Layman's Bible Commentaries; London: SCM, 1961), 69. Rust seems to miss the point that the time of the Judges may have been familiar to the implied reader without reference to a *book of* Judges. Other HB books point to it being a well-known historical period (2 Sam 7:11; 2 Kgs 23:22; 1 Chr 17:6, 10).

138 See, inter alios, LaCocque, *Ruth*; Zakovitch, *Rut*.

139 Arndt Meinhold, "Theologische Schwerpunkte im Buch Ruth und ihr Gewicht für Datierung," *TZ* 32 (1976): 129-37.

140 M. David, "The Date of the Book of Ruth," *OtSt* 1 (1942): 63.

141 Ronald M. Hals, *The Theology of the Book of Ruth* (Philadelphia: Fortress, 1969).

142 Cf. Susan Niditch, "Legends of Wise Heroes and Heroines," in *The Hebrew Bible and Its Modern Interpreters* (ed. Douglas A. Knight and Gene M. Tucker; Philadelphia: Fortress, 1985), 454.

143 Leon Morris, *Ruth: An Introduction and Commentary* (TOTC; Downers Grove: InterVarsity, 1968), 239.

144 C. J. Goslinga, *Joshua, Judges, Ruth* (trans. Ray Togtman, Bible Student's Commentary; Grand Rapids: Zondervan, 1986).

145 Gordis, "Love," 246.

Campbell compares Ruth to other novellas, and suggests a monarchical date.[146] Kirsten Nielsen also proposes a date during the Monarchy, but based on intertextuality, with allusions to the "patriarchal narratives."[147] In contrast, part of André LaCocque's argument for a post-exilic date is based on his thesis that the main point of the RN is "ultimately a commentary on the Law."[148] So his dating for Ruth, in the same way as the other scholars mentioned, rests upon the dating of other texts. He assumes an exilic or post-exilic dating for the prior texts, just as Campbell and Nielsen work from a premise of a monarchical dating for other "novellas."

4. Linguistic-Philological

It is often argued that the dating of Biblical Hebrew provides the most objective criterion to date the RN. According to this approach, language must take precedence over historical and theological arguments.[149] Standard Biblical Hebrew (SBH) is understood to be pre-exilic, while Late Biblical Hebrew (LBH) is post-exilic, with the exile as a transitional period.[150] Frederic Bush has been influential among Ruth scholars in his analysis of the SBH and LBH features found in Ruth.[151] According to Bush, there are ten features that are characteristic of SBH,[152] and eight features

---

146 Campbell, *Ruth*, 24.
147 Nielsen, *Ruth*, 12-17 *et passim*. These include women's stories dealing with infertility and triumph over it: Sarai and Hagar (Gen 16), Lot's daughters (Gen 19), Tamar (Gen 38).
148 LaCocque, *Ruth*, 19.
149 E.g., Avi Hurvitz, "Can Biblical Texts be Dated Linguistically? Chronological Perspectives in the Historical Study of Biblical Hebrew," in *Congress Volume: Oslo 1998* (ed. André Lemaire and Magne Sæbø; VTSup 80; Leiden: Brill, 2000), 144.
150 Major studies include Avi Hurvitz, *A Linguistic Study of the Relationship between the Priestly Source and the Book of Ezekiel* (CahRB 20; Paris: Gabalda, 1982); Robert Polzin, *Late Biblical Hebrew: Toward an Historical Typology of Biblical Hebrew Prose* (HSM 12; Missoula: Scholars Press, 1976); Mark F. Rooker, *Biblical Hebrew in Transition: The Language of the Book of Ezekiel* (JSOTSup 90; Sheffield: JSOT Press, 1990).
151 Those who accept his findings in whole or in part, and its significance for dating include: Linafelt and Beal, *Ruth & Esther*; Matthews, *Judges/Ruth*; Pressler, *Joshua, Judges, Ruth*; Sakenfeld, *Ruth*; Younger, *Judges and Ruth*.
152 These are: (1) the preference for אנכי over אני; (2) the prevalence of the ו-consecutive; (3) the use in temporal clauses of ויהי/והיה כ/ב instead of כ/ב plus infinitive or other substantive; (4) the use of כי instead of אשר to introduce a noun clause of a verb; (5) the predicate-subject rather than subject-predicate in substantival clauses introduced by כי or אשר; (6) the lack of the use of ל rather than את to mark the direct object; (7) the plene spelling of דויד instead of the defectively written דיד; (8) the use of בין...ובין, instead of בין...ל; (9) the failure of the final *nun* of the preposition מן to assimilate before an

that are characteristic of LBH.¹⁵³ Based on these findings he concludes that the author lived no earlier than the transitional period between SBH and LBH, that is, the late pre-exilic to post-exilic era. In his judgement, a date in the early post-exilic period seems more likely.¹⁵⁴

Bush argues that the appearance of a number of LBH features indicates that the book of Ruth is not pre-exilic. Recent research, however, casts doubt on the assumptions behind this. First, almost all the distinctive features of so-called "Late" Biblical Hebrew are also attested in "Early" Biblical Hebrew (EBH) texts.¹⁵⁵ For example, Bush's first LBH feature is the exclusive use of verbal suffixes rather than את plus pronominal suffix.¹⁵⁶ Yet this same preference is also a characteristic of EBH texts such as Nahum, Habakkuk, and long stretches of the "early" book of Kings.¹⁵⁷ Thus, to call the use of verbal suffixes "LBH" means only that they are well-attested in the definitely post-exilic books of Esther, Ezra, Nehemiah, Daniel and Chronicles, and not that they are only attested in a chronologically late period.¹⁵⁸ Their value as evidence for late dating of texts where they appear is thus minimal since they are not demonstrably late in a chronological sense.

One might suggest that the occurrence of so-called LBH linguistic features in EBH texts is due to later scribal updating of the texts. This argument, however, would hold both ways, since there is no reason why the few supposed LBH forms in Ruth are not themselves due to linguistic

---

articulated noun; (10) the sevenfold occurrence of second or third person dual morphemes of common gender. See Bush, *Ruth*, 22-24.

153 These are: (1) the preference for attaching the pronominal object directly to the verb rather than the direct object marker את/אות; (2) the direct attachment of the third feminine suffix to a plural verb ending in –û in contrast to SBH, which regularly attaches masculine pronominal suffixes with such verb forms to the direct object marker and has a similar preference for the same with feminine suffixes; (3) the preference for the preposition ל over אל before the indirect object following the verb אמר and in the phrase ל קרוב (Ruth 2:20); (4) the idiom נשא אשה (1:4) instead of לקח אשה (which is also present in 4:13); (5) the piel form לקים (4:7) instead of הקים, which may be classified as an "Aramaism"; (6) the form ונתן (4:7), reflecting the reduction in the use of the *waw*-consecutive in LBH; (7) the use of the idiom שלף נעל (4:7), which is probably a calque, a new expression created under Aramaic influence; (8) the use of the piel form of the verb שבר (1:13) instead of the SBH synonyms קוה and יחל. See Bush, *Ruth*, 24-30.

154 Bush, *Ruth*, 30. Based on the same understanding of the linguistic development of biblical Hebrew, Zevit also dates the book of Ruth to the early post-exilic period; Zevit, "Dating Ruth," 592-93.

155 Early Biblical Hebrew (EBH) is equivalent to Standard Biblical Hebrew (SBH).

156 Cf. Polzin, *Late Biblical Hebrew*, 28-31; Rooker, *Biblical Hebrew in Transition*, 86-87.

157 Ian Young, "Late Biblical Hebrew and the Qumran Pesher Habakkuk," *Journal of Hebrew Scriptures* 8 (2008): 15-16.

158 The historical setting of these books indicates a post-exilic date.

change in scribal transmission. A number of studies have presented detailed evidence that the language of biblical texts was demonstrably changed in textual transmission.[159] The argument that the current linguistic profile of MT Ruth reflects the language, and hence date, of the original author of Ruth is in serious tension with the findings of recent textual criticism.

Despite these important text-critical considerations, it is in fact demonstrable that so-called LBH linguistic features existed in the pre-exilic era. Despite the limited extent of the corpus of inscriptions from the pre-exilic period, a number of LBH features are found in them. Young, Rezetko and Ehrensvärd identify nine supposed LBH features in the Arad Ostraca from c 600 B.C.E.[160] It is noteworthy that these are more LBH features than Bush claims to find in the book of Ruth, even though Ruth contains more words in more varied linguistic contexts than the Arad corpus.[161] The appearance of these so-called LBH forms in the chronologically-definite pre-exilic inscriptions reveals that the claim to find LBH forms in biblical texts leads to no necessary conclusions about the date of those texts.

The fact that LBH features are found in EBH texts is not a new discovery; it is an accepted feature of the methodology of Avi Hurvitz. Hurvitz suggests criteria for identifying what he calls LBH features, but the decisive criterion for dating texts is the criterion of accumulation.[162] In other words, to be classified as LBH, a text must have a significant accumulation of LBH linguistic features. Hurvitz actually does not define more clearly how great a significant accumulation is, but recently Young, Rezetko and Ehrensvärd have developed a simple test of accumulation in which they sample 28 texts of 500 Hebrew graphic units in length. They found that every text investigated, whether EBH or LBH, has LBH linguistic features.[163] As Hurvitz's methodology suggests, the difference between passages is not the presence of LBH linguistic features, but rather

---

159 There is evidence for linguistic fluidity in the pre-stabilisation text of the Hebrew Bible, with individual linguistic elements being replaced in scribal transmission; see Ian Young, "Biblical Texts Cannot be Dated Linguistically," *HS* 46 (2005): 349-51; Ian Young, Robert Rezetko, and Martin Ehrensvärd, *Linguistic Dating of Biblical Texts* (London: Equinox, 2008), esp. 1:341-60; 2:100-01, and references therein.

160 Young, Rezetko, and Ehrensvärd, *Linguistic Dating*, 1:164-68.

161 The Arad corpus contains around 500 reasonably preserved words, whereas the book of Ruth contains 1280 words. Young, Rezetko, and Ehrensvärd's analysis of the Arad corpus is based on Y. Aharoni, *Arad Inscriptions* (Jerusalem: Israel Exploration Society, 1981).

162 Hurvitz's criteria are: (1) linguistic distribution; (2) linguistic contrast; (3) extra-biblical attestation; and (4) accumulation. See, e.g., Avi Hurvitz, "The Date of the Prose-Tale of Job Linguistically Reconsidered," *HTR* 67 (1974): 17-34; Hurvitz, *A Linguistic Study*.

163 Young, Rezetko, and Ehrensvärd, *Linguistic Dating*, 1:131-36.

that the core LBH texts exhibit a much higher accumulation of these features than the core EBH texts.

Bush's identification of supposed LBH features is inadequate as an argument for the lateness of the RN.¹⁶⁴ The important question is whether Ruth has an accumulation of LBH features greater than other generally accepted EBH texts. The fact that Bush identifies a total of eight features, whereas the pre-exilic Arad Ostraca have nine, or a core EBH text such as 1 Kings 22 has eight, indicates that Ruth's low accumulation of so-called LBH features is characteristic of a classification as an EBH text. In contrast, the lowest accumulation in a core LBH text is seventeen, for Esther 5:1–6:13a.¹⁶⁵ According to the accepted methodology for identifying LBH as used by Hurvitz, the RN is therefore in EBH, not LBH.

Yet the classification of Ruth as EBH has no obvious chronological significance. Texts with low accumulations of LBH features are well attested throughout the post-exilic period, e.g., Pesher Habakkuk from the first century B.C.E.¹⁶⁶ Young, Rezetko and Ehrensvärd argue on the basis of this evidence that EBH and LBH were co-existing styles of Hebrew, used by biblical authors, both early and late.¹⁶⁷ Whether their specific reconstruction is correct, the data presented here is enough to show that the appearance of a small number of links with so-called LBH is of no significance for the dating of Ruth.

D. Conclusions Regarding the Dating of the Book of Ruth

It has been shown that each of the four main arguments for dating the RN is subjective. This includes the previously almost inviolable argument based on linguistic factors. Each of the arguments is subject to the interpreter's presuppositions and interpretation of the available evidence. The aim of this discussion was to demonstrate that it is impossible to date Ruth with absolute certainty due to the many variables and the required interpretation of the available evidence. However, this does not mean that the task of determining the dating of the book of Ruth is a futile exercise; an interpreter can still weigh up the various factors to establish the most plausible date of composition.

---

164 It has been shown that these LBH features are commonly attested in EBH texts, and therefore it is doubtful that they are chronologically late.
165 Young, Rezetko, and Ehrensvärd, *Linguistic Dating*, 1:133.
166 Young, "Pesher Habakkuk," 1-38.
167 Young, Rezetko, and Ehrensvärd, *Linguistic Dating*, esp. 2:96-99. They suggest that EBH and LBH represent two tendencies among scribes of the biblical period: conservative and non-conservative.

In fact, an evaluation of the evidence produces two possible eras for the origin of the RN. An argument based on historical/chronological evidence requires a dating beyond the birth of David, but close enough to allow the readers to have familiarity with the circumstances and milieu of the period of the Judges. It also requires enough time to pass for an explanation of the custom involving the sandal to be necessary.[168] This evidence is equivocal: familiarity with the time of the Judges suggests a monarchic provenance, while an explanation for the custom involving the sandal suggests a later provenance.

Literary/stylistic evidence is also not decisive. The closing genealogy is integral to the overall chiastic structure of the RN, balancing the pseudo-genealogy that opens the book (1:1-5).[169] This being the case, it intimates a monarchic concern in general or a Davidic concern in particular. Within the Monarchic Period, the genealogy may indicate an apologetic concern for David's ancestry, including his Moabite strain. The turmoil following Solomon's death and the struggle to establish the legitimacy of the southern kingdom throughout the time of the divided monarchy seems a particularly germane time for this defence. Within the Persian Period, there is an absence of an Israelite king, so the RN could represent a royalist hope. Hence, either a monarchic or Persian provenance for the RN is possible.

Ideological/theological evidence slightly favours a Persian date. The acceptance of Ruth as a foreigner into the people of God is significant because it is both a prominent theme in the RN, and one that is found relatively infrequently in HB narrative. Hence, it points to a special concern during the time of composition of the RN. Although interaction with non-Israelites is present in accounts of both the Monarchic Period and the Persian Period, the closer interaction with foreigners in the Persian Period is slightly in favour of a Persian origin for the RN.

Overall, then, although the RN could have been composed in either the Monarchic or Persian Periods, a consideration of the above factors slightly favours an origin in the post-exilic period. Nonetheless, due to the tentative nature of this conclusion, the implied reader will, for the moment, be situated generally—from the late Monarchic to the Persian Period. I will state a firm position on the provenance of the RN, however, in Chapter Five, after deriving the emphases of the RN, and the Monarchic and Persian Periods, arising from a social identity approach.

---

168 Of course this assumes that the explanation is part of the "original text." But if the note on the sandal is a later gloss, it tells us nothing about the date of the text.
169 See, inter alios, Stephen Bertman, "Symmetrical Design in the Book of Ruth," *JBL* 84 (1965): 165-68; Bezalel Porten, "The Scroll of Ruth: A Rhetorical Study," *Gratz College Annual* 7 (1978): 23-49.

VIII. Summary and Conclusion

This chapter outlined the predominantly collectivistic or social orientation of the self in ancient Israel, and applied a social identity approach to form a model of ancient Israelite identity. It also discussed the centrality of narrative in identity construction, and how, in turn, narratives can influence identity and behaviour. An implied reader was also described and situated from the late Monarchic Period to the Persian Period. These methodological assumptions will form the lens through which to view the identity and actions of the three main protagonists in the RN in the next three chapters, as well as inform the investigation of the composition and reception of the RN in Chapter Five.

Boaz: Identity and Ethics

In this chapter I explore the relationship between the actions of Boaz and his identity. In the first section I will delineate the individual and social components of his identity as presented in the RN, and then in the second section I will illustrate how the components contribute to his actions. In the final section I will use these findings to analyse Boaz's actions (and inaction) from an identity perspective by comparing and contrasting them to those of his foil—Mr. So-and-So. I will then conclude with some implications for an implied reader.

I. The Identity of Boaz

A. Personal Component

The first description of Boaz apropos his personal self-component is that he is איש גבור חיל (Ruth 2:1). In the HB חיל has the basic meaning "strength, power," and is used in military (of an army), physical (of a man), material (wealth of a person), and moral (virtue of a person) senses.[1] In the context of the RN, the description of Boaz as איש גבור חיל would encompass the last two senses, and גבור implies that Boaz is a particularly fine example.[2] The implied author presents Boaz in chapter 2 as a wealthy landowner. Not only does he possess fields, he also has male servants and female servants, along with a foreman to direct them in their work.

Boaz is also presented as a morally upright man, who even greets his workers with a blessing: "YHWH be with you!" (יהוה עמכם). His reputation is supported by the response of his harvesters, who reciprocate his benediction (2:4). His treatment of Ruth and his workers throughout the chapter support his high moral standing. His careful oversight of his

---

1   See BDB, 298; *HALOT* 1:311-312; H. Eising, "חַיִל," *TDOT* 4:348-355.
2   H. Kosmala, "גָּבַר," *TDOT* 2:373, comments that גבור is an intensive form, and thus means "a particularly strong or mighty person who carries out, or has carried out great deeds, and surpasses others in doing so." Cf. BDB, 1368; *HALOT* 1:172. As Zakovitch, *Rut*, 108, comments, in the case of Boaz it also denotes "ein Mann mit Grundbesitz und einer angesehenen Stellung."

workers is suggested by his immediate recognition of Ruth, a new gleaner unfamiliar to him (2:5). Additionally, he provides food and drink for his workers along with Ruth (2:14), as well as ensuring he grants especial protection for Ruth—as a foreigner—by commanding his male servants not to touch her or rebuke her (2:9, 15-16). Thus, Boaz is presented as a wealthy man who is also honoured and respected by the people who work for him.

The second personal descriptor is the name בעז (2:1). An implied reader in the time of the late monarchy would be aware of the northern pillar in the Solomonic temple named בעז (1 Kgs 7:21; 2 Chron 3:17), and the majority of earlier translations and interpreters make a connection between בעז and "strength."[3] Considering the close apposition of בעז with איש גבור חיל in 2:1, the most appropriate translation is "a pillar of the community," which also conveys an allusion to the Temple.[4] This being the case, not only is Boaz described explicitly as "a man of great worth" (איש גבור חיל), it is also reflected in the symbolic meaning of his name.

B. Social Component

1. Non-Kin: Male Gender

In the RN the male servants are described as performing the strenuous work of harvesting, with the female servants gleaning after them (2:23). Although Boaz was involved in the oversight of the harvesting, the narrative does describe his involvement in the heavy physical labour of harvesting the barley and wheat crops. That he does winnow on the threshing floor after the harvesting is finished contributes to the picture of him as an older man, because winnowing is not as physically demanding.

2. Non-Kin: Elder Generation

Although the RN does not specify whether Boaz was a parent, it does present him both as a member of the elder generation[5] as well as

---

3   The transliterations of the name in LXX and Old Latin as *Boos* support this meaning; Hubbard, *Ruth*, 134. Cf. Robert Gordis, "Personal Names in Ruth - A Note on Biblical Etymologies," *Judaism* 35 (1986): 299.
4   So Fewell and Gunn, *Compromising*, 40.
5   So, e.g., Campbell, *Ruth*, 110-11; H. H. Rowley, "The Marriage of Ruth," in *The Servant of the Lord and Other Essays on the Old Testament* (Oxford: Blackwell, 1965), 192. *Pace* Sasson, *Ruth*, 85.

performing parental functions. As mentioned above, his tasks with regard to harvesting suggest he is less physically able. His description and presentation as "a man of great worth" and the symbolism of his name sustain this view. It is also suggested by Boaz's perspective of Ruth ("Whose young woman is this?" [למי הנערה הזאת; 2:5]), and his description of the rest of the characters in chapter 2 as "young women/men" (נערה and נער; 2:8, 9, 21). Boaz's elder status is confirmed when Ruth reveals she had chosen Boaz to act as a גאל although younger men (הבחורים) were available (3:10).

Additionally, his ability to procure ten elders of the town as witnesses, probably drawing them away from their current work, highlights his social standing in the town (4:2);[6] indeed, Rabbinic interpreters suggest he was one of the town elders.[7] If Boaz and Naomi's speech can be viewed as "old fashioned," this further augments their elder status.[8] Moreover, "my daughter" (בתי; 2:8; 3:10, 11) as Boaz's favourite form of address to Ruth reinforces the generational difference, indicating how Boaz primarily viewed Ruth. Naomi's use of בתי to address her daughter-in-law (1:11, 12, 13; 2:2, 22; 3:1, 16, 18) draws comparisons to Boaz's parental treatment of Ruth in protecting and providing for her (2:8-9, 14-16, 21; 3:15). In the context of the events that transpire on the threshing floor, בתי may also be understood in its further nuance—as a term of endearment indicating his affection for her. The shift in the meaning of the epithet בתי reflects the shift in the way Boaz views Ruth; his paternalistic approach segues smoothly to the romantic.

3. Kin: Clansman of Elimelech

It is pertinent that the kinship aspect of Boaz's identity is emphasised at a crucial juncture in the narrative. Chapter 2 commences with an aside from the author: "Now Naomi had a kinsman of her husband, a man of great worth, from the clan of Elimelech, whose name was Boaz" (2:1). Story time stops as the narrator flags Boaz's significance before he appears in the

---

6   Cf. Block, *Judges, Ruth*, 707.
7   The description of Boaz as an octogenarian, however, may be overestimating his age; *Midr. Ruth Rab.* 6:2.
8   So Campbell, *Ruth*, 25, 110. Myers, *Linguistic and Literary Form*, 20, suggests it could be a "relatively early dialectical peculiarity." Cf. Ian Young, "Evidence of Diversity in Pre-Exilic Hebrew," *HS* 38 (1997): 10, who interprets the unusual linguistic forms as indicating that Boaz and Naomi originated from Bethlehem, and Gow, *Ruth*, 195, who suggests it is a marker of a "rural dialect."

next scene.⁹ At the end of chapter 1 the implied reader is left with the question: who will be the one to reverse Naomi's emptiness? This pause, following directly from the previous chapter, then presents Boaz as the prime candidate for this task. Not only does Boaz have the material means to assuage Naomi's emptiness, he also has the moral fibre, suggesting that he would be willing to do so (as איש גבור חיל).

Moreover, as a "relative" (מודע;¹⁰ 2:1) he is further qualified to assist in ameliorating her destitution because he can potentially function in the role of גאל. The pivotal importance of this aspect of Boaz's identity is indicated by its repetition both at the beginning (2:1, 3) and end of the chapter, where Naomi points out:

> The man is a close relative of ours, he is one of our kinsman-redeemers (מגאלנו; 2:20).¹¹

The anticipation of an implied reader is raised further during the chapter, through Boaz's explanation of his generous actions toward Ruth:

> It has been fully revealed to me all that you have done for your mother-in-law after the death of your husband (2:11).

Boaz knows about Ruth's familial relationship to Naomi, and hence to him through the clan of Elimelech, albeit distantly and indirectly. At this stage in proceedings Boaz may not necessarily be treating Ruth well because she is distantly related by marriage. Indeed, his explanation is that it is in response to the kindness Ruth had shown Naomi. Nevertheless, as מודע from the same משפחה, Boaz is placed front and centre as the one to reverse Naomi's emptiness through his role as גאל. Hence, the anticipation felt by an implied reader after the introduction of Boaz as from the same משפחה as Elimelech is raised further by his actions in providing for Ruth and Naomi throughout chapter 2.

---

9   In narrative terms, this pause extends the discourse time and foregrounds the mediation of events by the narrator.

10 This meaning of מודע is clarified by its only other usage in the HB, Prov 7:4, where its feminine form (מודעת) appears in a parallel clause with "sister."

11 In the HB, a גאל is a family member with the following responsibilities: (1) to receive payment of atonement money (Num 5:5-8); (2) the redemption of blood, or to act as an "avenger of blood" (Num 35:9-28; Deut 19:4-13); (3) the redemption of relatives who have been sold into slavery to a foreigner (Lev 25:47-54); and (4) the redemption of property when land has been sold outside the family (Lev 25:24-25). In the context of the narrative, it seems unlikely that Naomi is using גאל in one of these technical senses. Here it is used more generally, in a way which parallels God's actions on behalf of his people. Cf. Ringgren, *TDOT* 2:352-353. Nonetheless, an implied reader might be considering how Boaz might act in one of the technical senses.

4. Kin: Israelite

Boaz's national identity as an Israelite is implicit to the RN. An Israelite enjoyed the privilege of an inheritance of land from YHWH, but it also involved providing for those who did not directly benefit from the usufruct of the land. In particular, the widow (אלמנה), the fatherless (יתום), and the alien (גר) form a marginalised social group[12] devoid of the provision and protection of an Israelite adult male.[13] Israelite law provides welfare measures for the *personae miserae* through the presentation of a triennial tithe composed of all produce harvested from the land (Deut 14:22-29; 26:12-15).[14] Additionally, every seventh year the land was to be left fallow, and its produce was to be left for the poor (אביני; Exod 23:10-11; cf. Lev 25:1-7).

In the RN, the last legal provision for the needy is found—gleaning. At harvest time an Israelite landowner was to leave a portion of his field, grapevine, or olive grove unharvested for the poor, the widow, the fatherless, and the alien to collect (Lev 19:9-10; 23:22; Deut 24:19-21). Yet the number of times this special provision is mentioned in the Law suggests this was not always followed by landowners (Exod 22:22-24; Lev 19:9-10; 23:22; Deut 10:18; 14:29; 16:11; 24:17). The repeated exhortation of the Prophets indicates this was an ongoing problem.[15] In the RN, this is reflected in Ruth's request to Naomi: "Please let me go to the field and glean among the ears of grain after him *in whose sight I may find favour*" (אשר אמצא חן בעיניו; Ruth 2:2). That is, she feels that she needs to gain permission from the harvesters or the landowner before being allowed to

---

12 The protection of the weak was a common concept in the ancient Near East, found in the literature of Mesopotamia and Egypt. See, e.g., F. Charles Fensham, "Widow, Orphan, and the Poor in Ancient Near Eastern Legal and Wisdom Literature," *JNES* 21 (1962): 129-39; Norbert Lohfink, "Poverty in the Laws of the Ancient Near East and of the Bible," *TS* 52 (1991): 34-50. The HB is distinctive, however, in its concern for the גר.

13 In addition to the provision of economic support, a male provided protection and legal representation. Thus, a lack of a male advocate also left this marginalised social group open to being exploited and defrauded. Cf. Ronald E. Clements, "Poverty and the Kingdom of God - An Old Testament View," in *The Kingdom of God and Human Society: Essays by Members of the Scripture, Theology and Society Group* (ed. Robin Barbour; Edinburgh: T&T Clark, 1993), 15-16.

14 The Levites are also included as beneficiaries because they were without inherited land (Deut 14:29; 26:12-13).

15 For instance, Isa 1:21-23; 10:1-2; Amos 5:11-15; 8:4-6; Mic 3:1-3; cf. Job 24:3, 21; Ps 94:6.

glean in a particular field.¹⁶ This background thus provides the context for the actions of Boaz as an Israelite landowner.

II. The Actions of Boaz

The connection between the identity of Boaz and his actions will now be examined. In particular, I will draw attention to how his actions are related to components of his identity. These actions will be analysed in order of their presentation in the RN.

A. Chapter 2

In chapter 2 Boaz is presented as exceeding the minimum requirements of the gleaning law. Not only does Boaz permit Ruth to glean in his field, she is also afforded extra protection and water (2:8-9). Ruth's response reveals that Boaz's generosity is beyond her expectations (2:10). Nevertheless, while Boaz exceeds the minimum requirements of the gleaning law in allowing Ruth to glean in his field, Jack Sasson insightfully points out that, at this stage, Boaz only exceeds "the 'correct' behavior expected of a *gibbôr ḥayil*" by a small margin.¹⁷ Following the introduction to Boaz at the beginning of the chapter, the implied readers would be anticipating more.

By the end of chapter 2, however, there is unequivocal evidence that he exceeds all expectations. Boaz makes four supplemental provisions in this chapter. First, during mealtime he provides her with enough food to eat until sated, and then provides extra to take away for her mother-in-law (2:14, 18). The provision of the meal for Ruth in itself reinforces his generosity, because as a foreigner gleaning in the field it is not expected that she would eat with the rest of the male harvesters.¹⁸ Second, after mealtime Boaz emphatically gives his young men two specific instructions: allow her to glean among the sheaves; and deliberately pull out some stalks

---

16   So most commentators, e.g., Block, *Judges, Ruth*, 652-53; Fewell and Gunn, *Compromising*, 35. *Pace* Bush, *Ruth*, 104.
17   Sasson, *Ruth*, 49.
18   Her reticence and surprise in response to the invitation is found within the text, yet her treatment as a special guest would have further increased her astonishment. Not only is she served the basic staple food that has been brought for the harvesters, she is also offered an accompaniment to enhance her dining experience. Furthermore, she is served roasted grain by Boaz himself (2:14). In a word, she does not eat the scraps as a beggar; she eats heartily as a special guest.

for her to pick up (2:15-16).¹⁹ Third, she is granted protection from the other workers (2:15-16). Fourth, Boaz's munificence towards Ruth is not just a singular gesture; she is invited to glean in his field until the end of the barley and wheat harvests (2:23).²⁰

Thus, Boaz's superabundant generosity confirms him as "a man of great worth." That is, his actions reflect the virtue of his personal character, one marked by compassion, kindness, and charity. This is brought into sharper relief when it is placed within the socioeconomic and cultural realities of his time, and to whom his actions are directed. For Ruth the Moabitess is a foreigner as well as a widow, and hence one living on the fringes of, and heavily dependent upon society.

In short, Boaz's actions may be understood to be the result of at least two aspects of his identity: his Israelite nationality and his personal identity as a pillar of the community. Based on the ancient Israelite identity model from Chapter One, these are the outermost and the innermost concentric circles, respectively. Yet Boaz hints at another aspect of his identity after Ruth exclaims

> "Why have I found favour in your eyes, that you should take notice of me, since I am a foreigner?"

> Boaz replied, "It has been fully revealed to me, all that you have done for your mother-in-law after the death of your husband; how you left your father and your mother, and the land of your birth, and came to a people you did not know previously" (2:10-11).

The motivation Boaz provides for his actions towards Ruth is as notable for what he does not reveal as what he does reveal. The stated reason for his action is clear enough: it is in response to what he has been told apropos Ruth's remarkable decision to leave her parents and her homeland to cast her lot with her mother-in-law in a strange land among a strange people. The implication is that he is impressed by her actions and in some way wants to repay her for her loyalty to her mother-in-law. That this idea of retributive justice is central to his thinking is revealed in his ensuing invocation that YHWH would richly reward her for her actions (2:12).

Yet concerning the question Ruth poses to Boaz, inferences that can be adduced from the narrative context are almost more revealing. For an

---

19   For a discussion of the emphasis of "even between the sheaves" deriving from its placement at the front of the clause, and "deliberately pull out some stalks" deriving from the use of the infinitive absolute with the finite verb (של תשלו), see Bush, *Ruth*, 126. A concrete measure of the extent of Boaz's generosity is the quantity of barley she takes home that evening—כאיפה (2:17). This is the equivalent to between thirty and fifty pounds.
20   For a discussion of Boaz's actions within the "hospitality protocol," see Matthews, *Judges/Ruth*, 227-28.

implied reader of the RN, there are at least three inferences. The first inference is that he is acting out of obedience to the gleaning law, which he maintains because he is איש גבור חיל. He cannot verbalise this reason because this would be acting contrary his virtuous character; this would constitute boasting. Nonetheless, an implied reader is led to understand this as one explanation for his actions (2:1), although it would be an incomplete answer. For though Boaz might provide generously for destitute and needy people who happen to wander onto his field, it would be difficult to imagine he would treat all *personae miserae* with such generous abandon.[21]

The second inference is that he has a romantic interest in Ruth. Danna Fewell and David Gunn, and Tod Linafelt even suggest that Boaz is sexually interested in Ruth from the start. According to these scholars, the first hint is found in Boaz's query of his foreman: "Whose young woman (נערה) is this?" From this query Fewell and Gunn infer that Boaz is sexually attracted to Ruth at first sight.[22] Linafelt adds that other uses of נערה in the HB have sexual connotations.[23] Within chapter 2, sexual overtones are found in Boaz's instructions to his נערים not to molest Ruth (2:9, 16), and in Naomi's instructions for Ruth to stay close to the נערות instead of the נערים (2:22). The foreman's description of Ruth as a Moabite נערה might also be an allusion "to a stereotyped view of Moabite women as sexually available and even aggressive."[24]

Fewell and Gunn, and Linafelt's reconstruction is unconvincing because it reads against the grain of the story. Although sexual attraction is possible, from the presentation of Boaz in the narrative this seems unlikely; rather, it would be better to view his interest at this early stage in their relationship as springing from a combination of admiration for her past actions and a concern for his workers. This would be consistent with the narrator's presentation of Boaz as איש גבור חיל, particularly its moral component. The dangers of molestation from the נערים (including sexual) thus serve to highlight Boaz's protection of Ruth, in addition to the providence of YHWH in directing Ruth to the field owned by Boaz.

Nonetheless, Fewell and Gunn, and Linafelt are correct in identifying the sexual tension in chapter 2, as well as chapter 3. Robert Alter points to

---

21 One might also suggest that if his reputation was so well known in the community, all needy people would be drawn to him, and so they would all be found gleaning in his field and eating together with him and his workers. But the only person described eating with Boaz, indeed, being personally served by him in the narrative, is Ruth.

22 Fewell and Gunn, *Compromising*, 40-41.

23 Linafelt and Beal, *Ruth & Esther*, 30-31. נערה also connotes a woman of marriageable age and situation (e.g., Gen 24:14, 16; Deut 22:15, 16; 1 Kgs 1:3, 4), a concubine (e.g., Judg 19), and possibly a prostitute (Amos 2:7); see H. F. Fuhs, "נער," *TDOT* 9:483-484.

24 Linafelt and Beal, *Ruth & Esther*, 31. See Gen 19:30-38; 25:1-5.

an allusion to the betrothal type-scene in chapter 2.[25] In contrast to the typical betrothal type-scene, however, Alter notes that the author rotates the version in the RN "180 degrees on the axes of gender and geography."[26] Hence, the allusion to the type scene flags the *romantic potential* between Ruth and Boaz to the implied reader. Throughout the chapter, the implied author is planting the seeds of relational development in the reader's mind, but there is no concrete evidence that Boaz is romantically, let alone sexually attracted to Ruth at this early stage in their relationship.

The third inference is that Boaz is obligated to provide for Ruth as a relative. Boaz's response to Ruth—"It has been fully revealed to me, all that you have done *for your mother-in-law*"—suggests he shows such open-handed generosity because she is a member of his clan. There are three possible factors, however, against Boaz feeling a kinship obligation towards Ruth. First, a widow without a son to bind her to the clan is a peripheral member of the clan at best; she is not a true blood relation of the kinship group. Second, Ruth is a נכריה from a country with whom Israel felt animosity. Third, Boaz had not even seen her previously, let alone met her. Yet despite these factors, that Boaz's actions at least in part spring from kinship obligation seems to be an inference the implied author wants the implied reader to draw. Boaz's relation to Naomi—from the same clan as her deceased husband Elimelech—is mentioned twice in the chapter prior to Boaz's response to Ruth (2:1, 3), and the foreman's description of Ruth as "the Moabitess who came back from Moab *with Naomi*" (עם נעמי; 2:6) highlights Ruth's relation to Naomi. Set within this context, Boaz's speech may be understood as a direct response to Ruth's emphasis on her foreignness:

Ruth: Why have I found favour in your eyes … since I am a foreigner (נכריה)?

Boaz: I've been told all about what you have done for your mother-in-law (חמותך) since the death of your husband (אישך).

Ruth cannot comprehend why Boaz would treat her with such generosity, especially since she is a foreigner. Boaz, of course, knows that she is a member of his clan through marriage. Yet his response is framed in such a way that he does not imply *to Ruth* that she is actually a member of his clan, not a foreigner. Concurrently, there is still enough evidence for *an implied reader* to infer that he is in effect correcting her false assumption

---

25 Robert Alter, *The Art of Biblical Narrative* (New York: Basic Books, 1981), 51-60.

26 Alter, *Biblical Narrative*, 58. In the standard betrothal type-scene the protagonist is a male, who goes to a foreign land, where he meets his future wife near a well (e.g., Gen 24, 29; Exod 2). For a recent re-examination of the betrothal type-scene, see Michael W. Martin, "Betrothal Journey Narratives," *CBQ* 70 (2008): 505-23(14-15).

regarding her nationality. Understood in this way, this produces a dramatic irony: the reader knows she is a fellow clansperson, whereas Ruth at this stage is in the dark.

While the first two inferences drawn from Boaz's response only serve to paint a more complete picture for his motivations, the third inference provides another component of his identity that contributes to his actions. His actions do not derive solely from aspects of his personal self-component, as either deriving from or upholding his reputation as איש גבור חיל, or because he has an especial interest in Ruth. Boaz's actions are also mobilised by an aspect of his social identity, as a fellow clansperson of Ruth.

B. Chapter 3

The elements of Boaz's identity introduced in chapter 2 are developed further in chapter 3. His actions in this chapter can be viewed as either consistent with his personal self-component, or as deriving from responsibilities associated with his social self-component.

The turning point and climax of chapter 3, and arguably the RN, occurs in the interchange between Ruth and Boaz on the threshing floor.[27] At the beginning of the chapter, Naomi physically and mentally prepares Ruth for the encounter on the threshing floor (3:1-5). Ruth follows her mother-in-law's instructions precisely (3:6), and then the decisive moment arrives when she speaks with Boaz (3:7-13). While there have been many proposals apropos Boaz's motivations and actions in this scene, the following analysis will focus on the aspect of identity.

Boaz's personal interest in Ruth was noted in our discussion of Boaz's actions in chapter 2. I argued that his actions towards Ruth primarily derived from kinship obligations, but I also mentioned that the narrator hinted at the possibility of romantic interest. The seed of possibility now comes into fruition under the firm inducement of Ruth (3:9):

Boaz: Who are you?

Ruth: I am Ruth, your maid-servant. Spread the corner of your garment over your maid-servant, for you are a kinsman-redeemer.

Some commentators understand Ruth's response as a sexual advance.[28] On the basis of comparison with biblical and extrabiblical uses of the idiom, it

---

27 Cf. Campbell, *Ruth*, 130.
28 E.g., D. R. G. Beattie, "Ruth III," *JSOT* 5 (1978): 41-43.

is better to understand this as a marriage proposal.²⁹ Indeed, this appears to be Boaz's understanding (3:10-12):

> Boaz: May you be blessed by YHWH, my daughter. You have made this last kindness greater than the first in that you have not gone after young men, whether poor or rich. And now, my daughter, do not fear. All that you have asked, I will do for you. For all my fellow townsmen know that you are a woman of great worth.

Boaz's response to Ruth's advance can be understood as his personal interest expressed in a manner consistent with other aspects of his identity. His initial response is consistent with his standing as a pillar of society in the moral sense. He reflexively prays that YHWH would bless her, and understands this proposal as an act of kindness greater than the first kindness. As most commentators suggest, the first kindness most likely refers to Ruth's loyalty displayed in her decision to assist her mother-in-law, and in the process forsaking the relative comfort of her homeland (cf. 2:11). However, it is less clear what is intended by the "last kindness."

On one level, Boaz seems delighted and even flattered that Ruth would choose him from among an array of younger eligible men (3:10).³⁰ On this basis Ruth is understood to be showing further kindness to him by selecting him, despite his more elderly status.³¹ Additionally, his description of her as "a woman of worth" (אשת חיל; 3:11) seems to reinforce this understanding of Boaz to Ruth's proposal: he views her as a woman who would make an ideal wife (cf. Prov 31:10-31), and the author hints that they are a suitable match (cf. 2:1).³² His subsequent actions in the remainder of chapter 3 reflect and reinforce the personal component of his identity. After their discussion Boaz advises Ruth to stay for the night and then makes sure she leaves before her presence could be noticed by anyone else. His provision of barley for Ruth to take back to Naomi can be understood in a number of ways,³³ including as a measure to preserve their

---

29 See especially Paul A. Kruger, "The Hem of Garment in Marriage: The Meaning of the Symbolic Gesture in Ruth 3:9 and Ezek 16:8," *JNSL* 12 (1984): 79-86, and also Campbell, *Ruth*, 123. Cf. Rashi's comment to 3:9.

30 Cf. Bush, *Ruth*, 181; Linafelt and Beal, *Ruth & Esther*, 57.

31 Boaz's self-reference is overly depreciatory. He is not too old to supervise in his field, and he is able to spend the night on the threshing floor. He is also respected by his workers as well as fellow townspeople. Moreover, he is characterised as "a man of great worth" (איש גבור חיל), both in moral and material senses.

32 Cf. Campbell, *Ruth*, 124-25; Fischer, *Rut*, 214-15. Contra Linafelt and Beal, *Ruth & Esther*, 58, who view it as "one more marker of the ironic reversal between this supposed 'man of strength' ... and supposed lowly servant" [*sic*].

33 Nielsen, *Ruth*, 79, simply understands it as further evidence of Boaz's kindness. On a thematic level, scholars suggest that the grain ("seed") symbolises offspring, and within this understanding there is a "filling" of Naomi's emptiness. Not only has Boaz provided

reputations in case she is discovered as she returns from the threshing floor (cf. 3:14).[34] Also deriving from his personal reputation is the understanding that Boaz sent this gift to Naomi as a sign of good faith, viz. that he will pursue the matter of marriage to its conclusion: either he would marry Ruth or ensure the nearer kinsman-redeemer does.[35] Naomi's response to Ruth's explanation for the provision of barley would support this understanding (3:18).

On another level, Boaz's speech indicates that he interprets this "last kindness" as relating to obligations deriving from his social self-component. Although commentators are divided over whether Ruth consciously links the request for marriage with the responsibilities of a גאל in its strictly legal sense, this appears to be how Boaz understands it. Yet in responding to Ruth's request Boaz chooses his words deliberately, ensuring he does not make any rash promises. Instead of declaring outright that he would marry her, he responds somewhat obscurely:

כל אשר תאמרי אעשה לך (All that you ask I will do for you; 3:11)

The meaning of this becomes clearer as he explains that there is a nearer kinsman-redeemer holding the priority of redemption (3:12). That Boaz draws a connection between redemption and marriage is evidenced in the promise he makes to Ruth (3:13):

If he will redeem you (יגאלך), good; let him redeem (יגאל). But if he is not willing to redeem you (לגאלך), as surely as YHWH lives, then I will redeem you (וגאלתיך).

The repetition of גאל in Boaz's speech ensures that Ruth does not miss the centrality of the concept, nor the implied reader.

Yet the exact form of redemption is not clear at this point in the narrative. Although Boaz is qualified to accept the responsibility of גאל, Ruth does not fit into the biblical legal categories of redemption (person or blood), even most broadly conceived. She does not fit under the category of land redemption either. Although it turns out that land is part of what Boaz has in mind, this would not be the understanding of an implied reader because there has been no previous mention of Naomi or Ruth owning property in the narrative.[36] Hence, at this stage in the narrative גאל

---

for Naomi and Ruth with food, the grain is seen to represent a down-payment for the provision of an heir for Naomi.

34   Cf. Hubbard, *Ruth*, 222; Josephus, *Ant.* 5.331 (Thackeray, LCL).

35   Cf. Bush, *Ruth*, 187; Campbell, *Ruth*, 138.

36   It is likely that the *historical* readers of the book of Ruth would have understood the nuance of "redemption" Boaz is employing here, since they would have been aware of the legal and social customs from which this text derived. Cf. Beattie, "Ruth III," 39-40, who states that in order for a story to function as a story it must be coherent, intelligible,

makes the most sense if it is still used in a general sense of "delivering a member of one's kinship group … from evil of any kind."[37]

As a response to Ruth's proposition, גאל thus refers to her long-term "redemption," which would be effected through her marriage to a kinsman-redeemer. As the narrative transpires, this is inextricably linked to the redemption of land. Yet Boaz still points out that the presence of a nearer kinsman-redeemer means the right of redemption must be first offered to him. Although Boaz has pledged a personal responsibility to Ruth, he does not let this override his social obligations to the nearer kinsman. In short, despite Boaz's newly aroused romantic interest in Ruth, his actions are still constrained by his social identity as a clansman.

C. Chapter 4

The relationship between components of Boaz's identity and his actions in chapter 4 revolve around the transaction at the town gate. Central to this transaction is Boaz's linkage of land redemption and marriage, the focus of which is his proposal to the nearer kinsman-redeemer, a famous *crux interpretum* in the book of Ruth (4:5):

"On the day you acquire the field from the hand of Naomi ומאת רות המואביה אשת המת קניתי/קניתה in order to maintain the name of the deceased on his inheritance."

The plethora of suggested readings of this verse and the lack of scholarly consensus indicates the difficulty in interpreting this verse. Debate centres on two key words: ומאת and קניתי/קניתה.

a) ומאת

There are three main proposals for understanding ומאת. The first emends ומאת to גם אתת[38] or גם את ("and"/"also").[39] This proposal is followed by the majority of interpreters.[40] Nonetheless, in principle, it would be preferable

---

credible, and self-sufficient. Since we are dealing with *implied* readers in this study, we are restricted to what can be derived from the text as encoded by the implied author.

37 Bush, *Ruth*, 137.
38 *BHS*.
39 E.g., Gillis Gerleman, *Ruth. Das Hohelied* (BKAT 18; Neukirchen-Vluyn: Neukirchener Verlag, 1965), 35; Paul Joüon, *Ruth: Commentaire philologique et exégétique* (Rome: Pontifical Biblical Institute, 1924), 83; Sasson, *Ruth*, 122.
40 For a list of those who favour גם את, see Donald A. Leggett, *The Levirate and Goel Institutions in the Old Testament* (Cherry Hill: Mack, 1974), 224, fn. 53, and those since

to maintain the MT if an acceptable translation can be derived from it.⁴¹ The second proposal is "and from" (את + מן + ו). This interpretation suggests the field is to be acquired (קנה)⁴² from both Naomi and Ruth. The main problem with this interpretation is that this would contradict 4:9-10, where Boaz declares he is acquiring the land exclusively from Naomi.⁴³ Additionally, while it is possible Naomi and Ruth possessed the rights over portions of the field,⁴⁴ it is unlikely that they are co-possessors of the undivided field of Elimelech.

The third and preferred reading for ומאת understands the מ in ומאת as enclitic. This is the best syntactic fit, as well as maintaining the integrity of the MT. An enclitic מ yields the translation "and/also" (את + מ enclitic + ו), which finds biblical corroboration in Neh 5:11.⁴⁵ Gary Rendsburg suggests that, syntactically, the ו + enclitic מ functions as an emphasising con-

---

1974 include Fischer, *Rut*, 229; Zakovitch, *Rut*, 157. Those who favour וגם את include Gerleman, *Ruth*, 35; Hubbard, *Ruth*, 237, fn. 8. Both these proposals obviously facilitate assimilations.

41   This is the approach adopted in *BHQ*, which indicates maintaining the MT. Yet the textual witnesses (LXX and Targum) and the translations (Vulgate, Old Latin, and Syriac) cited as support are all ambiguous at this point. So although the proposal in *BHQ* differs from its predecessor by not providing a suggested emendation to the MT, an ambiguous meaning is still hinted at through the supporting evidence.

42   קנה here corresponds to Boaz's declaration of Naomi's intention to מכר the land that belonged to Elimelech (4:3). מכר most commonly means "to sell," but in light of socio-legal customs surrounding land ownership in Israel deriving from YHWH's sole ownership of the land, it most probably does not denote an economic transaction involving the transfer of land for a sum of money; *pace* Campbell, *Ruth*, 145. מכר is most likely being used in its less common denotation of "hand over," as it is in Lev 25; cf. E. Lipiński, "מכר," *TDOT* 8:292; *DCH* 5:271. In Ruth 4:3 then, it means to hand over the rights to or usufruct of the land. Within this context, קנה means "to acquire" the rights of usufruct of the land. Cf. E. Lipiński, "קָנָה," *TDOT* 13:59.

43   Cf. Rudolph, *Ruth*, 59.

44   In light of biblical evidence, it seems unlikely that Naomi, as a widow, would inherit land from her deceased husband, especially since land is generally passed down within the father's house or clan on the male side. Indeed, as Raymond Westbrook, *Property and Family in Biblical Laws* (JSOTSup 113; Sheffield: Sheffield Academic, 1991), 65, notes, it is not clear that women could own property at all, since the few biblical references involve women with sons, who stand to inherit the land at maturity. The categorisation of widows with orphans and aliens as groups of people who require especial protection and provision suggests that widows did not normally inherit property (e.g., Deut 10:18; 24:19-21; 26:12-13, etc.). Thus, as some commentators propose, it seems likely that Naomi inherited the field of Elimelech only in the sense of usufructuary rights, and the right to transfer it within the clan of Elimelech. So, e.g., Bush, *Ruth*, 204; E. Lipiński, "Le mariage de Ruth," *VT* 26 (1976): 125-26. As a widow, Naomi probably held these rights until she passed the property onto a suitable heir, married again, or died.

45   Constance Wallace, "*WM*- in Nehemiah 5:11," in *Eblaitica: Essays on the Ebla Archives and Eblaite Language* (ed. Cyrus H. Gordon, Gary A. Rendsburg, and Nathan H. Winter; Winona Lake: Eisenbrauns, 1987), 31.

junction, and can be translated "indeed, even, verily, yea."⁴⁶ Hence, the acquisition of the field and the acquisition of Ruth are two separate transactions, with emphasis on the second transaction.

In sum, the first proposal with its variations and the third proposal can yield the same translation: "and/also," introducing a second transaction in addition to the acquisition of the land from Naomi. Thus, even if the enclitic מ were not accepted, the first proposal, as the next preferred option, would yield the same translation. Nonetheless, the third proposal is preferable because it maintains the integrity of the MT.

b) קניתי/קניתה

Although some recent scholars argue for the *ketib* reading קָנִיתִי ("I acquire"), the *qere* reading קָנִיתָה ("you acquire") is preferable. The following analysis will focus on a particular strand of the argument for the *ketib* reading over the *qere* reading: the underlying understanding concerning whether it is justifiable to attribute a levirate element to the transaction taking place in chapter 4. Ziony Zevit argues for the *ketib* reading on two grounds: legal and syntactic.⁴⁷

Legally, the *qere* reading links role of *gōʾēl* to that of levir and "implies that the latter was obligatory, facts about which Mr. Almoni was totally unaware."⁴⁸ The *qere* reading also assumes that the levirate law of Deut 25:5-10 was in effect, when, Zevit argues, there is no evidence in the narrative that this was in fact the case. He adds that even if the law was in effect, it does not fulfil the requirements of Deut 25.

In response to Zevit, I would suggest it is not that Mr. So-and-So is unaware of the connection, but that he is unaware of its full implications in the presented case. Indeed, there is biblical evidence for an intimate link between name, offspring, and inheritance (esp. Gen 48:6; Num 27:4; Deut 25:5-10; 2 Sam 14:7; Ps 113:9); the "name" of a man was primarily preserved through the inheritance of his property by his descendants.⁴⁹ Hence, Eryl Davies is correct in stating: "[B]y insisting that the kinsman should undertake the double obligation of marrying the widow and

---

46 Gary A. Rendsburg, "Eblaite *U-MA* and Hebrew *WM-*," in *Eblaitica: Essays on the Ebla Archives and Eblaite Language* (ed. Cyrus H. Gordon, Gary A. Rendsburg, and Nathan H. Winter; Winona Lake: Eisenbrauns, 1987), 38. While his discussion of ו + enclitic מ is compelling, our opinions diverge concerning the second clause of Ruth 4:5, and hence I disagree with his translation of ומאת with "but, however."

47 Zevit, "Dating Ruth," 598-99.

48 Zevit, "Dating Ruth," 598-99.

49 Cf. Bush, *Ruth*, 223.

redeeming the property, Boaz was simply making explicit what had always been implicit in the levirate duty."[50] A practical implication of this is when the alienated land belongs to a childless widow, redemption of it "triggers the levirate duty."[51] This is because the principle undergirding both institutions is the same: redemption restores to the family the property that is lost (or is at threat of being lost) by alienation; the levirate institution "restores a family to its property from which it is separated by extinction of the male line."[52]

In the RN, Mr. So-and-So appears to be aware of this close linkage; indeed, he does not respond by arguing that it is an invalid connection when it is presented to him.[53] What he is probably unaware of is with whom the levirate marriage will apply.[54] Correctly presuming that the widow will be Naomi, who is beyond childbearing age, he accepts, because this would be an attractive economic proposition. Yet when Boaz points out that the levirate obligation would apply to pre-menopausal Ruth,[55] Mr So-and-So refuses on the basis that this would impair his inheritance (4:6).[56] Hence, evidence points against Zevit's first objection to the *qere* reading.

---

50 Eryl W. Davies, "Ruth IV 5 and the Duties of the Go'el," *VT* 33 (1983): 233.
51 Westbrook, *Property*, 67. Cf. Herbert C. Brichto, "Kin, Cult, Land, and Afterlife - A Biblical Complex," *HUCA* 44 (1973): 15-16; David Daube, *Ancient Jewish Law: Three Inaugural Lectures* (Leiden: Brill, 1981), 38.
52 Westbrook, *Property*, 64.
53 Furthermore, neither do the elders overrule.
54 Cf. Davies, "Duties," 233-34.
55 In view of 1:19; 2:11; and 3:11, it is improbable that Mr. So-and-So was unaware of the existence of Ruth, and her relation to the clan of Elimelech. The substitution of Ruth for Naomi is the most likely factor that caught Mr. So-and-So off-guard and caused him to change his mind. So, e.g., Bush, *Ruth*, 232; Campbell, *Ruth*, 159; Rudolph, *Ruth*, 67. While it is presented within the narrative as an accepted practice, and so presumably also for the implied readers, there is no consensus regarding the basis for the substitution. Joüon, *Ruth*, 10, and Lipiński, "Le mariage," 127, suggest it is similar to the custom that allowed servants to be substituted for infertile patriarchal wives (e.g., Gen 16:1-3; 30:1-6, 9-13). Thomas Thompson and Dorothy Thompson, "Some Legal Problems in the Book of Ruth," *VT* 18 (1968): 98, suggest that as a daughter-in-law, Ruth was dependent on Elimelech's estate and was thus presumed to have "a claim on the estate for a potential heir." If this is the case, it would be expected that this principle would be common knowledge, and thus also known to Mr. So-and-So. Therefore, the most likely suggestion is that of Davies, "Duties," 233-34, who suggests that Naomi voluntarily renounced her right as widow due to her advanced age.
56 An explanation of how marriage to Ruth would impair his inheritance follows infra. The substitution of Ruth for Naomi also explains the necessity for the transaction to take place at the town gate. Considering that levirate marriage would be a moral, not legal obligation (especially to Ruth instead of Naomi), it is conceivable Mr. So-and-So could have objected to Boaz's proposal that he must marry Ruth if he accepts the privilege of

The second component of Zevit's first objection to the *qere* reading is that there is "no evidence in the narrative" the levirate law of Deut 25 was in effect. However, at least seven possible allusions to the levirate institution can be found in the RN (1:11-13; 2:20; 3:9-13; 4:7-8, 9-10, 11-12, 16-17).[57] Each allusion in isolation might not be sufficient evidence to establish the case for a link to the levirate institution, but taken as a whole, their cumulative force is strongly in favour of this interpretation. In large part, Zevit's objection to the presence of the levirate law in the RN is based on divergences from the specific wording and descriptions found in the levirate law (Deut 25:5-10). Thus, he asserts that even if the levirate law were in effect, it would be irrelevant since those involved were not "brothers dwelling together," and "nothing like" the sandal ceremony is described in Ruth.

Such a position derives from an understanding of the law as having a limited application: only describing the specific and comprehensive circumstances in which it can be applied. As Westbrook rightly comments, however, this is not a valid approach to ancient Near Eastern law.

> Ancient Near Eastern jurisprudence failed to develop the tools of legal logic necessary for the formulation of general principles, and consequently its "law codes" are not codes at all, but seldom more than collections of decisions in individual cases which, of course, refer only to particular aspects of the legal institution involved. The laws in Deuteronomy are no exception to this rule, and it applies all the more so to law in the narratives, where the writer assumes knowledge of the law on the part of the reader and only concerns himself with some unusual, and for that reason interesting, application thereof.[58]

As described above, there are two unusual aspects of the application of the redemption and levirate laws in the RN: (1) the levirate law is also triggered by the application of the redemption law; and (2) because the widow involved is post-menopausal, the task of producing a descendant passes to the widow who is still fertile. This is based on the inherent purpose of the levirate law to restore the name of the deceased in both name and person. Thus, while the narrative application may not follow the specifics of the law, it is still consistent with the principle(s) underlying the law.

This widening of the scope of application of the law based on its underlying principle(s) is also found in Gen 38. While the episode may derive from "a much earlier sociojuridicial stratum than the Pentateuchal

---

redeeming the land. A public forum provides the necessary social pressure to stifle any objections Mr. So-and-So might have about this substitution, as well as providing ratification of the final outcome by the elders.

57 See Block, *Judges, Ruth*, 674-76; Gow, *Ruth*, 143-82.
58 Westbrook, *Property*, 71. Cf. Thompson and Thompson, "Legal," 89.

legislation,"⁵⁹ its inclusion in the Pentateuch is instructive regarding the narrative application of law. In Gen 38 there are only two of the three conditions required for a levirate union under the levirate law: Onan is a brother from the same parents, and his brother Er dies without siring an heir. But the brothers were not living together on an undivided estate after the death of their father, since Judah is still alive. This case, then, broadens the possible application of the levirate law. It also highlights the importance of the levirate obligation (cf. Gen 38:26),⁶⁰ and by demonstrating the validity of its application to a father-in-law (Judah), the author presses for a much wider potential scope of application.⁶¹

Similarly, an examination of the redemption law within its broader context yields the understanding that "brother" (אח) not only denotes a male sibling with the same parent(s), but also the wider kinship group.⁶² The responsibility is laid primarily upon one of his brothers, then his uncles; his uncle's sons, and then any other blood relations (משאר בשרו; lit. "of the flesh of his flesh") from his משפחה (Lev 25:49). The clansmen responsible for the redemption of person are most likely the same group that is responsible for redemption of land.⁶³ Indeed, "brother" might even encompass all the "brothers of Israel."⁶⁴ Therefore, narrative corroboration with the levirate law (Gen 38) and the inner logic of the redemptive law (Lev 25) would militate against a restrictive, and point towards a more expansive application of the law in general.

---

59 Nahum M. Sarna, *Genesis* (JPS Torah Commentary; Philadelphia: JPS, 1989), 270.
60 Through the morally questionable actions of Tamar, the author demonstrates the lengths to which Tamar had to go in order to preserve the family line of Er. The outcome of her actions reveals that the principle of maintaining the family line overrides other considerations—in this case the morality of deceiving a father-in-law in order to become impregnated by him. This hierarchy of laws is illustrated in the levirate law itself, as it supersedes the law forbidding sexual contact or marriage with a brother's wife (Lev 18:16; 20:21). Cf. S. R. Driver, *A Critical and Exegetical Commentary on Deuteronomy* (3rd ed., ICC; Edinburgh: T&T Clark, 1901), 285.
61 Cf. Rowley, "Marriage," 175-76. There is also a provision for the father-in-law to take on the responsibility if there is no brother-in-law in Hittite Law § 193 (*ANET*, 196), or even if there is in MAL § 33 (*ANET*, 182).
62 This is the most likely usage of "brother" in Ruth 4:3—"male relative." Boaz's relation to the family of Elimelech has only been described in general terms throughout the narrative; he is a מודע ("relative" or "kinsman"; 2:1, 20; 3:2). Boaz's description of Elimelech as "our brother" instead of "my brother" would reinforce this understanding.
63 Cf. Gregory C. Chirichigno, *Debt-Slavery in Israel and the Ancient Near East* (JSOTSup 141; Sheffield: JSOT Press, 1993), 325; Jacob Milgrom, *Leviticus 23-27* (AB 3B; New York: Doubleday, 2000), 2194.
64 Sara Japhet, "The Relationship between the Legal Corpora in the Pentateuch in Light of Manumission Laws," in *Studies in Bible 1986* (ed. Sara Japhet; Jerusalem: Magnes Press, 1986), 77. This is also evidenced in some English translations of אחיך (Lev 25:25, 35, 39, 47), e.g., NASB ("a countryman of yours") and NIV ("one of your countrymen").

The second main basis for Zevit's objection to the *qere* is on syntactic grounds. He argues it compels "interpreting 'Ruth the Moabitess wife of the dead' as the direct object of the following verb, *qnyth*, and necessitates excising the *mem* from *m't* to yield the direct object marker *'t*."⁶⁵ As established supra, this would be the interpretation based on the most likely understanding of ומאת with an enclitic *mem*. Zevit further observes that this leads to an atypical ordering of constituents in the second half of the verse: Object + Verb + Modifier rather than Verb + Object + Modifier. He rightly suggests that its presence within the book of Ruth—generally with little syntactic difficulty—requires explanation, the most likely of which is to draw attention to the significance of the remark.⁶⁶

Although Zevit does not attribute any particular importance to Boaz's statement, I suggest this is a crucial point in the narrative. Indeed, it is the climax of this chapter,⁶⁷ and the tension generated is comparable to Ruth's proposal to Boaz on the threshing floor and his response in chapter 3. Tension is relieved in chapter 3 when Boaz affirms that he will undertake to do all she requests. Yet the conditional nature of his response— dependent upon the reaction of the nearer kinsman-redeemer—means the implied reader is eagerly anticipating the interchange between Boaz and Mr. So-and-So. When Mr. So-and-So accepts the right of redemption, the tension is raised further as the implied reader awaits Boaz's next gambit. It is into this context that Boaz's response to Mr. So-and-So is spoken.

Structurally also, the primary focus of this section is on Boaz's speech and Mr. So-and-So's reply (4:5-6).⁶⁸ In particular, the second part of Boaz's statement introduces Boaz's "master-stroke"—Ruth is part of a package deal with the land. On the background of the levirate allusions in the RN, and the inextricable connection between redemptive and levirate responsibilities within this especial set of circumstances, Boaz's statement can be understood as pointing out that the redemption of property triggers the levirate responsibility with Ruth, not Naomi. Therefore, this is the reason for the atypical ordering that places the emphasis on "Ruth the Moabitess, wife of the deceased."

---

65 Zevit, "Dating Ruth," 599.
66 Personal communication, dated 13/4/07.
67 Cf. D. R. G. Beattie, "Kethibh and Qere in Ruth IV 5," *VT* 21 (1971): 492; Hubbard, *Ruth*, 243.
68 Cf. Gow, *Ruth*, 79-80: "Verse 5 then becomes the hinge upon which the whole situation turns."

In short, while Zevit is correct to highlight the exegetical consequences of the *qere* reading, his interpretation does not capture the reading's true significance, based on the social, legal, and literary context.[69]

D. Summary

Drawing together the preferred readings of the two problematic words in Ruth 4:5 yields the translation:

> When you acquire the field from Naomi, also Ruth the Moabitess, the wife of the deceased, you acquire, in order to restore the name of the dead upon his inheritance.[70]

Thus, Boaz proposes that when the right of redemption for the field is to be acquired by the nearer kinsman-redeemer from Naomi, it also precipitates the parallel institution of levirate marriage to Ruth, not Naomi as presumed by Mr. So-and-So. Having established the inextricable connection between the obligations of land redemption and levirate marriage in the situation found in the RN, we are now in a position to examine the connection between the identity and actions of Boaz. This will be approached by means of a comparison with Mr. So-and-So because this will place Boaz's actions into sharper relief.

III. The Identity and Actions of Mr. So-and-So

The common social identity of Boaz and Mr. So-and-So as relatives from the Elimelech's clan grants them the privilege of redeeming the field from

---

[69] Zevit's case relies heavily upon the two objections to the *qere* reading presented and examined. This may have been due to limitations of space, or because this was only one component of his larger argument concerning the dating of the book of Ruth. Nonetheless, his only positive argument for the *ketib* reading is a general one, and I quote in full: "In this case, I suspect that both *ketib* and *qerî* reflect ancient m.s. variants and the *qerî* should not be considered a learned guess at the best way to read or interpret the *ketib*. Sometimes the *ketib* preserves a superior reading." For his references, see Zevit, "Dating Ruth," 598, fn. 38. While I concur that, in general, the *ketib* may sometimes and perhaps even mostly preserve a superior reading, it would be preferable, methodologically speaking, to evaluate each case on its own merits, including presenting a positive argument for the preferred reading. Examples of this are Beattie, "Kethibh and Qere in Ruth IV 5," 490-94, who argues for the *ketib* reading, and explains the *qere* as a misunderstanding deriving from Ruth 4:9, 10; and Linafelt, who argues on the basis of a chiasm he discerns in 4:5; Linafelt and Beal, *Ruth & Esther*, 68-69.

[70] The translation with the two preferred interpretive options is followed by a number of EVV, including NET, NASB, and NRSV. The only translation, to my knowledge, that takes the *ketiv* reading is the REB.

Naomi. The clearest point of differentiation between them is apparent after Boaz reveals that the attendant levirate obligation actually applies to Ruth. Mr. So-and-So's response is telling:

> I cannot redeem it for myself, as I might ruin my own inheritance (נחלתי). Redeem it for yourself; you may have my right of redemption (גאלתי), for I cannot redeem it (4:6).

His eagerness to accept the responsibility of land redemption indicates it was also a privilege (4:4). Although a financial sum had to be repaid to the current leaseholder, and there was the added burden of providing materially for Naomi, the usufruct of the land would offset this cost. Furthermore, if Mr. So-and-So already had children, the land would add to their inheritance. For these reasons, it is an attractive proposal. Yet when the levirate obligation is introduced, Mr. So-and-So reneges on his responsibility. Although his refusal is stated clearly ("I might ruin my inheritance"), the reason behind it, along with *how* the levirate responsibility might ruin his inheritance is not overt.

A number of suggested reasons for his refusal are less likely because they are primarily arguments from silence. (1) Mr. So-and-So's statement is simply "courteous circumlocution for the thought that he did not wish to marry Ruth."[71] This suggestion still does not provide an explanation for his statement. (2) Ruth's presence would cause too much friction with an incumbent wife.[72] (3) He is not able to maintain both his current property and the additional property.[73] The main factor against this understanding is he had already agreed to it before the added levirate stipulation. (4) Those who posit that his refusal is because Ruth is a Moabitess may be closer to the solution.[74] Indeed, Boaz mentions this aspect of Ruth's identity in his revised proposal to Mr. So-and-So (4:5). Ruth's foreign status is certainly a feature that the implied author highlights—but mainly in the first half of the narrative, as she first arrives in Bethlehem (1:22; 2:2, 6, 21). Its presence in the mouth of Boaz in 4:10 in addition to 4:5,[75] both cases in conjunction with her widow status, suggests that either the designation is used for legal precision,[76] or to recall her "doubly unfortunate" status—Ruth's non-

---

71 Frants Buhl, "Some Observations on the Social Institutions of the Israelites," *AJT* 1 (1897): 736. Cf. Joüon, *Ruth*, 84.
72 Targum to Ruth 4:6.
73 John Gray, *Joshua, Judges, Ruth* (NCBC; Grand Rapids: Eerdmans, 1986), 399.
74 E.g., *Midr. Ruth Rab.* 7:7, 10; Rashi. Zakovitch, *Rut*, 159, asserts that Mr. So-and-So cannot reveal his true reasons "weil sie auch auf Boas zutreffen würden, der bereits verkündet hat, daß er - falls er sich weigern sollte - bereit ist, Rut zu lösen."
75 Campbell, *Ruth*, 160, correctly notes that if it was only used at 4:5, the case for this understanding would be stronger.
76 Hubbard, *Ruth*, 243, 255.

Israelite ethnicity along with her tragic widowhood.⁷⁷ While this suggestion is not completely an argument from silence, the fact that this reason is not provided by Mr. So-and-So in response to Boaz's revised proposal (4:5-6) undermines the likelihood of it being the main reason for his refusal.

An attempt to draw an explanation from Mr. So-and-So's verbalised reason involves understanding *how* a levirate union with Ruth would impair his inheritance. Certainly, the maintenance of Ruth, Naomi, and any potential offspring he might sire along with the needs of any current family would add to his production requirements from his fields in the short term. Considering the extra burden of repaying the cost for the additional field, along with the erratic agricultural production in that geographical region, it is understandable that Mr. So-and-So would emphatically proclaim "I cannot!" (לא אוכל).⁷⁸ If, due to the aforementioned factors, he was to find himself overextended due to the upkeep for his enlarged number of dependents, he might enter the downward spiral of poverty described in Lev 25.⁷⁹ In this way, he might impair his landed inheritance during his lifetime. Thus, it appears his refusal is the most reasonable and prudent course of action.

Nonetheless, there are two factors mitigating the risk. First, Mr. So-and-So has at least one clansman who is איש גבור חיל in both senses of the word, and thus able and willing to assist him if he fell into economic straits, especially considering the concern he has already displayed for the widows. Second, it seems unlikely that he cannot afford the extra cost, because the only additional factor to his initial acceptance is that he would have to feed two widows in the short term, along with any offspring in the future. The usufruct of Elimelech's field should offset the additional demand. Thus, while the inability to meet production needs potentially leading to debt and the alienation of his land may be sufficient motivation, the aforementioned factors should diminish this concern for Mr. So-and-So.

Another consideration for Mr. So-and-So may be the fate of his inheritance after he passes away. At this point a consideration of his possible household circumstances is required, because his marital status, and more pertinently, the existence of offspring is not mentioned.⁸⁰ The majority of commentators presume he is married, or at least has his own

---

77   Campbell, *Ruth*, 160; Hubbard, *Ruth*, 256.
78   Mr. So-and-So does not say "I will not" but the stronger "I cannot." Cf. Morris, *Ruth*, 304.
79   See Milgrom, *Leviticus 23-27*, 2191-241.
80   Rashi, commenting on his name פלני אלמני, suggests he is called אלמני because he was a widower. He also suggests he had offspring.

children.[81] Although within his cultural context this would be a sound presumption, this is not known for certain. I will thus consider each possibility.

If, on the one hand, Mr. So-and-So does not have descendants, a levirate marriage with Ruth means that their first son, for all intents and purposes, belongs to Mahlon, not himself. Not only would the land he redeemed at his own expense be inherited by this son, so also would his own land unless he produces further children.[82] It would thus not only become an issue of property inheritance, but also of the perpetuation of his name upon his property. While his land would not be alienated from the clan if he produced one son, he would face personal extinction unless he had subsequent sons. Of course, for Mr. So-and-So there also lurks the possibility that Ruth has not already produced children because she is infertile. He would have known that Ruth could have been married for up to ten years without bearing children (1:4-5),[83] and also that her remaining reproductive time is limited. This would be advantageous if Mr. So-and-So already has offspring, but if he lacks an heir, the threat to his name and inheritance is further magnified.

If, on the other hand, he already has offspring, the situation would be substantially different. He would still bear the cost of redeeming the property in addition to the upkeep of Naomi, Ruth, and any offspring engendered with Ruth. Although the increased needs should be offset by the usufruct from the redeemed land, there is still the risk from unpredictable crop production. Additionally, once the first son matured, he would inherit the redeemed land. It may also be the case, as Eryl Davies and others suggest, that this son would further inherit a share of Mr. So-and-So's estate, diluting the inheritance for each of his own children.[84] While Mr. So-and-So may have considered this outcome, it is not certain it would apply because the firstborn son is reckoned as Mahlon's (cf. Deut 25:6). Even if this is not the case, there is still a considerable risk in

---

81 Including, inter alios, Josephus, *Ant.* 5.332 (Thackeray, LCL); Rudolph, *Ruth*, 67; Thompson and Thompson, "Legal," 98.

82 If he were a bachelor at this time and he were to have further children, then it most likely would be with Ruth. For although polygamy was permissible in ancient Israel, the cost of maintaining more than one wife was probably prohibitive, not to mention the family tensions it could cause, as illustrated in the patriarchal narratives (e.g., Abraham with Hagar and Sarah, and Jacob with Leah and Rachel). Both the narrative and legal texts draw attention to its undesirability. See, e.g., the discussion in Wenham, *Story*, 84-87.

83 It is not clear from וישבו שם כעשר שנים whether ten years refers to the total time beginning with the arrival of Elimelech's family in Moab, or to the length of the marriages before the sons died. Either way, Ruth is portrayed as barren at the beginning of the narrative.

84 E.g., Davies, "Duties," 234; Rudolph, *Ruth*, 67; Thompson and Thompson, "Legal," 98.

accepting the levirate responsibility for Mr. So-and-So and his household. To summarise, if Mr. So-and-So is single without offspring, levirate marriage to Ruth presents a greater long-term risk (to the perpetuation of his "name") than short-term risk (to his landed property while he is alive). If he is married with offspring, the levirate marriage presents a greater short-term than long-term risk.[85]

In a word, an examination of the potential reasons behind Mr. So-and-So's refusal to accept the levirate responsibility finds them reasonable, understandable and predictable. While the specific personal circumstances surrounding Mr. So-and-So's refusal of the responsibility are not clear, his general motivation is lucid enough: the preservation of his own inheritance. If he was single and without an heir, this situation would present the greatest "absolute risk" to the perpetuation of his "name."[86] If he was married with offspring, the "absolute risk" would be lower. His refusal in this case is the way a normal, responsible family man would be expected to act.[87]

Mr. So-and-So's actions can also be understood as stemming from a conflict between different components of his identity. Although his social identity as a member of the clan of Elimelech brings with it obligations as a redeemer, as the head of his "father's house" he has responsibilities to his own household. Furthermore, his clan membership presents another conflict—with his personal identity. Not only is the integrity of his household under threat, Mr. So-and-So could also foresee that his personal "name" was under the threat of extinction.

Hence, there is limited shame attached to Mr. So-and-So's refusal. This is evidenced in the sandal ceremony. While there are similarities with the sandal custom described in Deut 25:8-10, the divergences suggest that Mr. So-and-So's actions are not to be understood in the same light. His familial distance means he does not have the same degree of compulsion to act; indeed, Ruth does not have recourse to the same channels of coercion outlined in the law.[88] Moreover, the strongly shame-attaching rituals of

---

85 *Pace* Joüon, *Ruth*, 84, who avers that Mr. So-and-So is over-exaggerating the condition in which he would find himself; and Bush, *Ruth*, 246.

86 I designate the risk "absolute" because it is not conditioned by other factors; it is operating in a theoretical realm. This will be contrasted to "relative" risk infra.

87 Cf. Würthwein, *Megilloth*, 22, Hubbard, *Ruth*, 247. *Pace* Rudolph, *Ruth*, 67: "Er rechnete kühl und wirtschaftlich."

88 There is no indication that Ruth wants to take this course of action. Certainly she has been released from her duties to her family-in-law, and is not required to marry within the family (1:8-13; 3:10).

spitting and name-calling are not re-enacted in the book of Ruth because they are not appropriate.[89]

Nevertheless, in the RN his actions are set in contrast to those of Boaz. This is particularly evident in the structure of Mr. So-and-So's response to Boaz (4:6):

לא אוכל לגאול לי (I cannot redeem it for myself)

פן אשחית את נחלתי (as I might ruin my own inheritance)

גאל לך אתה את גאלתי (Redeem it for yourself; you may have my right of redemption)

כי לא אוכל לגאל (for I cannot redeem it)

The concentric structure highlights Mr. So-and-So's refusal. In the first and last clauses he reiterates his inability to redeem,[90] and in the third clause the transfer of his right to Boaz. These two complementary actions are brought into stronger relief by the emphatic syntactic form of his words in the first and third clauses.[91] Mr. So-and-So's primary consideration for himself is also underlined by his multiple self-references ("I" or "myself" used six times), compared with no references to those who would stand to gain or lose the most from the transaction—Ruth and Naomi.[92] The apposition of the second and third clauses clearly shows the transfer of the right of redemption from Mr. So-and-So to Boaz, along with the attendant risk. Whatever Mr. So-and-So's family circumstances might have been, one thing is clear: he was not willing to place himself or his immediate family at risk for the sake of the interests of his wider kinship group.

---

89 Contra Josephus, *Ant.* 5.335 (Thackeray, LCL), who adds that Ruth removed Mr. So-and-So's shoe and spat in his face.

90 The repetition of his refusal to redeem is emphatic; *pace* Zakovitch, *Rut*, 159, who views it as a marker of his uncertainty.

91 The "ethical dative" is used in both the first (לי) and third clauses (לך), further enhancing the contrast (See GKC § 119s), and the independent pronoun (אתה) in the third clause in apposition to the pronominal suffix places further emphasis on the transference of the redemption right (GKC §§ 135d-g); see Bush, *Ruth*, 229, 33. Hubbard, *Ruth*, 246, adds that the statement is made more emphatic by the same derivation of both the imperative (גאל) and its object (גְּאֻלָּה).

92 Although Mr. So-and-So does not specify an object for the redemption, he most likely has the land principally in mind, although the more general understanding of "redeem" in the RN allows for Naomi and Ruth as a secondary consideration. Cf. Bush, *Ruth*, 229; Hubbard, *Ruth*, 237-38, fn. 12.

IV. The Identity and Actions of Boaz

This is, of course, precisely the opposite with Boaz. His personal circumstances are not explicitly mentioned in the narrative. Millar Burrows assumes that Mr. So-and-So is married with children, and proposes that Boaz is in the same situation.[93] Most commentators, however, presume that Boaz is unmarried without children, with some averring that he is a widower.[94] Socio-historical considerations render this second reading more likely, given the presentation of Boaz as from an elder generation with his attendant social status. Naomi's choice of Boaz as husband for Ruth, combined with the probably low incidence of polygamy at time, is suggestive of Boaz's single status, with widowhood a plausible explanation. Furthermore, while the allusion to Perez (4:12) primarily refers to other factors,[95] the presence of *two* offspring from the union of Judah and Tamar (Zerah and Perez; Gen 38:29-30) at least suggests that Boaz does not already have an heir.

Thus, the people at the gate are wishing Boaz not just an heir to inherit the "name" of Elimelech, but also another heir to inherit his own "name." Moreover, the references to "your house" and "the offspring that YHWH will give you" (4:12) are probably best explained if Boaz was childless.[96] Nonetheless, although this is the most likely scenario (widower without children), it is possible any of Mr. So-and-So's reconstructed personal circumstances also apply to Boaz. The corollary is that all the attendant risks and benefits of accepting the redemptive and levirate responsibilities also fully apply to Boaz.

If Boaz is single and without an heir, this situation holds the greatest "absolute risk" for him to accept the redemptive and levirate responsibilities. Yet he is eager to assume this set of responsibilities. From an identity perspective, his actions reinforce and further enhance his personal reputation as "a man of great worth." His willingness to accept the extra responsibilities associated with the widows can be understood as a natural progression of the protection and provision he has already extended to them. If the normal, expected response is found in Mr. So-and-So, then Boaz acts beyond the requirements of his social identity.

---

93 Millar Burrows, "The Marriage of Boaz and Ruth," *JBL* 59 (1940): 452. Burrows understands the author's aim as enhancing the virtue of Boaz by contrast with the nearer kinsman. Cf. Gray, *Ruth*, 312.

94 Cf. Eryl W. Davies, "Inheritance Rights and the Hebrew Levirate Marriage: Part 2," *VT* 31 (1981): 259; Morris, *Ruth*, 312; Rowley, "Marriage," 192.

95 These include: (1) his prominence in the tribe of Judah; (2) the similar circumstances leading to his birth with those of Obed; and (3) his close connection with Bethlehem.

96 Morris, *Ruth*, 312.

Similarly to Mr. So-and-So, Boaz is willing to take on the redemptive obligation, normally a clansman's role. Yet in contrast to Mr. So-and-So, Boaz is willing to take on the additional obligation usually attached to particular members of a father's house—the levirs. Boaz, therefore, although more distantly related to Naomi and Ruth than Mr. So-and-So, willingly takes on the role usually assigned to a close household member. In the process of restoring or maintaining the lineage and name of Elimelech (4:10), he is simultaneously risking his own lineage and name. In this way, his actions can be understood as subordinating his personal identity for the sake of perpetuating the identity of a fellow clansman. Paradoxically, through his selfless actions his name is honoured and immortalised: he ultimately provides an ancestor in the line of King David. In contrast, Mr. So-and-So seeks immortality, but he is, ironically, left without even a personal name. Thus, although greater genetic distance means lower obligation, there is also greater potential honour.

Nonetheless, Boaz's personal interest in Ruth is a factor in his willingness to take the risk. Scholarship is polarised regarding the importance of this motivation. At one end of the spectrum are scholars such as Fewell and Gunn, who assert that Boaz is *primarily* motivated by self-interest, based on his personal attraction to Ruth. From their very first meeting, Boaz's words to Ruth in chapter 2 are understood to be "more than tinged with sexual overtones," indicating Boaz's unconscious longings.[97] These sexual longings surface on the threshing floor, where Ruth's "last kindness" (3:10) is interpreted as "keeping herself for Boaz and making a proposal of union with him."[98] By dawn, Boaz's main concern is for his standing in the community in light of the previous night's activities: the combination of his inebriation, waking to find his "feet" uncovered, and Ruth next to him leads him to conclude that he might have impregnated Ruth. His urgency and course of action ("weaving together the announcement of marriage into a proposal about property"), reflect his need to "redeem" his reputation.[99] Furthermore, Boaz uses the redemption of property as a "cloak" to cover his desire to marry Ruth.[100] According to Fewell and Gunn, Boaz's final action in the narrative, viz. sexual intercourse with Ruth, is most telling apropos his desire for her (4:13).[101] The divergence of Fewell and Gunn's interpretation of the specific texts from my own are clear from my previous analysis of the aforementioned

---

97   Fewell and Gunn, *Compromising*, 84-85.
98   Fewell and Gunn, *Compromising*, 86.
99   Fewell and Gunn, *Compromising*, 87.
100 Fewell and Gunn, *Compromising*, 88-92.
101 Fewell and Gunn, *Compromising*, 87.

passages.¹⁰² While Fewell and Gunn are correct to highlight Boaz's personal interest in Ruth, they end up overstating their case. From a social identity perspective, their reading effectively places Boaz's personal identity as the most salient self-component.

At the other end of the spectrum are scholars who maintain that Boaz's actions derive from a strong sense of altruism intermingled with social obligation, with little, if any consideration for his personal interest in Ruth. For instance, Bush is effusive in his praise of Boaz as a character whose conduct is marked by "gracious and loving kindness that goes beyond the call of duty," and "selfless generosity."¹⁰³ His actions transcend "the claims of self-interest."¹⁰⁴ Similarly, in his willingness "to sacrifice his own means, his own life for two impoverished widows," Robert Hubbard views Boaz as modelling the "extraordinary demands of ḥesed."¹⁰⁵ While scholars such as Bush and Hubbard are correct to note the importance of Boaz's social motivations, an examination from a social identity perspective yields a more complex motivational picture.

In relation to the non-kin aspect of his social identity, his status as an elder male is manifested in his general provision and protection for Naomi and Ruth. In broad terms, all of his actions also reflect and uphold the patriarchal structure in which he lives. Additionally, his actions can be understood to derive from the kin aspect of his social identity: as an Israelite, Boaz provides for Ruth, an underprivileged member of his society; as a clansman of Elimelech, he acts as גאל to restore the property of Naomi to the clan; finally, in direct contrast to Mr. So-and-So, he is also willing to act as a levir, taking up a role normally associated with the closest kinship group—the father's house. Thus, the evidence suggests that

---

102 In large part, these divergences are expected, resulting from a difference in reading strategies. Although both the approach of this study and that of Fewell and Gunn are influenced by reader-response theory, the main difference is that my approach is "text-controlled." The approach of Fewell and Gunn allows a reading "against the grain," or contrary to words of the characters, or statements of the narrator. This approach yields interesting and new insights into the text, and highlights how the gaps in the story can be interpreted in numerous ways. These readings, however, are difficult to validate as there is no agreed textual evidence from which to argue a particular position. One problem with this approach as applied to the RN is that it requires interpreting the text against the descriptions of the narrator and the overall actions of the characters; e.g., both Boaz and Ruth are presented as characters of integrity (2:1; 3:11), whose lives are marked by חסד (1:8; 2:20; 3:10). Fewell and Gunn's approach would thus require the functioning of an "unreliable narrator," a device not generally accepted as being present in the HB; cf. Meir Sternberg, *The Poetics of Biblical Narrative* (Bloomington: Indiana University Press, 1985), 51.

103 Bush, *Ruth*, 54-55.
104 Bush, *Ruth*, 52.
105 Hubbard, *Ruth*, 73.

Boaz's social self-component is influential in his actions. Instead of only originating from a concern for himself, his actions also originate from a concern for others—individuals as well as the community—and it is fitting that his legacy is on the national level (4:17-22).

To understand Boaz's actions as deriving exclusively from his social identity, however, would be an unbalanced reading. As established supra, the seed of Boaz's personal interest in Ruth was sown, then germinated while they interacted in his field. It then came to full fruition on the threshing floor. Thus, a significant impetus for his subsequent actions can be contributed to his personal interest in Ruth. Indeed, if his interest was not piqued by Ruth on the threshing floor it is very doubtful the transaction of chapter 4 would have taken place.

On balance then, motivations arising from Boaz's personal self-component are secondary to his social self-component. Although he is initially flattered by Ruth's selection of him, he is also cognisant of the wider implications of her decision for the family of Naomi (3:10). Furthermore, even when his romantic interest in Ruth is piqued on the threshing floor, he is still concerned to act in a way that is consistent with his social identity as a clansman (3:12-13). He does not let his personal interest override the normal community structures and processes. Moreover, when the time comes to legalising the transaction, his express concern is not only for himself, but also for his wider kinship group and the perpetuation of his clansman's name (4:9-10; cf. 4:5). The personal component of his identity is appropriately expressed; he still upholds his social obligations. Hence, the actions of Boaz can be understood to arise from both his personal and social self-components, with the social relatively more salient.

V. The Identity and Inaction of Boaz

On the basis of his altruism—a life characterised by חסד—many commentators view Boaz as a paragon of virtue, and thus a model to emulate. Other scholars, however, point out that his actions are not exemplary throughout the whole narrative. In particular, they claim that there is more he could have done regarding his kinship obligations in chapter 2. For example, Irmtraud Fischer asserts:

> Although [Boaz] has duty of redemption and recognizes the misery of the widows, he does not act, but generously tolerates gleaning, the right of the

poor.... [Ruth is] far better than the so-called "capable men" of one's own people, who first have to be challenged to perform their duty of solidarity.¹⁰⁶

Although overly critical of Boaz, Fischer's point is well taken. While Boaz provides generously for the widows beyond the legal requirements, by the end of the harvest season the predicament of Ruth and Naomi is essentially the same as before Boaz intervened. Since Ruth's gleaning in Boaz's field would have been complete, contact between them would markedly diminish, and along with it Ruth's prospects of finding a "home" and Naomi finding fulfilment for her "emptiness." This understanding is bolstered by Naomi's response to this situation in hatching her daring and dangerous plan for Ruth; if Boaz had taken steps to secure their ongoing provision and protection, Naomi's initiative would have been unnecessary. Thus, critics argue that Boaz is to be faulted on the basis of his lack of initiative with regards to the widows.¹⁰⁷

A consideration of this criticism requires an examination of the possible reasons behind Boaz's inaction. Some scholars suggest Boaz considered marriage to Ruth an insuperable risk to his reputation and inheritance. For instance, Fewell and Gunn suggest that marriage to Ruth as a Moabite woman has a "conventional value" that is "decidedly negative."¹⁰⁸ Wilhelm Rudolph posits that the reckoning of the first son of a Boaz–Ruth union to Mahlon might have deterred Boaz from pursuing Ruth.¹⁰⁹ For the same reasons as provided against Mr. So-and-So's refusal on the basis of her ethnicity, along with Boaz's description of Ruth as אשת חיל, this suggestion is unlikely. Certainly, these factors do not hinder him after she proposes.

A more probable reason can be inferred from Boaz's own statement: there is a nearer kinsman who has a prior right of redemption (3:12-13).¹¹⁰ As a person particularly mindful of his social obligations, Boaz was not willing to contravene the mores of his community by usurping another's privilege. This may be a valid and sufficient reason for Boaz not to pursue a marriage with Ruth. Furthermore, there are no indications that Boaz was under any *legal* compulsion to act, because he was not the nearest kinsman.

---

106 Irmtraud Fischer, "The Book of Ruth: A 'Feminist' Commentary on the Torah?," in *Ruth and Esther: A Feminist Companion to the Bible (Second Series)* (ed. Athalya Brenner; Sheffield: Sheffield Academic Press, 1999), 47.
107 E.g., Anthony Phillips, "The Book of Ruth - Deception and Shame," *JJS* 37 (1986): 1-17, and Daube, *Jewish Law*, 38: "[Boaz] is studiously cautious, takes no steps to accomplish a real change in their situation. He first meets Ruth at the beginning of the barley harvest: both it and the wheat harvest go by and he still is just supportive, tender—distant."
108 Fewell and Gunn, *Compromising*, 87.
109 Rudolph, *Ruth*, 53.
110 Leggett, *Levirate*, 207.

These factors notwithstanding, scholars are right to point out there rested upon him a *moral* obligation to take some initiative on the basis of his established personal relationship with Ruth and Naomi. Thus, David Daube suggests he could have assisted the widows by putting it to Naomi that if no closer relation approaches her, he could redeem the field.[111] And Fewell and Gunn assert that he should have pressed the nearer kinsman to shoulder his responsibility.[112]

Yet an exploration of the reasons behind Boaz's inaction from a social identity perspective presents a more nuanced picture. If Boaz's inaction partly stemmed from his social identity, it also partly stemmed from his personal identity. For if, as I argued supra, the redemptive and levirate roles are inseparable in this particular and unusual circumstance, the operation of this principle would mean the person who assumes the redemptive responsibility would have to marry the dowager—Naomi. If Boaz's most likely personal situation is accepted (single and heirless), and the possibility of polygamy ruled out, his hesitation can be understood as stemming from his personal identity: this course of action precludes the possibility of producing a descendant to perpetuate his "name."

This being the case, it may be argued that Boaz should have encouraged Mr. So-and-So to exercise his right of redemption. But if this were to occur, Mr. So-and-So is likely also to end up marrying Naomi, and in doing so, the "name" of Elimelech would be extinguished because Naomi cannot produce further sons (1:11-13). On the basis of his acute sense of kinship obligation—a component of his social identity—it is unlikely Boaz would allow this to occur. Thus, the personal and social components of Boaz's identity have conspired to place him in a bind, making it impossible for Boaz to assist the widows without extinguishing Elimelech's and his own post-mortem identity. Even Boaz's inaction is consistent with his identity. His only means of escape is for Naomi to remove any possibility of a levirate marriage to her, which occurs through her sending Ruth to the threshing floor. This concept of Ruth substituting for Naomi is reinforced by the womenfolk of the town when they ascribe Obed to Naomi (4:17).

---

111 Daube, *Jewish Law*, 38.
112 Fewell and Gunn, *Compromising*, 87.

VI. An Assessment of Boaz's Actions from a Social Identity Perspective

From the perspective of social identity theory, Boaz is more likely to accept the redemptive and levirate roles under the circumstances. In regards to his personal self-component, he has adequate reasons to want to marry Ruth. To compare with Mr. So-and-So, whom most commentators assume already has a family, and if Boaz is heirless, it actually would be more beneficial for Boaz to marry Ruth. In regards to his relational self-component, and in contrast to Mr. So-and-So, he already has an established dyadic relationship with Ruth. Furthermore, his established relationship with both Ruth and Naomi renders him morally responsible for securing their ongoing provision. For all these reasons, there is less uncertainty associated with Boaz acting than for Mr. So-and-So. Indeed, there are significant positive reasons to do so.

Yet, just like Mr. So-and-So, Boaz also held a right of refusal. Although the risk for Boaz may have been lower than for Mr. So-and-So, there is still lingering doubt surrounding Ruth's fertility. Moreover, what if she is only able to bear one son? For the first son of the union is to be reckoned as Mahlon's, and if Boaz was childless, there would be no-one to perpetuate his own name. So while the risk associated with Boaz's acceptance is lower relative to Mr. So-and-So's, his willingness to proceed can still be viewed as virtuous, because there was no legal obligation for him to act. His action can be seen as an act of *hesed*, in the sense that he acts outside the domain of duty. If, as some commentators suggest, the family situations of Boaz and Mr. So-and-So are the same, this would place Boaz's actions in an even more virtuous light.

From the perspective of social identity theory, Mr. So-and-So acts as expected under the circumstances. After being given a strong situational prime to act according to his relational self-component as a member of the clan of Elimelech (4:3-4a), Mr. So-and-So quickly accepts the opportunity to enlarge his estate by redeeming Elimelech's land (4:4b).[113] Yet when Ruth is revealed as part of the transaction (4:5), she presents a conflict between his personal and relational identity self-components. When he

---

113 Priming procedures affect the accessibility of concepts, including self-components. For a general review of priming procedures, see Robert S. Wyer and Thomas K. Srull, "Human Cognition in Its Social Context," *Psychological Review* 93 (1986): 322-59. For studies finding that priming procedures can stimulate the retrieval of self-components, see, e.g., Brewer and Gardner, "Who Is This 'We'?," 83-93; David Trafimow et al., "The Effects of Language and Priming on the Relative Accessibility of the Private Self and the Collective Self," *Journal of Cross-Cultural Psychology* 28 (1997): 107-23.

declines on the basis that it would ruin his own inheritance (4:6), this can be understood on a personal level: it might threaten the perpetuation of his own name. If, as most commentators assume, he is already the head of his own father's house, the decision to marry Ruth might also impair his estate for his current family. And since he is not already in a relationship with Ruth, his current kinship group is more accessible, and consequently has a greater comparative salience. Furthermore, there are hints in the narrative that Ruth is still considered a foreigner, a member of an outgroup, and consequently one to be suspicious of.

VII. Summary and Conclusions

I have shown that Boaz's actions in the RN are primarily influenced by his social identity; his personal identity plays a secondary role. That he is viewed as an exemplary figure by an overwhelming majority of scholars can be understood from a social identity theory perspective: he goes beyond what is expected of him according to group norms—he subordinates his personal identity in acting for a collective goal. In doing so, he paradoxically reinforces his personal reputation as "a man of great worth." Boaz's actions were brought into sharper relief in contrast with Mr. So-and-So's actions. If Mr. So-and-So represents the normal, expected response, then, on the whole, Boaz's response represents the extraordinary. In this way he is correctly understood as an exemplary figure, a person characterised by חסד.

The presentation of Boaz as an ideal Israelite challenges the identity of an implied reader of the RN; indeed, the positive outcome of Boaz's actions would have provided strong motivation to follow his example. Nonetheless, in relation to the group norms found in the laws of the HB, the actions of Boaz would be unsettling in regards to identity. For the implication is that group norms not only involve following the strict prescriptions of the law, but also going beyond the specifics of the law. Boaz not only fulfils the law *qua* an Israelite (gleaning law) and *qua* a clansman (redemption law), he goes beyond the requirements of the law *qua* a levir (levirate law), although he is not actually a levir. If the law circumscribes acceptable and unacceptable behaviour for Israelites, the promotion of Boaz's actions in the RN means the requirements are essentially open-ended.

For an ancient Israelite is to act in whatever ways are dictated by the particular situation, guided by this principle: act in a way that furthers the cause of the kinship group. The general nature of this principle makes it more difficult to determine appropriate behaviour in new and ambiguous situations than following the specific details of a particular law. This is against the usual function of a norm, which is to simplify complex situations by determining appropriate actions for group members. Therefore, if the Mosaic Law functions as a boundary maintaining and reinforcing Israelite identity,[114] the application of the law in the RN reduces its effectiveness.

Additionally, this level of kinship obligation would have been particularly demanding for two reasons. First, the implications of Boaz's actions in the RN broaden the scope of obligation. In particular circumstances, the levirate law applies not only to a brother who shared a father, but also to more distant relatives; this is consistent with the trajectory of the Tamar and Judah narrative. Although the degree of obligation is still relative to genetic proximity, the application of this law which has breached the confines of the smallest social unit (father's house) to include a unit with a greater pool of members now means that the obligation potentially applies to a significantly greater number of relatives. Within the context of a collectivist society, this would have added to the variety of demands on individuals, which were already diffuse.[115]

Second, the kinship obligation was demanding because it was inescapable. In individualist societies people often withdraw from inconveniently demanding social groups, but this is not an option for members of a collectivist society. Even if the society makes costly demands on an individual, she cannot withdraw from her kinship group.[116] The result is a person either accepts the obligation, or he refuses the obligation and accepts the consequences. These choices are associated with either honour or shame, the degree of which is determined by kinship proximity. Given that persons on the allocentric end of the spectrum readily accept group norms, the RN is probably directed at those on the allocentric end, by providing cognitive or affective education through narrative.

---

114 Cf. The OT Pseudepigraphal work the *Letter of Aristeas*, 139, which describes the law as given by God to fence "us about with impregnable palisades and with walls of iron, to the intent that we should in no way have dealings with any of the other nations."

115 This is in contrast to individualist societies, in which demands by ingroups on individual contributions are highly segmented, requiring contributions only at a certain time and place or of a certain kind. Cf. Harry C. Triandis et al., "Individualism and Collectivism: Cross-Cultural Perspectives on Self-Group Relationships," *Journal of Personality and Social Psychology* 54 (1988): 324.

116 To a great extent individuals are attached to their kinship groups by force of necessity; the relative sparsity of material resources means they are dependent on their groups for survival. Emotional security is also primarily derived from kinship groups.

Hence, by demonstrating the supremacy of social identity over personal identity through the person of Boaz, the author of the RN aims to motivate his readers to contribute to wider kinship group goals. And in some circumstances, this may involve acting beyond the strict requirements of the law.

Ruth: Identity and Ethics

The stability of Boaz's identity stands in contrast to the transformation of Ruth's identity. At the beginning of the RN she is a Moabitess, by the end she has become incorporated into Israel. In this chapter I explore this transformation in Ruth's identity, and the place of her actions in this transformation. Although her change in national allegiance is the central change, I also analyse her actions once she arrives in her adopted country from the perspective of identity. This chapter will conclude with some implications of Ruth's transformation for an implied reader.

I. The Transformation of Ruth's Identity

A. Moabite Stereotype

One of the most prominent descriptions of Ruth is as a Moabitess, a member of a negatively viewed outgroup according to social identity theory.[1] Within this theory, stereotypes are generalisations about people based on dyadic relationships or group membership. As outlined previously, it is the understanding that each member of a particular group shares the same qualities.[2] Hence, a specific group member is assumed to be, and treated as, identical to other group members. While ingroup stereotyping is generally positive, the stereotypes of outgroups tend to be negative.[3]

From the aetiology of Moab and the overall history of relations between Israel and Moab as presented in the HB, the stereotype of a

---

1   If the frequency of a reference can be accepted as a general indication of emphasis, then after her proper name (12 times) or pronominal particles, prominence is given to "my daughter(s)" (11 times in total; including usage by Naomi [1:11, 12, 13; 2:2, 22; 3:1, 16, 18] and Boaz [2:8, 3:10, 11]), "Moabitess/the Moabitess" (7 times; 1:4, 22; 2:2, 6, 21; 4:5, 10), "daughter(s)-in-law" (7 times; 1:6, 7, 8, 22; 2:20, 22; 4:15), "wife/widow of the dead/Mahlon" (3 times; 1:4; 4:5, 10), "the woman" (3 times; 3:8, 14; 4:11), "wife [of Boaz]" (twice; 4:10, 13), "young woman" (twice; 2:5; 4:12), and "woman of worth" (3:11).
2   See "The Social Identity Approach" in Chapter One.
3   Both forms of stereotyping strengthen the sense of belonging for members of the ingroup.

Moabite is predominantly negative for an implied reader. Israel viewed the Moabites as relatives (cf. Deut 2:8-9), but held them with disdain as a result of their incestuous origins (Gen 19:30-38).[4] They were to be excluded from the assembly of YHWH because of their wrongdoings against Israel (Deut 23:3-6).[5] The rationale given in the HB is that they were not hospitable to Israel when they came out of Egypt, and they had hired Balaam to curse Israel (Num 22-24). While Israel was at Shittim, the Israelite men joined in worshipping the Baal of Peor with Moabite women, which may have involved sexual immorality (Num 25:1-3).[6] Both the cultic centre Beth Peor and the worship of the Baal of Peor became symbols of religious apostasy (Deut 4:3-4; cf. Josh 22:17; Ps 106:28; Hos 9:10).

Closer to the historical literary setting of the book of Ruth, the defeat of Israel at the hands of the Moabite king Eglon and the subsequent subjugation of Israel for eighteen years illustrates the intermittently hostile relations between the two countries (Judg 3:12-30).[7] During the judgeship of Jephthah, Israel again turned away from YHWH by worshipping the gods of Moab along with the gods of other nations (Judg 10:6). Apart from a short period in which Israel may have enjoyed cordial relations with Moab,[8] the overall depiction of Moab is as a negative outgroup.[9] Hence, while some scholars explain Elimelech's sojourn in Moab on the basis of friendly relations between the countries,[10] or geographical or genealogical proximity, it is unlikely the implied reader would view his sojourn in the

---

4 According to Gen 19, the Moabites descended from Moab, the son of Lot's elder daughter by drunken Lot.

5 The Moabites were still excluded from the assembly after the return from exile (Neh 13:1).

6 Numbers 25:1 states that "Israel began לזנות with the Moabite women." The verb זנה in the HB is used literally, as in "to commit fornication," and figuratively, as in "to engage in idolatry." These different nuances are reflected in the interpretation of Num 25; e.g., Martin Noth, *Numbers* (OTL; London: SCM, 1968), 196; Baruch A. Levine, *Numbers 21-36* (AB 4A; New York: Doubleday, 2000), 283.

7 Ten thousand Moabite men died when YHWH raised up Ehud to deliver Israel (Judg 3:29).

8 King David asked the king of Moab for refuge for his parents in 1 Sam 22:3-4.

9 Cf. Isa 15-16; Jer 48; Ezek 25:8-11; Amos 2:1-3; Ezra 9:1; Neh 13:1.

10 E.g., Bush, *Ruth*, 67; Campbell, *Ruth*, 59; Zakovitch, *Rut*, 77.

same light.¹¹ For some commentators, this is underlined by the fate of Elimelech and his sons.¹²

From the outset, therefore, an implied reader would have viewed Ruth with suspicion; she would have been stereotyped as a member of an outgroup. This stereotyping is also associated with particular psychological or moral characteristics and their evaluations.¹³ In the light of the history of Israel's dealings with Moabite women, it is likely that the implied reader would have stereotyped Ruth as immoral—both cultically and sexually.

B. Change of Allegiance

From an identity perspective, however, the RN shows how Ruth becomes a member of the ingroup. The first and most crucial step in her incorporation is her pledge to Naomi, which can be understood as a change of allegiance (Ruth 1:16-17). While most of Jewish tradition views Ruth's commitment to Naomi's God as an expression of conversion,¹⁴ it may be better to view her decision as a step in her "judaization,"¹⁵ a process that will also eventually incorporate her religious conversion.

Shaye Cohen describes three elements of conversion to Judaism deriving from the period mid-second century B.C.E. to the fifth century C.E.:
1. Practice of the Jewish laws
2. Exclusive devotion to the God of the Jews
3. Integration into the Jewish community.¹⁶

Although the elements refer to a later period than the RN, they are helpful for understanding Ruth's change of allegiance. The second element is fulfilled on the road to Bethlehem. While Ruth's pledge centres on her loyalty to Naomi, she also pledges her allegiance to Naomi's country and God (1:16-17). That Ruth is to be understood as turning away from her

---

11 Cf. Hubbard, *Ruth*, 87; Sakenfeld, *Ruth*, 19-20. The Moabite stone provides extrabiblical evidence of the hostility between Israel and Moab. It celebrates a number of military victories by Mesha, king of Moab, during the time of Omri. See J. Andrew Dearman, ed., *Studies in the Mesha Inscription and Moab* (Atlanta: Scholars Press, 1989), 93-95.

12 See *Midr. Ruth Rab.* 2:10; Rashi's comment to Ruth 1:1, 3; Charles P. Baylis, "Naomi in the Book of Ruth in Light of the Mosaic Covenant," *BSac* 161 (2004): 420-22.

13 Kathleen Ethier and Kay Deaux, "Hispanics in Ivy: Assessing Identity and Perceived Threat," *Sex Roles* 22 (1990): 437.

14 See, e.g., *Midr. Ruth Rab.* 2:22; Targum to Ruth 1:16. Ruth is viewed as the paradigmatic convert to Judaism. Some recent proponents of this view include Gow, *Ruth*, 37; Hubbard, *Ruth*, 120; Nielsen, *Ruth*, 49-50.

15 So Gerleman, *Ruth*, 20, and followed by Nielsen, *Ruth*, 50.

16 Shaye J. D. Cohen, "Crossing the Boundary and Becoming a Jew," *HTR* 82 (1989): 26.

Moabite gods can be inferred from Naomi's statement that Orpah has returned "to her people and her gods" (1:15). From the monotheistic perspective of the Israelite storyteller, Ruth's commitment is not to worship YHWH in addition to other gods; rather, she entrusts herself completely to Naomi's God.[17] If she had used "God" (אלהים) in her formula, one might suggest that she is invoking Chemosh, the Moabite deity.[18] But as a reflection of her identification with her newly adopted God, Ruth appeals to YHWH to curse her should she renege on her vow (1:17).[19] The retrospective summary at the end of the chapter then serves to underline her change of allegiance: it is not only Naomi returning home, it is Ruth also (1:22).[20]

The first and third elements, and hence her full conversion, are completed upon her return to the land of Israel. In Bethlehem, she applies and follows the pertinent Israelite laws to her advantage, and by the end of the narrative she is integrated into the Israelite community. Hence, while it may be difficult to determine the genuine nature of Ruth's religious commitment at the time of her pledge to Naomi, her subsequent actions provide adequate evidence of her conversion. On this basis, her conversion to the Israelite religion is complete.

Some commentators, however, reject the notion that conversion is represented by Ruth's vow. For instance, Campbell argues that the focus in Ruth's words is upon "human loyalty and self-renouncing fidelity," with her devotion to YHWH almost "buried in her pledge."[21] For Campbell, there is no conversion, but "simply a living out of the way of Yahweh."[22] While I agree the focus of Ruth's vow is on her devotion to Naomi, this is not mutually exclusive of her devotion to YHWH. Indeed, Ruth realises that YHWH is inseparable from the person of Naomi (1:16-17).[23]

---

17 Sakenfeld, *Ruth*, 33.
18 LaCocque, *Ruth*, 54.
19 For a similar vow of loyalty from a foreigner towards an Israelite (Ittai the Gittite to David), see 2 Sam 15:21.
20 The relative clause ("she who returned from the country of Moab"; השבה משדי מואב) functions to emphasise Ruth's "return," a prominent theme in Ruth 1; see esp. Werner Dommershausen, "Leitwortstil in der Ruthrolle," in *Theologie im Wandel* (ed. Johannes Neumann and Joseph Ratzinger; Munich-Freiberg: Wewel, 1967), 394-407. Of course, it is only Naomi and Orpah who in reality return home. As such, Ruth's return to Judah highlights the remarkable nature of her action as a foreigner and anticipates her acceptance into Israel; Bush, *Ruth*, 96. Cf. H. -J. Fabry, "שוב," *TDOT* 14:478, who suggests her "return" may be symbolic of conversion.
21 Campbell, *Ruth*, 80. Cf. Mark S. Smith, "'Your People Shall Be My People': Family and Covenant in Ruth 1:16-17," *CBQ* 69 (2007): 242-58.
22 Campbell, *Ruth*, 82.
23 Cf. LaCocque, *Ruth*, 52.

Similarly, her act of חסד in following Naomi can be viewed as her expressing an ethical ideal of her new religion. Moreover, instead of her devotion to YHWH being hidden within her pledge to Naomi, it is preferable to view it as the central statement of chiasm. Murray Gow notes that Ruth's speech has a symmetrical structure, with "Your people shall be my people, and your God my God" (עמך עמי ואלהיך אלהי) occupying the central position.[24] Consequently, the placement of Ruth's vow of allegiance to YHWH highlights its importance.

Adele Berlin also rejects the idea of Ruth's conversion. She comments that during the time of Ruth, there was "no formal procedure or even the theoretical possibility for religious conversion." Instead, Ruth simply "adopts the people and God of Naomi."[25] Although there might not have been a formal procedure for religious conversion, the RN describes Ruth's clear turning away from a foreign god to serve YHWH exclusively. Furthermore, evidence from elsewhere in the HB suggests there were some who were not only incorporated into the people of Israel, they also rejected their gods to follow the God of Israel. This can be seen in HB texts broadly contemporaneous with the book of Ruth.[26] In his analysis of the גר ("resident alien") in Deuteronomy, Kenton Sparks distinguishes between two types of non-Israelite גר: those who were on the social periphery of Israelite society and assimilated into it, and those who chose to maintain an independent sense of identity.[27] The former participated in the religious life of Israel, including festivals (e.g., Deut 16:11, 14) and covenant renewal (Deut 29:11; 31:12), while the latter was similar to the non-assimilating "foreigner" (נכרי).

The presence of foreigners within Israelite society who had transferred their religious affiliation to Israel's God is also found in other HB texts (Exod 12:39, 43-49; Josh 6:25; 2 Sam 11:3; 15:19-23). Thus, both legal and narrative texts reinforce the possibility of incorporation of individuals and families into Israel. Deuteronomy and the instance of Rahab in particular (Josh 6:25) point to the concept of conversion. While it might not have been specifically named as such, it was akin to the same process.

---

24 Gow, *Ruth*, 36-37.

25 Adele Berlin, "Ruth," in *HarperCollins Bible Commentary* (ed. James L. Mays; San Francisco: Harper & Row, 2000), 241. Cf. Rudolph, *Ruth*, 43.

26 Although there is no consensus regarding the dating of both books, the majority of critical scholars date the composition/redaction of Deuteronomy from the time of Josiah to the exile, while the book of Ruth is dated from the mid-monarchy to the post-exilic period. On this basis, there is significant overlap between the books.

27 Kenton L. Sparks, *Ethnicity and Identity in Ancient Israel: Prolegomena to the Study of Ethnic Sentiments and Their Expression in the Hebrew Bible* (Winona Lake: Eisenbrauns, 1998), 240-41.

Another way of understanding Ruth's transformation is in reference to Arnold van Genep's phases of a rite of passage. This is defined as "rites which accompany every change of place, state, social position, and age":
1. Separation
2. Margin (or limen[28])
3. Aggregation.[29]

Ruth's departure from Moab and the transfer of her allegiance to Naomi renders Ruth a liminal person. Within this process, Ruth has now separated herself from her Moabite land and community. Her transitional state is underscored by the physical location of her vow: on the road between Moab and Israel. Physically and metaphorically she is on the border of two national identities. As a liminal person, she is "neither here nor there; [she] is betwixt and between the positions assigned by law, custom, convention, and ceremonial [sic]."[30] The narrative of Ruth charts her progress to the final phase of aggregation or incorporation, in which she once again reaches a stable state. In this state, she has clearly defined rights and obligations vis-à-vis others; she is expected to behave "in accordance with certain customary norms and ethical standards binding on incumbents of social position in a system of such positions."[31]

C. Ruth's Journey to Aggregation

Although Ruth's change of identity on the national kinship level is the most prominent transformation, there are also other aspects of her social identity that undergo change. These identities can be classified vis-à-vis her relation to Naomi and Boaz.

1. Identities Relating to Naomi

Ruth's obligations to Naomi primarily stem from her identity as a daughter-in-law. Her devotion to Naomi on this basis is manifest from chapter 1, and her loyalty to Naomi is set in starker relief when compared to the decision of Orpah, her sister-in-law (1:14-15). Similarly to the situation with Boaz and Mr. So-and-So, Orpah chose the expected and

---

28 "Threshold" (Lat.).
29 Arnold van Gennep, *Les rites de passage* (Paris: Nourry, 1909), as quoted in Victor W. Turner, *The Ritual Process: Structure and Anti-Structure* (London: Routledge & Kegan Paul, 1969), 94.
30 Turner, *The Ritual Process*, 95.
31 Turner, *The Ritual Process*, 95.

most expedient path, while Ruth chose the more difficult path in following her mother-in-law, even though she had been released from her kinship obligations (1:8-15).[32] Ruth's vow of loyalty to Naomi establishes a kinship tie that transcends the death of the male who had connected them (1:16-17). As Mark Smith observes: "This relationship represents a family tie closer than that expressed by the formal status of former in-laws."[33]

Upon arrival in Bethlehem Ruth begins to work out what her obligations to Naomi entail in her newly adopted country. Owing to necessity, and deriving from her non-kinship identity as a member of the younger generation, she asks Naomi for permission to glean in the fields (2:2).[34] Her identity as a widow provides her the right to glean in the field. She does so, and brings her gleanings back to share with her mother-in-law (2:18). Her devotion to Naomi, expressed in chapter 1, and now enacted in chapter 2, reflects a closer relationship between Ruth and Naomi: not daughter-in-law, but daughter.[35] This is especially intimated to the implied reader by the discordant juxtaposition of the two terms in 2:22: "Naomi said to Ruth her daughter-in-law, 'It is good, my daughter.'" The implied author stresses their relation by marriage through both the narrator ("daughter-in-law"; 2:20, 22; and "mother-in-law"; 2:18, 19 [twice], 23) and Boaz ("mother-in-law"; 2:11).

Naomi's perception of Ruth as "daughter," however, is a more accurate rendering of the more intimate level of their interaction (2:2, 22). Without a centralised system of welfare and support for the elderly, the younger generation, in particular sons, were responsible for providing care and security for their dependent parents in their infirmity.[36] In the absence of sons, it would be expected that any remaining daughters would fulfil this role. In providing for her mother-in-law, then, Ruth is going beyond what

---

32 The conventional judgement upon Orpah's action is either neutral (expedient) or negative (abandoner). More recently, some feminist scholars have viewed her more positively, drawing strength from her example; see, e.g., Laura E. Donaldson, "The Sign of Orpah: Reading Ruth through Native Eyes," in *Ruth and Esther: A Feminist Companion to the Bible (Second Series)* (ed. Athalya Brenner; Sheffield: Sheffield Academic Press, 1999), 144.

33 Smith, "Family," 247.

34 Some recent commentators understand אלכה־נא as an expression of firm resolve; e.g., Linafelt and Beal, *Ruth & Esther*, 25; Sakenfeld, *Ruth*, 39. However, the use of a cohortative and the נא suggests subordination, and hence a polite request for permission or approval; e.g., GBH §114a; GKC §108c; Ahouva Shulman, "The Particle נָא in Biblical Hebrew Prose," *HS* 40 (1999): 57-82.

35 Cf. Kristin M. Saxegaard, "'More than Seven Sons': Ruth as Example of the Good Son," *SJOT* 15 (2001): 265.

36 In ancient Israel, most daughters would leave their family to join the family of their husband; cf. Fischer, *Rut*, 253.

is required of her as a daughter-in-law;[37] she is taking on a role normally associated with direct offspring, although she is neither son nor daughter.

In fact, by the end of the narrative the chorus of womenfolk recognise Ruth as being worth more than seven sons (טובה לך משבעה בנים; 4:15), the ideal number in HB thought.[38] By this stage, not only has she supported Naomi for the short-term, she has also ensured Naomi's long-term security by marrying into the clan of Elimelech. Additionally, she has provided a descendant to perpetuate the name of her deceased husband. This is a feat that, conspicuously, her own sons could not achieve.[39] Ruth's offspring is described as a "redeemer" (גאל)[40]—one who restores Naomi's life and who will sustain her in her twilight years (4:14-15).

Ruth's central and indispensable role in Obed's birth means that she is also a "redeemer" for Naomi. Through Ruth's actions Naomi's life is restored: from empty and bitter to fulfilled and satisfied (cf. 1:3-5, 21 with 4:15-17).[41] Hence Ruth, a character whose actions display a superabundant love for her mother-in-law (4:15), is appositely described as being worth more than the ideal number of sons. From a state of liminality she not only learns to fulfil her role as a daughter-in-law in a strange land, she also takes on the additional role of a son. Her actions, which ultimately produce a descendant for Naomi, not only "re"-establish her (and her mother-in-law) in the clan of Elimelech, it also incorporates her into wider Israelite society (4:17-22).

2. Identities Relating to Boaz

The transformation of Ruth vis-à-vis Boaz proceeds through a series of stages. At the beginning she is an unidentified worker in Boaz's field. In response to Boaz's question, the foreman informs him of her identity in relation to Naomi: she is the Moabitess who returned with her (2:6). The foreign aspect of her identity is prominent in the foreman's thinking as well as her own (2:6, 10). Yet her self-identification as a "foreigner" (נכריה; 2:10) is strictly incorrect considering the events that have taken place. Within the HB, נכריה generally denotes the stranger who is only

---

37 Cf. Berquist, "Role," 27-28.
38 See 1 Sam 2:5; 1 Chron 3:24; Job 1:2; 42:13; Jer 15:9.
39 Berlin, *Poetics*, 88.
40 Syntactically and contextually, this is the best understanding, as held by the overwhelming majority of commentators. A small minority, however, maintain that it refers to Boaz. For a discussion, see, e.g., Bush, *Ruth*, 253-54; Leggett, *Levirate*, 255-59.
41 The use of the same verbal root שוב in 1:21 and 4:15 forms an inclusio that provides closure for the story; cf. Campbell, *Ruth*, 164, 68.

temporarily in the country, a foreigner who has not given up his/her original home.[42] From chapter 1, however, it is clear that Ruth has severed all connections with her homeland. Thus, the use of נכריה probably reflects Ruth's extreme self-consciousness about her alien status. Perhaps she also uses the term because it would be less likely to invoke hostility to refer to herself as a נכריה instead of a גר.[43] It would also be consistent with an implied reader's current perception of her as foreign, with the associated connotation of being dangerous or hostile.[44] As such, it would be expected that Boaz would treat her with at least some caution; hence, Ruth's surprise at Boaz's indifference to her Moabite origin.

Yet Boaz's explanation for his favour towards Ruth reveals that he views her as more than just a foreigner, a stereotypical Moabite, or a potential victim of abuse[45] (cf. 2:8-9, 15-16, 22). He is aware of the loyalty she has shown her mother-in-law (2:11), whom he knows is a member of his own clan by marriage. Although Ruth's social identity as a Moabite is prominent in her first interaction with her newly adopted community, Boaz already perceives her as an individual. Her identity is not only linked to her familial bond (daughter-in-law of Naomi) or to her nationality (Moabite). He already views her as one who has performed noteworthy deeds in her own right, and as one who is now already in the process of aggregation into a new people. Thus, it is appropriate for Boaz to call upon YHWH to bless her for her actions because she has identified herself with this new deity (2:12). Even in this opening interaction, Boaz is instrumental in the transformation of Ruth's identity. She is no longer to be perceived as a "foreigner" with minimal privileges, but as an "immigrant" or semi-assimilated foreigner (גר). As one who has severed her ties with her homeland, she joins the Israelite community as one with a range of rights and privileges comparable to an Israelite native.[46]

---

42 Michael Guttmann, "The Term 'Foreigner' (נכרי) Historically Considered," *HUCA* 3 (1926): 1. Cf. B. Lang, "נכר," *TDOT* 9:427.
43 Matthews, "Social Identity," 51.
44 This added connotation is attested within the HB (e.g., 2 Sam 22:45-46; Neh 9:2; 13:30). Cf. Mary T. Douglas, *Purity and Danger: An Analysis of Concepts of Pollution and Taboo* (London: Routledge & K. Paul, 1966), 94-98.
45 Recent readings view the harvest field with its male workers as a potential source of danger for Ruth. See, e.g., Michael Carasik, "Ruth 2,7: Why the Overseer Was Embarrassed," *ZAW* 107 (1995): 493-94; Fischer, *Rut*, 172-73; David Shepherd, "Violence in the Fields? Translating, Reading, and Revising in Ruth 2," *CBQ* 63 (2001): 444-62.
46 For a discussion of the differences between a נכרי and a גר see, e.g., B. Lang, "נכר," *TDOT* 9:426-427; Frank A. Spina, "Israelites as *gerim*, 'Sojourners,' in Social and Historical Context," in *The Word of the Lord Shall Go Forth: Essays in Honor of David Noel Freedman in Celebration of His Sixtieth Birthday* (ed. Carol L. Meyers and Michael P. O'Connor; Winona Lake: Eisenbrauns, 1983), 323.

Boaz's perception of her identity is rapidly absorbed by Ruth. As a member of Israelite society, she responds to him with an appropriately deferential tone. She calls him "my lord" (אדני), and humbly describes her identity as "your maidservant" (שפחתך), even though she is mindful that she is not even on par with his servant girls (2:13b). Nonetheless, she still takes the initiative to mention that she hopes to remain in his favour (2:13a). Her wish is shortly granted, when at mealtime (לעת האכל)[47] she is invited (גשי הלם)[48] to sit with the other Israelite gleaners and partake of the same food (2:14). After the meal, the further privilege of gleaning among the sheaves is extended to her (2:15). All these special benefits of membership in the Israelite community reinforce her understanding of her changing identity. As she continues to work in Boaz's field, she stays close to his servant girls and is identified with them (2:22-23; 3:2). Her liminality is reducing as she is now a member of this group in the Bethlehem community.[49] Concurrently, her social status is rising in parallel with her integration into Israelite society.

The centrality of Boaz in the transformation of Ruth's identity is particularly manifest in the episode on the threshing floor. He has already played a key role in her understanding of her identity and place within Israelite society through their interaction in his field. Her change in clothing as she approaches the threshing floor marks the end of her liminal phase of mourning after her husband's death,[50] and consequently, her availability for marriage to Boaz (3:3).[51] Her response to Boaz's request to identify herself is revealing of her self-understanding: "I am Ruth, your servant" (אנכי רות אמתך; 3:9). Neither she nor anyone else had used her first name previously. But she now confidently asserts her personal name,

---

47 This is based on the MT division, which joins this phrase with the preceding words of the narrator, instead of the words of Boaz that follow (as in the LXX). The originality of the MT is followed by most modern commentators, including Bush, *Ruth*, 125; Campbell, *Ruth*, 102. Hence, there is a chronological separation between verses 13 and 14.

48 This phrase suggests that Ruth was keeping her distance; Block, *Judges, Ruth*, 666. Although she had found Boaz's favour, she was not presuming upon it.

49 Matthews, *Judges/Ruth*, 230.

50 The parallel between Ruth's triad of actions in washing, anointing herself, and putting on an outer garment in 3:3 and the similar actions of David in 2 Sam 12:20, which signalled the end of his mourning period for his son, indicates that Ruth's actions imply the end of her mourning for the death of her husband; cf. Zakovitch, *Rut*, 136; Bush, *Ruth*, 152. *Pace* Sakenfeld, *Ruth*, 54.

51 Although Ruth is presented attractively to Boaz, the suggestion that her preparations are those of a bride for marriage, e.g., Sasson, *Ruth*, 66-68, or more commonly, for the purpose of seducing Boaz (e.g., Hubbard, *Ruth*, 201-02; LaCocque, *Ruth*, 91; Zakovitch, *Rut*, 136) cannot be sustained from elsewhere in the HB; for discussion and references, see Block, *Judges, Ruth*, 683; Bush, *Ruth*, 150-52.

which is congruent with the level of intimacy of their relationship, having been established over a whole harvest season—a period of some seven weeks.[52]

The use of her personal name is also consistent with the personal nature of their meeting.[53] No longer a non-descript foreigner working in the field, nor a worker from the lowest social rung, she now openly identifies herself as his "servant" (אמה; 3:9), as distinct from her previous self-identification as a "maidservant" (שפחה; 2:13). Although some scholars attribute the difference to stylistic variation,[54] Sasson convincingly argues that the term שפחה applied to females belonging to the lowest rung of the social ladder,[55] while אמה represented women who could advance to the status of wives or concubines.[56] Hence, in her twofold assertion of her identity as a "servant" she is implying that she is now qualified to marry Boaz.

On this basis, in addition to her social identity as a relative from his clan, she requests that he act upon his responsibility as a kinsman-redeemer and take her hand in marriage. Significantly, her phraseology ("spread the corner of your garment [כנפך]"[57] over me"; 3:9) recycles words Boaz used to indicate her initial assimilation into Israelite society (2:12). Previously he perceived that she sought refuge under the wings [כנפים] of YHWH by aligning herself with him and his people. Now Ruth uses these words in her marriage proposal,[58] which, if successful, will usher in the final stage of the transformation of her identity.

The importance of Boaz in Ruth's incorporation into Israelite society is also evident in her terminal identity. When Boaz successfully procures the right to marry Ruth, her identity as Boaz's wife means she is publicly and concretely bound to the wider Israelite society (4:10, 13).[59] No longer is she identified as a widow and a foreigner, no longer is she a member of the underprivileged. She is now the wife of Boaz, and furthermore, on the scale of moral worth is on equal terms with him (2:1 cf. 3:11). The

---

52 Cf. Deut 16:9-12. Campbell, *Ruth*, 108.
53 Fischer, *Rut*, 210.
54 E.g., Campbell, *Ruth*, 123; Zakovitch, *Rut*, 141.
55 Although a שפחה could be presented by a sterile wife to her husband to bear a child on her behalf, this would not change her status; Sasson, *Ruth*, 53.
56 The usage of both terms in 1 Sam 25:41 highlights their difference: Abigail is an אמה but wants to put herself in a subordinate position vis-à-vis David, so she refers to herself as a שפחה; A. Jepsen, "Amah und Schiphchah," *VT* 8 (1958): 293-97(95).
57 Lit. "wing" or "extremity," which in this context refers to the skirt or corner of Boaz's garment; cf. BDB, 489.
58 For the idiomatic usage of "to spread one's wings over someone," see Deut 23:1 [22:30]; 27:20; Ezek 16:8; Mal 2:16. See also Kruger, "Hem," 79-86.
59 Hubbard, *Ruth*, 256-58.

consummation of their marriage and the birth of a son also signals the culmination of Ruth's aggregation into Israelite society. They function as her rites of aggregation, publicly transferring upon her the status and honour of Israelite wife and mother.[60] Her genetic infusion into the line of Israel renders her a legitimate builder of the "house of Israel" (4:11). The benediction of the happy throng at Bethlehem's town gate that Ruth be identified alongside the matriarchs of Israel is fulfilled beyond their furthest imaginings: she becomes a forebear of the most esteemed Israelite king of all (4:17-22).

D. Summary

The RN charts Ruth's integration into her chosen ingroup: from her initial identity as a Moabite foreigner, she attains the status of an Israelite matriarch; from a state of liminality, she reaches the final state of incorporation into Israelite society. This is achieved through her interaction with Naomi and Boaz. From our identity paradigm, the discussion has focused solely on social aspects—both non-kin (female from younger generation) and kin (Moabite, member of the same clan as Boaz, and from Elimelech's father's house).

II. The Personal Component of Ruth's Identity

Although the social component of Ruth's identity is prominent in the narrative, the personal component is also clearly presented. The above description of the transformation of Ruth's identity through her social interaction with Naomi and Boaz may give the impression that Ruth was a passive participant. Nothing would be further from the truth. In fact, personal components of Ruth's identity—especially her initiative and her חסד—play a crucial role in her transformation.

---

60 Cf. John G. Peristiany, "Introduction," in *Honor and Grace in Anthropology* (ed. John G. Peristiany and Julian A. Pitt-Rivers; Cambridge: Cambridge University Press, 1992), 2: "Rites establish consensus as to 'how things are' and thus they fix legitimacy. Hence ritual is the guarantor of the social order, conveying honor, not only in the formal distribution of the dignities on ceremonial occasions, but also in the sense of making manifest the honorable status of the actors."

A. The Initiative of Ruth

Ruth shows initiative in each of the chapters in which she is present. Her first and foundational display of initiative is her commitment to Naomi. Despite the urgings of her mother-in-law to return to her mother's house, and despite the lead of her sister-in-law who does return, she takes the initiative to follow her mother-in-law. In this act she displays willingness to defy convention and shun the safety of the familiar—she forsakes her land, people, and gods for those of Naomi (1:16-17). Her tenacity in clinging to her mother-in-law is reflected in her well-known speech of devotion. The strong affection and loyalty Ruth has for Naomi is reflected in the use of דבק (1:14; cf. Gen 2:24; 34:3),[61] and the use of Ruth's vow in modern marriage ceremonies taps into the level of commitment Ruth has for Naomi. Yet her willingness to defy convention on the road to Bethlehem is not a one-off action. Her willingness to marry a foreigner from Israel suggests it is a stable character trait. Initiative is a prominent component of her personal identity.

In chapter 2 Ruth shows initiative by asking permission to glean in the fields outside Bethlehem. Acutely aware of their need for nourishment and the lack of a provider within the household, Ruth displays resourcefulness in seeking physical provision. It is not stated whether Ruth knew she had the right to glean under Israelite law, or whether gleaning was a privilege extended to the underprivileged generally in the ancient Near East.[62] Whatever the case may be, she at least was aware of the provision to glean in a field, and that permission was required to glean in a particular field. This permission is granted by the foreman of Boaz's field, and her request is relayed to Boaz (2:7).[63] In turn, Boaz secures an ongoing supply of food for her, as well as physical protection within his field (2:8-9, 14-16). He explains that his actions are in response to Ruth's faithfulness to Naomi

---

61 Cf. Phyllis Trible, *God and the Rhetoric of Sexuality* (Philadelphia: Fortress, 1978), 197, fn. 13; G. Wallis, "דָּבַק," *TDOT* 3:80-81.

62 References to gleaning in Sumerian and Egyptian texts may indicate that the practice was not uncommon; see David L. Baker, "To Glean or Not to Glean..." *ExpTim* 117 (2006): 406.

63 This is based on the meaning of עמד in the phrase ותבוא ותעמוד מאז הבקר ועד עתה as "to remain, stay." See BDB, 764; *HALOT*, 841; Bush, *Ruth*, 118. So NASB. Hence, the foreman is indicating that he gave permission for Ruth to glean, and she has been working until the present time (the arrival of Boaz). For nineteen different interpretations of this phrase, see Daniel Lys, "Résidence ou repos? Notule sur Ruth ii 7," *VT* 21 (1971): 497-99, and for a recent interpretation of Ruth 2:7, see Jonathan Grossman, "'Gleaning among the Ears'–'Gathering among the Sheaves': Characterizing the Image of the Supervising Boy (Ruth 2)," *JBL* 126 (2007): 703-16.

(2:11). In short, Boaz rewards Ruth for the primary initiative she displayed towards Naomi.

Ruth displays further initiative in her conversation with Boaz in chapter 2. Her first words to Boaz may be understood as a reflexive response to his surprising generosity (2:10), but her second speech in response to Boaz's explanation for his largesse reveals her enterprising character. Instead of simply expressing gratitude for Boaz's gracious provision, she states:

> May I continue to find favour in your eyes, my lord. For you have given me comfort and have spoken kindly to your maidservant, though I do not have the standing of one of your maidservants (2:13).

Ruth's response is well crafted. She begins by acknowledging the favour Boaz has shown her. Immediately sizing him up as a person who draws satisfaction from pleasing others, she emphasises the effect he has on her emotional state—providing her comfort (נחמתני), and reassuring her heart (דברת על לב).[64] In this way she has formed a self-perpetuating cycle: his action leads to her happiness, which leads to his satisfaction, which feeds his motivation to please her more. This is all couched in terms that underline her humility and submissiveness as a supplicant.[65] Moreover, there is a subtle request nestled in her response: not only does Ruth acknowledge the favour Boaz has already shown, her use of אמצא indicates her wish to remain in his favour. In 2:10 she uses the perfective מצאתי, now in 2:13 the imperfective indicates his present and ongoing favour. The cohortative sense of אמצא in this context means that she is, in effect, asking that he maintain his generosity towards her, or even show generosity beyond his current display.[66] It is thus not surprising that Boaz displays further munificence towards her both at mealtime and afterwards (2:14-16).

---

[64] Comfort (נחם) in this instance has the connotation of reassurance or relief from distress. Campbell, *Ruth*, 100-01, notes three meanings for דברת על לב in the HB: (1) to persuade or entice a woman; (2) to comfort or relieve; and (3) to reassure or encourage. The second and third meanings are most pertinent in this context, and overlaps with the first clause. The context does not favour the first meaning; *pace* Linafelt and Beal, *Ruth & Esther*, 37.

[65] Ruth addresses Boaz as "my lord" (אדני), and refers to herself as "your maidservant" (שפחתך).

[66] In its context the cohortative sense would fit best, since she has found his favour (2:10), and now wants to maintain his favour because she has found it very beneficial (2:13). Her response functions as both a wish that Boaz's generosity continue, as well as expressing gratitude for Boaz's kindness; so Campbell, *Ruth*, 100; Hubbard, *Ruth*, 168, and NIV, NRSV. Other scholars interpret Ruth's phrase solely as an expression of gratitude; e.g., Bush, *Ruth*, 123-24; Rudolph, *Ruth*, 47, and NJPS, NET.

Ruth's final display of initiative is on the threshing floor (chapter 3). When Naomi outlines the plan for Ruth to follow, Ruth's response is: "All that you say I will do" (כל אשר תאמרי אעשה; 3:5).[67] The word order of her response suggests her intention to follow Naomi's plan, which is corroborated by the proleptic narratorial summary: "So she went down to the threshing floor and did just as[68] her mother-in-law commanded her to do" (3:6). Given the careful presentation of Ruth as precisely following the instructions of Naomi, it is somewhat startling to find she does not seem to do this.

Rather than wait for Boaz to tell her what to do, she asks him to marry her because he is a kinsman-redeemer (גאל; 3:9). And the way she expresses her proposal underscores her initiative: the use of כנף in her proposal, a word used previously by Boaz in conversation with her adds extra incentive for him to accept her request. For Boaz had prayed that she would be richly rewarded by YHWH for taking shelter under כנפיו (2:12). By reusing the same word, she is essentially asking him to act as the human agent through whom YHWH would answer his prayer.[69] Not only does Ruth seize the initiative when it is presented to her, she uses the opportunity to maximise the possibility he would answer in the affirmative.

Ruth's proposal is not evidence, however, for an alteration to Naomi's plan. Adele Berlin, for instance, views Ruth's actions as a misunderstanding of her mother-in-law's instructions: "Naomi sent her on a romantic mission but she turned it into a quest for a redeemer."[70] Rather, Ruth's proposal is best understood as her taking the initiative when a small opening is provided by Boaz's enquiry: "Who are you?" (3:9). She replies by telling him who he is and what he is to do.[71] For Naomi's plan only sketches the steps Ruth is to take up to the point of conversation with Boaz, and does not provide the words she is to speak. Furthermore, as Katharine Sakenfeld notes, by beginning with a question rather than telling Ruth what to do, "Boaz has moved the encounter away from Naomi's anticipated scenario."[72] Indeed, Ruth's words are consistent with the overall aim of the scheme: to provide Ruth with security through a marriage partner (3:1; cf. 1:9). Hence, Ruth's words are best understood as the climactic culmination to the actions she has already taken immediately

---

67 In this context the imperfect form of אמר indicates an action (Naomi's command) that, although just completed, still has an effect lasting into the present; see GKC § 107h.
68 Heb. בכל, with כ taken as the *kaph veritatis*; see, *IBHS*, § 11.2.9b.
69 Cf. W. S. Prinsloo, "The Theology of the Book of Ruth," *VT* 30 (1980): 337.
70 Berlin, *Poetics*, 90. Cf. Zakovitch, *Rut*, 141, who suggests that Ruth disobeys Naomi's command.
71 The reversal is also noted by, inter alios, Campbell, *Ruth*, 121; LaCocque, *Ruth*, 97.
72 Sakenfeld, *Ruth*, 57.

prior to and during the encounter on the threshing floor. They do not contravene the express plan of her mother-in-law; instead, they reveal Ruth's determination and ability for independent thought in seizing the initiative within the small window of opportunity presented to her by both Naomi and Boaz.

Nonetheless, in her initiative Ruth is careful not to transgress the legal and social boundaries of ancient Israel. Through her actions she shows that she is aware of cultural norms and skilfully manoeuvres herself within these. Apropos Naomi, she paradoxically opposes her parental authority in chapter 1. Yet if this is understood as her desire to not leave her mother-in-law abandoned and vulnerable, it reflects a strong sense of filial piety towards her. She is willing to contravene her mother-in-law's command in order to uphold a higher overarching ethical principle. In chapter 2, her initiative is motivated by the need to provide for her elderly parent, and she gleans in the field within the provision of the law. At the beginning of chapter 3, it is Naomi who takes the initiative. Under these circumstances, Ruth willingly follows her mother-in-law's plan, while concurrently adding her own personal initiative. In short, her interactions with Naomi provide evidence of her grasp of filial and legal requirements; these form the boundary within which she is able to move, and which she manipulates according to her discretion.

Apropos her interactions with Boaz, she also remains within social and legal boundaries. She immediately realises he is a generous landowner who could possibly become a personal benefactor. Her subtle request to him in chapter 2, given in an overtly deferential tone, reflects her understanding of the workings of a patriarchal society and the power invested in the male members. Once she is informed that he is in fact from among their kinsman-redeemers (2:20), this morsel of information is quickly integrated into her thinking and used to her advantage in chapter 3 (3:9).[73]

In her initiative, however, Ruth does not overstep the social boundaries of her time. The patriarchal social structure is evident in the RN: Boaz's enquiry of his overseer presupposes that each woman is the responsibility of, and therefore under the authority of a man (2:5);[74] the main actors at the scene at the town gate are male—those involved in the legal case and the elders who adjudicate the case, and pronounce their blessing on the final outcome (4:1-12); the male perspective is prominent as the situation is described with overt male concerns, such as patrilineality (4:5, 9-10). Ruth is aware of this, and works the patriarchal system to her advantage. She knows the responsibility to care for needy family members is invested in a

---

73   When outlining her plan, Naomi only describes Boaz as a "kinsman" or "relative" (מדעת; 3:2; cf. 2:1). Ruth takes the initiative of calling him a "kinsman-redeemer" (גאל; 3:9).

74   Trible, *Sexuality*, 176.

male clansman—the kinsman-redeemer. Armed with this knowledge, she does not hesitate to challenge him to take up his responsibility; Boaz is simply a reactor to her (and Naomi's) initiative (3:9-13).[75] Ruth's proposition is certainly bold, but it still derives from a role inherent in her society. Although her initiative challenges the boundaries of her patriarchal society, her conformity to its rules reveals her care in moving within them.

Neither does Ruth overstep the boundaries of the law in her interaction with Boaz. The majority of commentators understand Ruth's request for marriage (3:9) as evidence that she is adding the levirate responsibility to those of the kinsman-redeemer: at least part of her motivation is to provide an heir for Mahlon through a levirate union.[76] As Bush points out, however, this view is problematic for three reasons.[77] (1) The expressed sole purpose of the plan is the provision of "home and husband" for Ruth (3:1-4). Naomi does not mention the provision of an heir for Elimelech and Mahlon. (2) The previous usage of גאל (2:20) was in its general non-legal sense. Since nothing has changed from that point in the narrative until chapter 3, it is unlikely Ruth is now using גאל in its legal sense of asking Boaz to redeem land. (3) Ruth does not identify herself as "wife of the deceased," or "wife of Mahlon," implying she must raise an heir for her deceased husband's property. Rather, she calls herself an אמה, one who is socially eligible for marriage. Sakenfeld adds another reason against reading a reference to property or offspring: it presupposes that Ruth has a technical knowledge of Israelite laws, which would be unlikely for a new immigrant.[78] Hence, it is better to understand Ruth's use of גאל in its more general sense of "kinsman who has a responsibility for the well-being of fellow family members." This usage of גאל makes better narrative sense: Ruth is requesting marriage apart from any reference or allusion to levirate marriage or land redemption.

In short, Ruth's interactions with Boaz convey a strong sense of her understanding of both the patriarchal and kinship structure of her society, and the rights and obligations deriving from these. She also stays within the bounds of the law. In all her actions Ruth plays by the rules of her society, being careful not to break them. Even as she works within the system, however, her initiative as a reflection of her quiet determination is unmistakable.[79]

---

75 Cf. LaCocque, *Ruth*, 96.
76 These include Gray, *Ruth*, 395; Matthews, *Judges/Ruth*, 234; cf. Rashi's comment on 3:9.
77 Bush, *Ruth*, 168-69.
78 Sakenfeld, *Ruth*, 61.
79 Cf. Fischer, "The Book of Ruth," 33: "The book of Ruth shows how to take seriously the real social system as well as the women's independent concept of living."

B. The חסד of Ruth

Closely related to the first component of Ruth's personal identity is her characteristic virtue of חסד. Gordon Clark describes this rich and distinctly Hebrew term as "a beneficent action performed, in the context of a deep and enduring commitment between two persons or parties, by one who is able to render assistance to the needy party who in the circumstances is unable to help him- or herself."[80] Most scholars would agree that חסד is mostly expressed in the context of a relationship, but differ on which aspect to emphasise: obligation or benevolence. Sakenfeld, for instance, notes that the actor has "a privately and even publicly recognized responsibility to do *ḥesed* because of the relationship in which he stands."[81] Yet after an examination of all the texts within which חסד is used, Francis Andersen presents a correction to this understanding: "The formal, legal side of *ḥesed* as obligation and duty has been exaggerated. It is incidental and marginal. The heart of the matter is a generous and beneficial action, not at all required. The action often does not follow custom. In fact, it often requires breach of custom, violation of duty."[82] Understood in this way, חסד is aptly used by both Naomi and Boaz to describe Ruth's actions.[83]

Naomi prays that YHWH would reward her daughters-in-law with חסד, just as they had shown to her and her family (המתים ועמדי; 1:8). The חסד of Ruth and Orpah to which Naomi refers is the care and hospitality they had demonstrated to her family during their sojourn in Moab.[84] Boaz also praises Ruth for two acts of חסד. As established in Chapter Two, Ruth's first act of חסד refers to her abandonment of her homeland and her people in order to care for her mother-in-law (cf. 2:11). But the reason for her choice of Boaz for a marriage partner as a greater act of חסד than the first is not as easily discerned. On the basis of their previously established

---

80 Gordon R. Clark, *The Word Hesed in the Hebrew Bible* (JSOTSup 157; Sheffield: Sheffield Academic Press, 1993), 267.

81 Katharine D. Sakenfeld, *The Meaning of Hesed in the Hebrew Bible: A New Enquiry* (HSM 17; Missoula: Scholars Press, 1978), 234. Cf. Nelson Glueck, *Hesed in the Bible* (trans. Alfred Gottschalk; Cincinnati: Hebrew Union College Press, 1967), 55: חסד operating between persons is "conduct in accord with a mutual relationship of rights and duties or conduct corresponding to a mutually *obligatory* relationship" (emphasis added).

82 Francis I. Andersen, "Yahweh, the Kind and Sensitive God," in *God Who is Rich in Mercy: Essays Presented to Dr. D. B. Knox* (ed. Peter T. O'Brien and David G. Peterson; Sydney: Lancer, 1986), 44.

83 It is difficult to find a single English equivalent to חסד. From the foregoing discussion, translations emphasising obligation are inappropriate; e.g., *HALOT* 1:336-37. Those translations emphasising goodness or kindness capture the sense better; e.g., BDB, 338-39. While "loving-kindness" is probably the closest approximation, I will continue to use חסד in lieu of an English equivalent.

84 Cf. Sakenfeld, *Ruth*, 25; Zakovitch, *Rut*, 89.

relationship, it would seem to be an understandable, if not natural choice; this would hardly represent an act of חסד.

An understanding of this enigmatic statement can be drawn from the narrative context.[85] His statement that Ruth was free to choose from all the eligible bachelors in town reveals that she was under no obligation to marry a relative of her deceased husband (3:10). Indeed, she was released from all familial responsibilities (1:8-9). Hence, in one sense, Ruth's marriage to any Israelite could be viewed as an act of חסד because it makes permanent her relationship with Naomi in Israel, and thus her continued provision for her.

Yet Boaz's description of Ruth's action as one of חסד also needs to take into account two other factors: his status in comparison to other potential grooms; and his kinship relation as a kinsman-redeemer. Her choice of Boaz can be considered an act of חסד because she sets aside personal preferences. As Boaz notes, she could have chased after a host of young men, either poor or rich (3:10). That is, she could have married for love or money, but she chose loyalty to Naomi and her family instead.[86] Given Boaz's elderly status, Zakovitch even suggests that Ruth acts independently of her heart's desire (*Herzensbegehrens*).[87] As noted in Chapter Two, though, Boaz speaks in an overly deferential tone. He may be older than other potential marriage partners, but he also has some attractive qualities.

Nonetheless, from Ruth's perspective a younger groom would have been more beneficial. If she still wanted to retain the kinship benefits, she could have chosen the other kinsman-redeemer, who was probably younger than Boaz.[88] In a small community, it seems unlikely Naomi and Ruth would have been unaware of Mr. So-and So's presence (cf. 1:19; 2:6; 3:11). Although, as a younger man, he would probably be more concerned to secure his financial stability, at least he would have a longer timeframe in which to provide for Ruth.[89] If this is a pertinent consideration, it provides a reason for her proposal being an act of greater חסד: choosing Boaz means there is a higher chance she would be widowed again before her children are self-sufficient.[90]

---

85 A discussion of the "last kindness" in relation to Boaz's identity and his actions was presented in Chapter Two. This present discussion focuses on the significance of "the last kindness" for Ruth's character.
86 Hubbard, *Ruth*, 214-15.
87 Zakovitch, *Rut*, 142.
88 See the discussion in Chapter Two.
89 See the comparative anthropological evidence from contemporary kinship-based societies in Timothy M. Willis, *The Elders of the City: A Study of the Elders-Laws in Deuteronomy* (Atlanta: SBL, 2001), 238-50.
90 Cf. Willis, *Elders*, 264-65. One strand of Jewish thought has Boaz dying on the day after the wedding; *Ruth Zuta* 55, as mentioned in Louis Ginzberg, *The Legends of the Jews*

Boaz's subsequent response reveals that his appraisal of her action as a greater act of חסד is also essentially connected to his role as a kinsman-redeemer (3:11-13). Although Ruth may not have linked marriage with any legal responsibilities of a kinsman-redeemer, this is clearly how Boaz understands her request. His concern for the ranking of kinsman-redeemers and the priority held by the nearer kinsman belies a technical legal usage of גאל (3:12-13). That Boaz has in mind more than just marriage can be inferred from what he does *not* say. For, as Beattie observes, he could have said, "If [the nearer kinsman] will not marry you, I will."[91] Ruth simply requested marriage, but Boaz sees the wider consequences of her request—eventually involving the redemption of land, and the perpetuation of Mahlon's line. For these reasons Boaz considers Ruth's marriage request an act of greater חסד than her previous act.

חסד then, is a core personal attribute of Ruth. It is manifest in her actions in Moab as well as Bethlehem. As the motivating factor for her actions, her initiative can be viewed as arising from her חסד for Naomi; they are not risky behaviours undertaken for their own sake. Indeed, Campbell even suggests that initiative may be an essential component of חסד in some circumstances: "[*H*]*esed* has to do with creating circumstances in a relationship wherein change can take place. Both Naomi and Boaz need to be changed, and Ruth is the one who can do it, chooses to do it, and takes initiatives to do it."[92]

Furthermore, her acts of חסד are a major factor in Boaz's considering her "a woman of worth" (אשת חיל; 3:11). It is particularly germane that Boaz, himself a "man of great worth" and one characterised by חסד, is able to describe her actions as suffused with חסד. In short, as a consistent feature of Ruth's behaviour, חסד is a stable character trait, a central component of her personal identity.

C. Summary and Conclusions

Ruth's initiative and חסד are two of her most prominent character traits. Her actions are a reflection of these aspects of her personal identity, and are central to the transformation of her identity. A concrete illustration of the outcome *sans* these aspects of her personal identity is found in Orpah. Ruth's primary designation in the RN reflects her social identity as a

---

(trans. Henrietta Szold, Paul Radin, and Boaz Cohen, 7 vols., vol. 4; Philadelphia: Jewish Publication Society of America, 1928), 34.

91 Beattie, "Ruth III," 45.

92 Edward F. Campbell, "Naomi, Boaz, and Ruth, *hesed* (חסד) and Change," *Austin Seminary Bulletin* 105 (1990): 74.

Moabite. Aspects of her personal identity are crucial to the transformation of this social identity. Yet the initiatives she takes spring from her חסד towards her mother-in-law, Naomi. Thus, her actions can only be understood within her wider social identities. Her actions can truly be categorised as acts of חסד because she ventures beyond the obligations deriving from her social identities.

From the perspective of self-categorisation theory (SCT), the relative salience of social identity is dependent upon personal, social, and situational factors. As members of a relationship-based collectivist society, key close relationships are the central determinant of identity salience and subsequent action. At the beginning of the RN, both Ruth and Orpah shared the same social and situational factors. As daughters-in-law, they were members of the same ingroup with a close kinship tie to Naomi. On the road leaving Moab, Naomi had released them both from any familial obligation. The difference in the subsequent actions of Ruth, then, can be attributed to personality factors, specifically her חסד towards Naomi. It is this aspect of her personal identity that renders her social identity more salient, leading her to act with initiative to express her חסד towards her mother-in-law. In social identity terms, her חסד corresponds to the individual cultural orientation of allocentrism. When faced with making a decision between personal and collective goals, Ruth subordinates the former to the latter.

III. The Impact on the Identity of an Implied Reader

A. Ruth as Reinforcement

The incorporation of Ruth into Israelite society produces a dynamic tension for an implied reader. At first blush, it would seem her assimilation simply reinforces the identity of an ancient Israelite. After all, this singular Moabite absorbs Israelite custom and Law; she embraces the requirements of Naomi's people and God. Ellen van Wolde asserts that Ruth stops being a foreigner when she chooses Naomi, her people, and her God.[93] Similarly, Victor Matthews comments that no further trace of Ruth's Moabite heritage is mentioned in the text.[94] Her grand disavowal of Moab and her vow of wholehearted allegiance to Israel sets in train a series of events leading to her ultimate assimilation into Israelite society, punctuated by her contribution to the Royal Line.

---

93 Wolde, "Texts in Dialogue with Texts," 28.
94 Matthews, "Social Identity," 50.

The quality of Ruth's character as fundamentally marked by חסד, and her actions leading to her establishment as a matriarch distinguish her as a worthy member of Israel. In this respect, the intertextual allusions reinforce her place within Israelite society. Her decision to leave her native country to follow Naomi can be viewed as parallel to the journey undertaken by Abram (Gen 12:1-9); indeed, Ruth's action may be evidence of even greater faith than the Israelite patriarch.[95] Furthermore, although she may be descended from Lot (Gen 19:30-38), she distances herself from her ancestry by not behaving like Lot's eldest daughter on the threshing floor.[96] At the end of the RN Ruth is linked with the patriarchal mothers Rachel and Leah (4:11; Gen 29-30), with the suggestion that Ruth stands in continuity with that line.[97] She is also compared with Tamar (4:12; Gen 38), but presented as more virtuous: Tamar resorts to deception, Ruth openly reveals her identity (Ruth 3:9);[98] Tamar is compelled into sexual relations, Ruth maintains her sexual purity.[99] Hence, it is only with slight overstatement that Nielsen comments: "Ruth is … depicted not just as a new and better version of Tamar, but also as a new and better version of Abram."[100] Ultimately, then, her conversion and personal character reinforces the Israelite sense of identity.

This affirmation of Israelite identity is the presupposition of the vast majority of commentators, as reflected in the most commonly ascribed purposes for the book. The long-held consensus and recently revived view is that the book of Ruth was primarily written as a polemic against the enforcement of endogamous marriage (Ezra 10; Neh 13:23-27).[101] Specifically, it was written to protest the reforms of Ezra and Nehemiah against interracial marriage in the post-exilic period. Another commonly asserted purpose is that it contains propaganda promoting the Davidic dynasty. David is either glorified through his pious ancestry,[102] or is exonerated by explaining his non-Israelite blood.[103] Both of these views are predicated upon the downplaying or evacuation of the foreign aspect of Ruth's identity. Although Ruth was originally a foreigner, through her

---

95 Abram left his native land with a trust in God's promise, whereas Ruth left without any promise from God regarding her future; so, e.g., LaCocque, *Ruth*, 53.
96 Cf. Nielsen, *Ruth*, 68; Zakovitch, *Rut*, 51. For correspondences between the RN and Gen 19:30-38, see Zakovitch, *Rut*, 49-51.
97 Hubbard, *Ruth*, 259.
98 Cf. LaCocque, *Ruth*, 92.
99 For further correspondences between the RN and Gen 38, see Zakovitch, *Rut*, 52-54.
100 Nielsen, *Ruth*, 16.
101 For discussion and references, see "The Dating of the Book of Ruth" in Chapter One.
102 E.g., Joüon, *Ruth*, 2; Carl F. Keil and Franz Delitzsch, *Biblical commentary on the Old Testament* (trans. James Martin; Edinburgh: T&T Clark, 1872), 466.
103 E.g., Gerleman, *Ruth*, 6-7; Gow, *Ruth*, 137-39, 205-06.

transformation she is, for all intents and purposes, an Israelite. Her exemplary actions in exceeding kinship obligations and the specific requirements of Israelite law ironically present her as an ideal Israelite. This unreserved promotion of Ruth renders her a more than acceptable marriage partner and dynastic ancestor.

The shedding of the foreign element in Ruth's identity, however, means she poses no threat to the national psyche and personal Israelite identity. Indeed, by the end of the narrative, not only is she incorporated into the people of Israel, it seems her identity is subsumed within it. If the benediction of the elders and townspeople at the town gate is reflective of national sentiment (4:11-12), then Ruth's prime value to Israel is in her reproductive capacity.[104] There is a reversal of the transformation of her identity: she is de-identified to "the woman" (האשה; 4:11), her description on the threshing floor (3:8, 14), then to "the young woman" (הנערה; 4:12), her first description by an Israelite (2:5). The development of her identity is unravelled as she once again becomes faceless and nameless, and thus harmless to Israelite identity. At the end of the narrative, she is excluded in favour of a focus on the patrilineal descent of King David (4:18-22).[105] Ruth takes the journey to Israel, but in the end, the path to transformation only seems to end in subjugation. Consequently, no adjustment is required on the part of Israel as the host nation, only maintenance of the Israelite identity *status quo.*

B. Ruth as Challenge

Upon further examination, the presence of Ruth also presents a challenge to Israelite identity. For although Ruth is finally incorporated into the people of God, she cannot remove all vestiges of her "foreignness." Throughout the narrative, there are hints that the transformation of her identity is neither as smooth nor as complete as understood by most scholars. The difficulty facing an immigrant is implicit in Naomi's speech to her daughters-in-law on the road to Judah. Naomi is a pragmatic woman: she knows that it would be better for her daughters-in-law to be provided for by their parents and that it would be easier for them to remarry in Moab than in Israel (1:8-9). She knows the difficulty facing a migrant entering a new country and culture because the experience is still raw in her own memory. Indeed, it would require a special display of חסד

---

104 Cf. Linafelt and Beal, *Ruth & Esther,* 75.
105 Richard Bauckham, "The Book of Ruth and the Possibility of a Feminist Canonical Hermeneutic," *BibInt* 5 (1997): 31-32.

for her daughters-in-law to be truly accepted into the Israelite community, like the חסד her daughters-in-law showed her family in Moab (1:8).

The repetition of Ruth *the Moabitess* provides further evidence for her continued status as an "other." This description of Ruth is mostly found upon her first interaction with Israelite society (1:22; 2:1, 6, 21). The implied author wants to highlight her foreignness at the beginning of the narrative, which would have closely mirrored the implied reader's initial perspective of her.[106] Yet the continued use of this designation by Boaz in the last chapter suggests an element of her foreignness remained (4:5, 10). Although, in Chapter Two, I maintained that its presence in the legal context primarily indicates legal precision or her underprivileged socioeconomic status, from the perspective of an implied reader it also serves to reinforce her alien origin. It is ironic that the appellation is placed on the lips of Boaz, the one character who especially overlooks their ethnic and socioeconomic differences. Although the final references to Ruth in the narrative point to some degree of integration into society by removing her outlandish designation,[107] its double presence earlier in the chapter indicates some ambivalence towards her final identity.

Understood within this framework, there is some validity in Bonnie Honig's suggestion that when Naomi takes Obed from Ruth, it "signals the community's continuing fear of Ruth's foreignness. Ruth the Moabitess cannot be trusted to raise her son properly, in the Israelite way."[108] In some sense Ruth remains a Moabite in Israelite society—one perhaps viewed with suspicion or even prejudice, yet also celebrated by her adopted culture.

Modern research into immigration, primarily deriving from the discipline of psychology, provides some insight into her degree of incorporation into Israelite society. Although, according to van Gennep's "rite of passage" model, Ruth reaches the final stable state of aggregation, recent immigration theories suggest that this is still largely a dynamic state. Understood within a cross-cultural psychology framework, the process leading to a final state is called acculturation, which is "the dual process of cultural and psychological change that takes place as a result of contact between two or more cultural groups and their individual members."[109] An

---

106 Cf. Dorothea Harvey, "Book of Ruth," in *Interpreter's Dictionary of the Bible* (ed. George A. Buttrick; Nashville: Abingdon, 1962), 133: "The adjective 'Moabitess' appears at least twice in connection with Ruth where the plot does not demand the title (2:2, 21)."
107 In 4:13 she is simply "Ruth," and in 4:15 she is Naomi's "daughter-in-law."
108 Bonnie Honig, "Ruth, the Model Emigrée: Mourning and the Symbolic Politics of Immigration," in *Ruth and Esther: A Feminist Companion to the Bible (Second Series)* (ed. Athalya Brenner; Sheffield: Sheffield Academic, 1999), 60.
109 John W. Berry, "Acculturation: Living Successfully in Two Cultures," *International Journal of Intercultural Relations* 29 (2005): 698.

influential model outlining the process of acculturation is the multidimensional model proposed by John Berry, which contains four strategies:
1. integration (selective adoption of features from the host society, retention of features from own cultural identity, and importance of positive relations with the host society);
2. assimilation (cultural identity is not maintained, only positive relations with the host society are important);
3. separation (only maintaining cultural heritage is important, interaction with the host society is avoided); and
4. marginalisation (neither cultural maintenance nor interaction with host society).[110]

As a result of an analysis of the psychological responses to acculturation, Berry proposes that immigrants undergo a process of change in at least six areas of psychological functioning (language, cognitive styles, personality, identity, attitudes, and acculturative stress). After some initial changes, the individual reaches a state of conflict, at which time an adaptation strategy is reached. Berry argues that the four acculturation strategies are not discrete, static strategies; individuals may switch from one strategy to another.

According to this model, Ruth's approach as an immigrant to Judah would be classified as the assimilation strategy. Her transfer of allegiance to Israel indicates her willingness to take on Israelite cultural identity. Furthermore, her willingness to abide by Israelite societal norms signifies her desire to maintain positive relations with her host society. But the process of acculturation is still a long-term process, perhaps even extending beyond an individual's lifetime to the next generation.[111] This is because adaptation involves changes in virtually all aspects of life. Hence, despite Ruth's best efforts to assimilate into Israelite society, to a large extent she will still maintain elements of her originating country. For instance, her complexion or physical attributes may distinguish her immediately, then her mannerisms and use of the Hebrew language (e.g., pronunciation and grammar)[112] would also betray her Moabite origin. Even with maximal cultural adaptation, she can never completely assimilate into Israelite society.

---

110 John W. Berry, "Acculturation as Varieties of Adaptation," in *Acculturation: Theory, Models, and Some New Findings* (ed. Amado M. Padilla; Boulder: Westview, 1980), 9-25.
111 Berry, "Two Cutures," 699.
112 Ironically, Ruth's speech does not display any linguistic peculiarities, in contrast to the speeches of the native Hebrew speakers Boaz and Naomi. Cf. Campbell, *Ruth*, 25.

This persistence of Ruth's foreignness presents a challenge to the identity of an ancient Israelite. Deriving in part from its importance as a description of the Davidic ancestry, the RN has been established as an essential national story. Hence, its repetition as an oral tale and then as part of the canon of the HB ensures that it has a permanent and ongoing influence on Israelite identity. Although Ruth's identity is transformed through interaction with Israelite society, the influence is not only unilateral; she also has an impact on her host society. Acculturation, as a process that entails contact between two groups, results in a change in both parties.[113] Although the immigrant group experiences the greatest change, the non-dominant group still influences the dominant host group.[114] Thus, the RN results in a bilateral modification of identity.

On a literary level, the acceptance of Ruth as a foreigner is facilitated through the implied author's use of point of view. Berlin notes that Ruth is the focus of an implied reader's interest point of view.[115] That she is present or assumed to be present in almost every scene feeds the reader's interest. As such, a reader intently follows the transformation of Ruth's identity, from a member of an outgroup to a member of the Israelite ingroup. By being involved in this process through observing Ruth, a reader is then more predisposed to accepting a foreigner into their midst. In spite of her despised Moabite origins, by the end of the RN a reader is more open to accepting Ruth as a fully-fledged member of the people of God, along with the challenges her presence entails.

The first challenge to Israelite identity is in the modification of Israelite norms vis-à-vis the acceptance of non-Israelites.[116] The acceptance of Ruth *qua* foreigner promotes the value of openness towards outsiders; non-Israelites are to be accepted into the people of God. This suggested influence of the book of Ruth is not novel, mentioned as it is by many scholars throughout history as a purpose for writing the RN. Bringing a social psychological perspective to the text, however, provides insights into *how* these norms may be modified in Israel as an ingroup, and in doing so, produce a change in Israelite social identity.

Social identity theory yields a pertinent perspective on intergroup processes between immigrants and host societies. Within this theory, group membership is a vital component of social identity, and people strive to attain or maintain a positive identity by engaging in favourable

---

113 Robert Redfield, Ralph Linton, and Melville J. Herskovits, "Memorandum for the Study of Acculturation," *American Anthropologist* 38 (1936): 149.
114 John W. Berry, "A Psychology of Immigration," *Journal of Social Issues* 57 (2001): 616.
115 Berlin, *Poetics*, 84.
116 Norms are values defining acceptable attitudes for group members, and thus function to stamp the members with a distinctive identity

comparisons between their ingroups and various outgroups. Consequently, ethnocentrism is an inevitable consequence of social identification: all outgroups are judged according to the standards and customs of the Israelite ingroup.[117] A closely related area of social psychological research describes the process by which ethnocentrism may be modified. The Intergroup Contact Hypothesis suggests that negative attitudes held by an ingroup towards outgroups are caused by a lack of knowledge about that group.[118] When individuals of two groups come into positive, personal, and cooperative contact with each other, their acquaintance will lead to an elimination or reduction in prejudices. Gordon Allport outlined four conditions that need to be met in order for the contact to be successful: (1) the interaction takes place between individuals with equal status in the situation; (2) the authorities support the contact; (3) common goals; and (4) no competition between groups.

All of these conditions are satisfied to some degree in the RN: Ruth is presented as an equal to Boaz, especially on the basis of virtue; the elders, as authorities within the text, support the contact; the common goal is presented as the perpetuation of a kinship line; and there is an absence of competition. Under these conditions mutual attitudes and interaction will become more positive, for instance, through a growing recognition of similarities.[119] In addition to these cognitive factors are affective factors, which may have a greater influence on reducing prejudice.[120] Furthermore, the Intergroup Contact Hypothesis suggests that both indirect (having an ingroup acquaintance who has an outgroup acquaintance) and direct (having personal interaction with an outgroup acquaintance) contact reduces prejudice at comparable levels.[121] Since the presence of Ruth in the ingroup community would involve both forms of contact, it would thus be expected that there would be a magnified reduction in the level of

---

117 Gordon W. Allport, *The Nature of Prejudice* (Cambridge, MA: Addison-Wesley, 1954), 42: "[A] certain amount of predilection is inevitable in all in-group memberships."

118 Allport, *The Nature of Prejudice*; Thomas F. Pettigrew, "Intergroup Contact Theory," *Annual Review of Psychology* 49 (1998): 65-85.

119 This process is explained in the Similarity-Attraction Hypothesis, which states that when one perceives another to be similar to oneself on various characteristics (for instance, attitudes and values), this other will be positively evaluated. See Donn E. Byrne, *The Attraction Paradigm* (New York: Academic, 1971).

120 Affective factors include increased ability to empathise with outsiders, and a reduction of intergroup threat and anxiety. See Linda R. Tropp and Thomas F. Pettigrew, "Differential Relationships between Intergroup Contact and Affective and Cognitive Dimensions of Prejudice," *Personality And Social Psychology Bulletin* 31 (2005): 1145-58.

121 Thomas F. Pettigrew et al., "Direct and Indirect Intergroup Contact Effects on Prejudice: A Normative Interpretation," *International Journal of Intercultural Relations* 31 (2007): 411-25.

prejudice towards Moabites.¹²² An ancient Israelite, as a member of a social group, would have innately understood the intergroup dynamics in play; hence, the satisfaction of multiple criteria would have strongly motivated positive relations with Ruth and the outgroup she represents. In these ways the presence of Ruth in the Israelite community would lead to openness and acceptance of Moabites as well as outsiders in general, and consequently a change in group norms and social identity.

The second challenge to Israelite identity—the basis for membership into the people of God—is closely linked to the first challenge. The previous discussion established that Ruth's foreign status challenges the Israelite group norm of intolerance towards outsiders. Nonetheless, not all foreigners are granted membership. Ruth is not simply presented as a foreigner; in literary terms she is not a "flat" character. That she is viewed as a "round" character partly derives from her virtuous actions and personality—a life marked by חסד.¹²³ Thus, the quality of her character is an essential basis for her incorporation into Israelite society. The way this presents a challenge to Israelite identity can be framed as a question: if Ruth *qua* foreigner can be accepted, what is the basis of membership into the people of God? This leads to the existential question: what is the essence of an Israelite?

The basic presumption of an implied reader would have been that membership within Israel is solely on the basis of ethnicity or descent. The inclusion of Ruth turns this understanding on its head: a person can be identified as a member of Israel by individual choice, just as Ruth chose to align herself with Israel. Orpah's decision to the contrary underscores this understanding. This assertion of self-determination, however, is to be held in tension with the all-causality of YHWH as also presented in the book of Ruth. As Hals points out, the "hidden hand of God" can be found throughout the narrative.¹²⁴ Nonetheless, within the framework of God's providence it is also the case that God acts through the choices and actions of individuals.¹²⁵ The actions of the protagonists are testament to this.

Ruth's subsequent actions reveal the genuine nature of her commitment and the norms of membership in the people of God. Similarly

---

122 For a recent application of the contact hypothesis to the migration context, see Alberto Voci and Miles Hewstone, "Intergroup Contact and Prejudice toward Immigrants in Italy: The Mediational Role of Anxiety and the Moderational Role of Group Salience," *Group Processes & Intergroup Relations* 6 (2003): 37-54.
123 Flat characters are constructed around a single, non-developing idea or quality, whereas round characters do not have these restrictions; see, seminally, Edward M. Forster in *Aspects of the Novel* (New York: Harcourt, Brace and World, 1927).
124 Hals, *Ruth* .
125 Cf. Pressler, *Joshua, Judges, Ruth*, 264; Sakenfeld, *Ruth*, 14-16.

to Boaz, the quality of Ruth's personal character is paraded as an example to follow. חסד is a prominent characteristic in both their personal identities. This leads both characters to go beyond the obligations inherent in their social identities. This moral virtue is presented as a group norm: all members of Israel are to liberally manifest חסד in their lives.

Additionally, Ruth's actions demonstrate how to exercise initiative appropriately. Although not all members of Israelite society would possess the same enterprise and determination, Ruth's decisions show that these qualities are essential under certain circumstances. Without her initiative it is unlikely the events in the RN would have developed so positively. Yet her initiative issued from her חסד for Naomi; this aspect of her personal identity acted in concert with her social identity. Hence, initiative is appropriate when it derives from חסד. In sum, the presence of Ruth *qua* virtuous foreigner challenges Israelite identity by destabilising their understanding of the essence of an Israelite. The presence of Ruth within the people of God challenges the view that membership is based solely on nationality—choice and quality of individual character is just as, if not more important than genetic descent.

IV. Summary and Conclusions

Ruth's identity is transformed from a Moabite to an Israelite; a member of an outgroup to an integral member of the ingroup. Although the stereotypical understanding of a Moabite would have been negative, by the end of the narrative Ruth is presented as an integrated member of Israelite society. Nevertheless, as Berlin suggests, there remains an underlying tension "between foreignness and familiarity."[126] For although Ruth is incorporated into the people of God, she still retains aspects of her country of origin. But this is a productive tension: her presence challenges ingroup norms towards outsiders, and leads to soul-searching vis-à-vis the essence of an Israelite.

The transformation of Ruth's identity is primarily through interaction with the two other main characters—Boaz and Naomi. This once again highlights the essential interdependence between members of a relation-based collectivist culture, such as ancient Israel. As Ruth relates to Boaz and Naomi within this society, her personal character traits are manifest, in particular her initiative and her חסד. These, as aspects of her personal identity, are central to the transformation of her social identity. The appropriate expression of her personal identity within the context of her

---

126 Berlin, *Poetics*, 88.

social identity thus presents an implicit example for an implied reader. Properly motivated action is important, and can even lead to a change in social identity.

On a philosophical level, the example of Ruth contributes to an understanding of the interaction between identity and ethics. Boaz's actions were shown to primarily proceed from his social identities. Although Ruth's actions are consistent with her social identity, they primarily derived from aspects of her personal identity, and lead to a transformation of her identity. Ruth's choices led to a change in her person. Her original and foundational choice to follow Naomi sets in train a series of choices deriving from this, and changes her identity: from a Moabite to an Israelite, from a daughter-in-law to better than seven sons, from a widow of Mahlon to a wife of Boaz, from an anonymous gleaner to a progenitor of David. In this way, choices leading to action can have an impact on identity. The direction of influence between identity and ethics is not only unilateral, it is bilateral. In many ways identity shapes or even constrains ethics, but ethics can also alter identity.

Naomi: Identity and Ethics

Social identity theory highlights the key influence of social groups on a person's identity. Yet there are circumstances in which people may lose their attachment to their social groups, and hence elements of their social identity. What effect might this have on overall identity? Naomi's situation is an ideal test case: she loses *all* practical connections to her kinship groups through the loss of her husband and sons. In this chapter, I examine the effect of this loss of social identity, and the working of Naomi's personal identity on the regaining of her overall identity. This will culminate in a discussion of some implications of Naomi's actions on the identity of an Israelite implied reader.

I. The Loss of Naomi's Identity

A. Social Component

1. Kin: Israelite

This aspect of Naomi's identity contains three phases: an Israelite in her home country; to Israelite sojourner in Moab; to Israelite repatriate. Each of these phases contains an amount of stress. This stress stems in large part from adaptation and adjustment to a new environment, and this even includes returning home. In fact, social psychological studies suggest that sojourners may experience more adjustment difficulties on returning home than entering a new culture.[1] Of particular relevance to Naomi's situation is the finding that return to a home country may be more difficult for singles and those who sojourn for an extended period.[2] Repatriation is also more difficult for those lacking support from family and friends upon

---

1 See, e.g., Nancy J. Adler, "Re-Entry: Managing Cross-Cultural Transitions," *Group & Organization Studies* 6 (1981): 341-56; Cecil G. Howard, "The Returning Overseas Executive: Cultural Shock in Reverse," *Human Resource Management* 13 (1974): 22-26.
2 J. Ben Cox, "The Role of Communication, Technology, and Cultural Identity in Repatriation Adjustment," *International Journal of Intercultural Relations* 28 (2004): 201-19, esp. 215.

return. All of these factors would have made Naomi's return home particularly challenging.

A significant part of her stress is tied up with issues of identity. As a sojourner in Moab, her identity was stable—a member of an outgroup. Upon her return to Judah, she must adapt again to the attitudes and behaviours that function as identity descriptors for an Israelite in Israelite society. She must respond to a new environment, one that, although initially familiar, has undoubtedly changed in the ten years she has been absent. She must absorb again the social rules and cues that were second nature to her when she left, along with the communication system and behavioural norms. Additionally, her external appearance may make integration more complicated by betraying her prolonged sojourn in Moab. The discomfort upon her return may be mutual, as hinted at by the womenfolk of the town: "Is this Naomi?" (1:19). Although her initial nation of origin was Israel, her experience abroad has changed her understanding of her identity, as well as the understanding of the members of her home country. No longer aggregated into her community, she is now a member of a new outgroup: repatriate.[3] In short, from the moment Naomi decides to return to Judah she is a liminal person, a state that continues until she achieves social status and reintegration as an Israelite at the end of the narrative.

2. Kin: Clan of Elimelech

Because an Israelite clan is patrilineal, the death of Naomi's husband and sons means that her connection to an Israelite clan is precarious. As one who married into Elimelech's clan, Naomi was to some extent an outsider in her adopted clan,[4] although adaptation to the new household might have been lessened if the marriage was arranged within clans (cf. Num 36:6-9).[5] Indeed, it is only when a woman produces a son that she is concretely and irrevocably part of the clan; she has contributed to the building up of the clan.[6] Conversely, if a woman is left as a widow without sons, she can be

---

3   Cf. Nan M. Sussman, "The Dynamic Nature of Cultural Identity Throughout Cultural Transitions: Why Home Is Not So Sweet," *Personality and Social Psychology Review* 4 (2000): 355-73(65).

4   Cf. Edmund R. Leach, *Culture and Communication* (Cambridge: Cambridge University Press, 1976), 74.

5   From a pragmatic point of view, they would have shared a common cultural and territorial heritage. See Meyers, "Family," 36.

6   Cf. Leach, *Culture*, 74-75.

sent back to her father's house (בית אב; e.g., Gen 38:11; Lev 22:13), or mother's house, as Naomi refers to it in the RN (בית אמה; 1:8).[7]

Hence, this leaves Naomi (and her daughter-in-law) in an insecure position: she is no longer tangibly connected to Elimelech's clan.[8] The narrator's introduction of Boaz is suggestive of this situation (Ruth 2:1). His mention at the beginning of the chapter raises hopes that he might be a suitable patron. He is not Naomi's direct relative, however, but the relative of Naomi's (deceased) husband. Direct kinship obligations are deflected by the description of Boaz as a מוֹדַע ("relative"; *qere*),[9] rather than his later description as a גאל (kinsman-redeemer; cf. 2:20; 3:9, 12)—one with more defined kinship responsibilities. Although Boaz is a relative, the implication is that the benefits of clan membership are no longer freely available; she may need to work hard to eke them out.

3. Kin: Father's House and Non-Kin: Wife to Widow

For Naomi, the loss of Elimelech and her sons severed her connection to a father's house. Practically, it meant the loss of a provider and protector, as well as leaving her without an advocate in legal proceedings, and hence, legal status.[10] Carolyn Leeb describes אלמנה, the biblical "widow," as "a post-menopausal woman whose husband has died and who has no secure attachment to a household headed by an adult male, in which she can be protected and represented."[11] Naomi is not described by this term in the RN; indeed, she is not given a term related to her status after the death of

---

7   From Naomi's perspective, she is encouraging her widowed daughters-in-law to return to their mothers, instead of their mother-in-law; cf. Porten, "The Scroll of Ruth," 36. The use of "mother's house" provides a glimpse into the power held by women in the household sphere (cf. Gen 24:28; Song 3:4; 8:2); see Amy-Jill Levine, "Ruth," in *The Women's Bible Commentary* (ed. Carol A. Newsom and Sharon H. Ringe; London: SPCK, 1992); Carol L. Meyers, "'To Her Mother's House': Considering a Counterpart to the Israelite *bêt'ab*," in *The Bible and the Politics of Exegesis: Essays in Honour of Norman K. Gottwald on His Sixty-Fifth Birthday* (ed. David Jobling, Peggy L. Day, and Gerald T. Shepherd; Cleveland: Pilgrim Press, 1991), 39-51.

8   The fragility of this relationship is illustrated in the fictional story of the Wise Woman of Tekoa (2 Sam 14:1-7).

9   Either the *ketib* (מְיֻדָּע; "close acquaintance, friend") or the *qere* reading is possible, with the *ketib* drawing especial attention to the social isolation of Naomi; cf. Fischer, *Rut*, 157. The *qere* is preferable, however, in light of its only other occurrence in the HB, Prov 7:4, where it appears opposite "sister."

10 Cf. Pnina Galpaz-Feller, "The Widow in the Bible and in Ancient Egypt," *ZAW* 120 (2008): 231. Nonetheless, widows and divorced women could undertake vows when there was no man to assume responsibility for them (Num 30:10[9]).

11 Carolyn S. Leeb, "The Widow: Homeless and Post-Menopausal," *BTB* 32 (2002): 162.

Elimelech. Nonetheless, it would seem her circumstances render this a suitable descriptor. This is certainly the case at the beginning of the narrative. She is post-menopausal, and has no attachment to a father's house. The narrator has already painted her situation as hopeless and destitute even before she herself despairs at her situation (1:21).

However, Naomi is not a true אלמנה for two reasons, both of which are revealed as the narrative develops. First, she still owns property, which renders her an attractive marriage prospect (4:3). The decision process of Mr. So-and-So is testament to this: he first accepts Boaz's proposition to buy Elimelech's former plot of land based on the assumption it would be bundled with a marriage to post-menopausal Naomi (4:4). It is only when Boaz reveals that the marriage would in fact be with fertile Ruth that Mr. So-and-So retracts his acceptance (4:5-6).

Second, although Naomi has returned from Moab without any male family members, she still has a determined and resourceful daughter-in-law. Ruth's presence is not appreciated or even acknowledged upon arrival in Bethlehem, as Naomi frames her complaint purely in the singular (1:19-21).[12] It does not take long, however, for Ruth to prove her worth to Naomi (2:1). Ultimately, it will be through Ruth that Naomi's situation is redeemed, and her identity as a full-fledged member of Israelite society restored.[13]

Nonetheless, at the beginning of the RN Naomi's circumstances render her an outsider. Within the patriarchal structure of ancient Israel, she is a member of a disadvantaged group. Lacking a connection to a father's house, she is effectively without social identity, and thus condemned to the fringes of Israelite society. As Pnina Galpaz-Feller notes, "[The widow] is referred to as miserable and as a lowly element in the society where she

---

12 Cf. Bush, *Ruth*, 96. Ruth is also virtually ignored by the womenfolk of the town; cf. Mira Morgenstern, "Ruth and the Sense of Self: Midrash and Difference," *Judaism* 48 (1999): 133.

13 Although Naomi is not given a designation after the death of Elimelech, Ruth is called "the wife of the dead man" (אשת המת; 4:5), and "the wife of Mahlon" (אשת מחלון; 4:10). These designations are appropriate, for since there is still inheritable land available for the son whom Ruth bears, there is the sense in which she is still married to Mahlon, and thus still a member of his kinship group. Furthermore, she is still able to draw upon the kinship obligations present within the Levirate law; see Paula S. Hiebert, "Whence Shall Help Come to Me? The Biblical Widow," in *Gender and Difference* (ed. Peggy L. Day; Minneapolis: Fortress, 1989), 125-41. For these reasons, Ruth cannot be legitimately designated an אלמנה. Similarly, if Naomi were to be given a "widow" term, אשת המת would be the most suitable.

dwells."¹⁴ Her lowly position within society also renders her vulnerable to exploitation by "more fortunately placed persons."¹⁵

4. Summary

Every aspect of Naomi's social identity has been abrogated. Instead of regaining her identity as a fully-fledged Israelite upon her return to Israel, her sojourn in Moab now means that she is a member of an outgroup: repatriate. More importantly, the loss of her husband and two sons effectively severs her ties to her former clan and a father's house. Consequently, she is without provision, protection, and representation. With "no remaining value to society and no one on earth to protect her," she is powerless and vulnerable.¹⁶ Although not fully accurate, an implied reader can empathise with Naomi when she exclaims that YHWH has brought her back "empty" from Moab (1:21).

B. Personal Component

1. Name

The loss of the crucial social aspects of Naomi's identity thus leaves her feeling hollow and empty on an individual level. This is particularly evidenced upon her return to Bethlehem, when the womenfolk of the town exclaim: "Is this Naomi?" (1:19). Within this rhetorical question there might be nestled an element of delighted surprise, of being glad to see her back.¹⁷ However, an element of disbelief probably predominates.¹⁸ For the passing of a decade would have aged her skin and facial features, and her clothing would have taken on a Moabite style. Yet there is probably a more sinister element to their disbelief. As Naomi arrives they would have immediately noticed the absence of her family members. She left Bethlehem with a husband and two sons, she now returns with only a foreign girl. No-one wants to ask the question but Naomi senses what is on their minds, as she affirms that she went away "full" (מלא) but now

---

14 Galpaz-Feller, "Widow," 234.
15 Clements, "Poverty," 16. Clements lists some channels of exploitation: legal manipulation; debt slavery; abuse of land tenure; and movement of boundary stones.
16 Leeb, "Widow," 162.
17 Campbell, *Ruth*, 75.
18 Cf. LaCocque, *Ruth*, 55; Sakenfeld, *Ruth*, 35.

YHWH has returned her "empty" (ריקם; 1:21).[19] No doubt, the years of grief over the death of her husband and sons, along with the subsequent deprivation would have also left her looking worn and haggard.[20]

The change in Naomi was not only external, it was also internal, as symbolised by the rejection of her name. If a personal name is a reflection of character and personality instead of simply an identifier, then "Naomi" (נעמי) was no longer suitable for her.[21] With a prominent citizen as a husband, and two sons in her household, she could easily live up to her name. Now deprived of all that could make her "pleasant," she feels only bitterness, and hence the personal identifier "Mara" (מרא) is more appropriate for her current situation and state of mind (1:20).[22] מרא is not only appropriate because the Almighty (שדי)[23] has embittered her life, but also because it has associations with misfortune (Job 3:20; 7:11; 10:1; 21:25) and even death (1 Sam 15:32; Isa 38:17).[24] In a similar way to Job, Naomi recognises that she suffers under the direct hand of the Almighty (Ruth 1:20 cf. Job 27:2). Hence, to continue to call her Naomi would have been akin to mockery. The rejection of her name had been anticipated by her claim that YHWH had made her life more bitter than those of her daughters-in-law (כי מר לי מאד מכם;[25] 1:13). Now her name is publicly changed, and along with it, her personal identity.

In effect, Naomi rejects her former identity because it is so far removed from her current experience. She does not enjoy the benefits that flow from her former social identities of Israelite, member of the clan of Elimelech, and particularly as a wife, mother, and a member of a father's house. Instead of a person with high social standing, she is now a childless widow and a marginalised repatriate. Thus, to continue to call her Naomi would remind her of her social status, and thus heighten the pain associated with her current condition. It is only when she regains her social standing at the end of the RN that she is comfortable with her former identity again.

---

19 The Midrash emphasises this contrast by interpreting "full" to indicate she was pregnant when she left Judah (*Midr. Ruth Rab.* 3:7).

20 Cf. Morris, *Ruth*, 262; *Midr. Ruth Rab.* 3:6: "In the past, [Naomi] used to go in a litter, and now she walks barefoot.… In the past she wore a cloak of fine wool, and now she is clothed in rags.… Before her countenance was ruddy from abundance of food and drink, and now it is sickly from hunger."

21 Cf. BDB, 1027; *IDB* 3:500-508.

22 מרא probably derives from מרר, meaning "bitter." Cf. BDB, 600; *HALOT* 2:638.

23 שדי is an appropriate title for YHWH in this context because of its association with power (e.g., Ezek 1:24; Ps 68:15[14]). See G. Steins, "שַׁדַּי," *TDOT* 14:418-446; Morris, *Ruth*, 264-68.

24 Fischer, *Rut*, 151. Cf. Campbell, *Ruth*, 76-77.

25 This translation takes the מן of מכם in a comparative sense; so, e.g., Campbell, *Ruth*, 70-71; Zakovitch, *Rut*, 94.

Yet her rejection of her former identity not only reflects her present feeling, it also serves to promulgate and entrench her in her situation. For in rejecting her former name, she is also alienating herself from her former community, the women who used to form her close social network.[26] By demanding that they not call her Naomi any longer, she is effectively saying she is not the same woman they knew a decade ago. Hence, they cannot relate to her as they used to. Owing to her loss of husband and sons, with the resultant loss of social status, perhaps there is a sense that she cannot relate to them, or, conversely, that they cannot relate to or empathise with her experience. It may be a combination of these, with the outcome being that she isolates herself from all societal contact. By keeping her social group at arm's length, she ends up perpetuating her marginal status.

Thus, Naomi's new name "Mara" not only symbolises the way she feels but also corresponds to her liminal phase. This period of transition began with the death of her husband and sons, and is compounded by her decision to leave Moab for Judah. As Victor Matthews observes, Naomi is "doubly liminal based on physical location and social status."[27] The end of her liminal phase, leading to her final state of aggregation within Israelite society, is marked by the reacceptance of her former personal name (4:14-17).

II. The Regaining of Naomi's Identity

If the loss of Naomi's personal identity is a direct result of the loss of the primary social aspects of her identity, then it follows that a restoration of these social aspects should lead to a restoration of her personal identity. In the following section, I demonstrate that this is indeed true for Naomi. I will examine how this unfolds by again focusing on the two components of her identity: social and personal.

---

26 For a discussion of the significance of informal women's groups in ancient Israel, see Carol L. Meyers, "'Women of the Neighbourhood' (Ruth 4.17): Informal Female Networks in Ancient Israel," in *Ruth and Esther: A Feminist Companion to the Bible* (ed. Athalya Brenner; Sheffield: Sheffield Academic Press, 1999), 110-27.
27 Matthews, "Social Identity," 2.

A. Social Component

1. Non-Kin: Mother-in-law

Although the loss of Naomi's kinship identities was a key contributor to her feeling of emptiness, she still retained a non-kin social identity that would ultimately lead to the revitalisation of her personal identity—mother-in-law. She remains a mother-in-law for the majority of the RN, yet this is not the way she had envisaged it. Indeed, if her plea for her daughters-in-law to return home was heeded by both her daughters-in-law (1:8-13), she would have been, in practicality, no longer a mother-in-law. Ruth stubbornly refuses to abandon her, however, so her identity as a mother-in-law is maintained as they return together to Bethlehem.

Soon after their arrival, Naomi is pressed to act in her capacity as a mother-in-law. In response to Ruth's request, Naomi grants her permission to glean in the fields (2:2). As noted in Chapter Three, Ruth takes the initiative to glean, although Naomi would have been more familiar with local gleaning procedures. The reason for Naomi only playing her role as a mother-in-law reactively, rather than proactively, by suggesting that Ruth go out to glean, is not explicit in the narrative. Following closely after her expression of bitterness and despair, however, it seems likely that she is still absorbed in this state of mind. Indeed, she only breaks her dark silence by responding to her daughter-in-law's request minimally, by uttering only two words: לכי בתי ("Go, my daughter").[28] There is no express appreciation[29] or approval of Ruth's enterprise, no warning of the possible dangers (cf. 2:22), and no directions given to a field of one who might be more amenable to her request to glean. Although Naomi retains her identity as a mother-in-law, at this stage in the narrative she does not actively play her role by directing Ruth.

Upon Ruth's presentation of her gleanings, however, Naomi is immediately energised in her role as mother-in-law. Observing that Ruth has brought back enough for both of them to eat for more than a week (כאיפה שערים;[30] 2:17), she realises that her daughter-in-law had found the favour of an exceedingly generous landowner. This shakes Naomi out of her inert state, as she excitedly enquires after his identity (2:18-19). When she finds out that it is Boaz, one of their kinsman-redeemers (2:20), one

---

28 Cf. LaCocque, *Ruth*, 63, who suggests that the brevity of Naomi's response expresses her despondency: "the two women had arrived at the bitter end—at subsistence."
29 Fischer, *Rut*, 165.
30 כ is best understood as a *kaph veritas*, instead of as a mark of approximation; so Campbell, *Ruth*, 104; Bush, *Ruth*, 132-33. Either way, it was an extraordinarily large amount of grain from one day's work.

can sense her bitterness lifting. She now actively instructs Ruth to follow Boaz's orders to stay in his field, and reinforces his warning against gleaning in another field (2:22). The potential in the relationship Ruth had secured with Boaz now provides the impetus for Naomi to take on fully the responsibilities of a mother-in-law.

Naomi sheds her social identity as a mother-in-law, however, as the narrative develops. There is a growing level of intimacy between Ruth and Naomi: just as Ruth functions beyond her role as a daughter-in-law in providing for Naomi as a son or daughter, so Naomi begins to respond to Ruth as a mother instead of a mother-in-law. Although Naomi's initial acknowledgement of Ruth as a daughter is essentially devoid of warmth (2:2),[31] she now at least acknowledges Ruth's existence (cf. 1:21). Evidence that Naomi begins to treat Ruth as a fully-fledged family member is found in Naomi's description of Boaz—"a close relative of *ours*, one of *our* kinsman-redeemers" (2:20).[32] As Johanna Bos notes, by the end of chapter 2, "all indications are that Naomi is beginning to wake up to the presence of Ruth and to the responsibility as well as the promise of this presence."[33] In particular, Naomi is taking on the responsibility of a parent.

Naomi's understanding of her identity as a mother finds full expression in chapter 3. In seeking a marriage partner for Ruth, she is performing a task usually associated with parents.[34] Her reasoning for the Threshing Floor Scheme reaffirms that she no longer views Ruth just as a daughter-in-law: "Is not Boaz *our* relative?" (מדעתנו; 3:2). By the end of the narrative, the mother-daughter relationship is clearly manifest to all, as expressed by the womenfolk of the town who symbolically call her the mother of Obed (4:17). Just as "Mara" corresponds to Naomi's liminal phase on a personal level, her identity as a "mother-in-law" corresponds to her liminal phase on a social level. It is a transitional identity, a stepping-stone for Naomi on her path to full integration into Israelite society.

2. Kin: Clan of Elimelech

While Ruth has the greatest impact on the revitalisation of Naomi's identity, Boaz also has a significant impact, albeit more indirectly. Through the actions of Ruth, Naomi's life is restored and her identity regained. Not only does Ruth exceed her role as a daughter-in-law in providing for

---

31 In the context of 2:2, בתי has an element of cordiality, along with the sense of a generation and authority gap; cf. Fischer, *Rut*, 165.
32 Cf. Linafelt and Beal, *Ruth & Esther*, 42.
33 Bos, "Shadows," 59.
34 E.g., Gen 21:21; 24:33-53; 38:6; Judg 14:2-3.

Naomi's physical needs, she also takes on the additional role of a son in producing descendants for Naomi, and perpetuating the name of Elimelech. Indeed, without Ruth, it seems likely that Naomi would have remained in her destitute state, the name Mara permanently attached to her. In turn, Boaz is indispensable in his role as Ruth's benefactor: he provides protection for Ruth, and the grain she brings back for Naomi. And through Ruth's marriage to Boaz the ongoing and permanent blessings flow through to Naomi. Thus, the revitalisation of Naomi's identity is through a combination of the actions of Ruth and Boaz: if Ruth is the conduit of blessing for Naomi, then, at least on a human level, Boaz is the source.[35]

Boaz's intervention is a crucial step in Naomi's regaining the kinship aspect of her identity. Although Boaz might not have been exclusively motivated by familial factors, for Naomi, Boaz's generosity meant that he still recognised her as a member of his clan. For the death of her husband and sons meant that she lost all concrete and definite connections to the clan. So Naomi's description of Boaz's action as one of חסד is apt (2:20)—it is an act of kindness extending beyond any obligations attached to their clan solidarity. The significance of Boaz's actions for Naomi is that the social component of her identity is now slowly reappearing. Her husband, sons, and the security of attachment to a father's house are still lacking, and are, in a sense, irreplaceable. Yet now at least through Boaz she is reconnected to the clan of Elimelech.

3. Kin: Israelite

Naomi's restoration to the clan of Elimelech also gives her a connection to the larger Israelite kinship group. Her newfound connection to a kinship group, although tenuous at this stage, also implied the beginning of the restoration of her status as an Israelite. Moreover, the relationship Ruth has developed spurs Naomi to think more like an Israelite. She places Boaz within the wider context of her social group as *one of* her kinsman-redeemers (2:20), she evaluates Boaz's proposal on the background of her knowledge of local hazards (2:22), finally culminating in her Threshing Floor Scheme, in which she draws upon her local knowledge of winnowing customs, and the traditional nocturnal behaviour of Israelite men on the threshing floor (3:2-4). With all these actions, her membership in the repatriate outgroup is beginning to lapse, as she begins to think and act more and more as an Israelite.

---

35 The implied author promotes YHWH's sovereignty and providence, without downplaying the importance of human initiative and action.

B. Personal Component

1. The Initiative of Naomi

The revitalisation of the social component of Naomi's identity prompts her to become more proactive. When she realises harvesting has ended, and along with it the potential for Ruth to obtain long-term provision through Boaz, she takes decisive action by formulating a scheme to find "security" for Ruth (3:1-4). Based on her judgement of Boaz's character, she is emboldened to send Ruth to Boaz with a daring plan to secure her long-term provision and protection. Ruth has won a connection to a kinsman-redeemer, now Naomi plots the best course of action to precipitate a marriage between Ruth and Boaz. No longer content to be passive in her role as a mother-in-law, she now grasps the initiative.

Initiative as a personal character trait of Naomi's has been revealed previously, and is now reactivated by her reforged kinship connections. Although she is withdrawn and passive in her role as mother-in-law upon her return to Bethlehem, there are two instances of her initiative prior to her return. The first instance is her decision to return to Bethlehem from Moab upon hearing that YHWH had broken the famine in Judah (1:6). Having sojourned in Moab for ten years, and established social networks in the foreign country, it may have been tempting to remain in Moab. Yet her judgement and timing prove to be impeccable, as they arrive in Bethlehem at the commencement of the harvest season (1:22). The second instance of her initiative is her determining the best course of action for her daughters-in-law. Taking into consideration the relative youthfulness of Ruth and Orpah, along with the obstacles that would face them as foreigners in Bethlehem, she releases them to remarry in Moab (1:8-9). Now with the reinstatement of the social component of her identity through the actions of Ruth and Boaz, a feeling of hope replaces her oppressive sense of grief and bitterness, as she takes leadership in directing her daughter-in-law.

The extent of her initiative is evident in her Threshing Floor Scheme, which is without precedent in the HB. Scholarship is divided into three main groups over whether it was a customary marriage request. One group remains agnostic regarding the issue.[36] The second group suggests it may have been an accepted custom at the time,[37] or it was "an Israelite but not Moabite procedure" because Naomi had to explain it to Ruth.[38] The third

---

36 E.g., Leggett, *Levirate*, 205; Morris, *Ruth*, 287.
37 E.g., Joyce G. Baldwin, "Ruth," in *The New Bible Commentary: Revised* (ed. Donald Guthrie and J. Alec Motyer; London: InterVarsity, 1970), 281.
38 Morris, *Ruth*, 284, and tentatively Hubbard, *Ruth*, 205.

group suggests it is culturally inappropriate.³⁹ Within the context of the RN and the HB, the last group appears the most likely.

The lack of similar episodes in the HB makes it difficult to discern with any certainty, but the circumstances surrounding the encounter suggests it would not have been a regular occurrence. The danger associated with sending a woman alone beyond the safety of the town walls under the cover of darkness to a male domain surely would have precluded it from being common practice (cf. Song 5:7).⁴⁰ Furthermore, a number of factors point to the impropriety of the encounter: the sexual undertones surrounding the ambiguous use of מרגלת, שכב, ידע, and בוא;⁴¹ the association of threshing floors with licentiousness (cf. Hos 9:1);⁴² and the intertextual allusions to biblical passages in which sexual intercourse does take place (Gen 19; 38).⁴³

The implied author presents a picture of immense sexual temptation for Boaz, especially with somnolence and possibly alcohol impairing his judgement (3:3). As Pressler notes, the secrecy of their encounter and Ruth's lack of a male legal advocate means that there were few barriers preventing Boaz from taking advantage of Ruth without assuming further responsibility for her or Naomi.⁴⁴ Boaz was most likely not drunk,⁴⁵ but his "mellower-than-usual" condition still indicates another obstacle for Ruth to overcome.⁴⁶ A number of scholars suggest that sexual intercourse occurred between Boaz and Ruth while he was intoxicated,⁴⁷ but such a reading is

---

39   E.g., Pressler, *Joshua, Judges, Ruth*, 284-85; cf. Harris, Brown, and Moore, *Joshua, Judges, Ruth*; LaCocque, *Ruth*, 81-87.
40   Song of Songs 5:7 describes the watchmen finding the woman and physically beating her. Some commentators understand this act of abuse as deriving from the watchmen taking her to be a harlot; e.g., Othmar Keel, *The Song of Songs* (CC; Minneapolis: Fortress Press, 1994), 195. For a discussion of different interpretations of this verse, see J. Cheryl Exum, *Song of Songs* (OTL; Louisville: Westminster John Knox, 2005), 197-200.
41   For a discussion of these double entendres, see, e.g., Campbell, *Ruth*, 131-32.
42   Hubbard, *Ruth*, 201.
43   For further discussion, see, e.g., LaCocque, *Ruth*, 81-97; Nielsen, *Ruth*, 13-17.
44   Pressler, *Joshua, Judges, Ruth*, 287.
45   וייטב לבו does not necessarily mean that Boaz was inebriated. It can also have the connotation of "a positively elevated exuberance" (e.g., 1 Kgs 8:66; Prov 15:15; Eccl 9:7); so Campbell, *Ruth*, 121. Cf. Zakovitch, *Rut*, 140: "freilich nicht bis zur Trunkenheit." Furthermore, since a period of time had lapsed from when he had fallen asleep to when he was startled (3:7-8), the effects of alcohol would have diminished.
46   Campbell, *Ruth*, 122.
47   E.g., Calum M. Carmichael, "'Treading' in the Book of Ruth," *ZAW* 92 (1980): 257; Phillips, "The Book of Ruth," 14. Cf. Fewell and Gunn, *Compromising*, 86-93.

against the grain of the text.⁴⁸ Linguistically, the phrasing of Boaz's request, for Ruth to "remain tonight" (ליני הלילה; 3:13 cf. 1:16) rather than "lie down" (שכב), is devoid of any sexual undertone and thus reinforces the understanding that sexual intercourse did not take place.⁴⁹ From a narrative perspective, as Ellen van Wolde notes, chapter 4 would be superfluous if the marriage was already consummated in chapter 3.⁵⁰ The description, "So Boaz took Ruth, and she became his wife. And he went to her" (4:13), would be out of order.⁵¹ Hence, it is preferable to understand the literary devices as evoking the sexual tension and temptation felt by the characters.⁵² As virtuous characters, they are able to overcome the sexual temptation on the threshing floor, and thus emerge as "the antithesis of the lawless characters" common to their historical period.⁵³

It seems likely, then, that the lack of similar episodes in the HB is not because they were unrecorded, but because it occurred infrequently, if at all, due to the dangers inherent in such a scheme. However, based on her knowledge of Boaz's lofty reputation and reliable character, along with her observation of Boaz's recent conspicuous partiality towards Ruth, Naomi was willing to take a gamble, confident that Boaz would act consistently with his character. In short, although Naomi's initiative is without parallel in the HB, it is a plan based on sound judgement.

Nonetheless, Naomi's scheme may be open to the charge of being unnecessary or even inappropriate. Based on her understanding of Boaz's generous nature and reliable character, why was such a risky and dangerous scheme necessary in the first place? Why did she not try to approach Boaz, either directly or through the town elders?⁵⁴ Although a satisfactory answer from the narrative remains elusive, there are a number of indications that the implied author wants an implied reader to

---

48   Some commentators argue that since the author presents Ruth and Boaz as characters of integrity, it would be expected that their actions on the threshing floor would be consistent with this description of their character; e.g., Bush, *Ruth*, 155-56; Campbell, *Ruth*, 132. This argument, however, is somewhat circular.
49   Cf. Campbell, *Ruth*, 137-38; Zakovitch, *Rut*, 144.
50   Ellen van Wolde, *Ruth and Naomi* (London: SCM, 1997), 84-85. Van Wolde adds that if they had sexual intercourse, the scene at the gate would have been "shamefully misleading."
51   Wolde, *Ruth and Naomi*, 85.
52   Moshe J. Bernstein, "Two Multivalent Readings in the Ruth Narrative," *JSOT* 50 (1991): 17-20.
53   Harry J. Harm, "The Function of Double Entendre in Ruth Three," *JOTT* 7 (1995): 23. Cf. Schadrac Keita and Janet W. Dyk, "The Scene at the Threshing Floor: Suggestive Readings and Intercultural Considerations on Ruth 3," *BT* 57 (2006): 17-32.
54   Hubbard, *Ruth*, 204.

understand that Naomi's scheme was necessary, and hence appropriate under the circumstances.
1. Naomi and Ruth's hopes for obtaining long-term security were fast-fading with the end of harvesting.
2. None of the kinsman-redeemers (including Boaz) had assumed ongoing responsibility for the widows by this stage.
3. While Boaz had been presented as a suitable marriage partner for Ruth, there were many possible impediments to their union, including the presence of a nearer kinsman-redeemer, their age difference, Ruth's Moabite status, and her observance of a mourning period for her deceased husband.
4. Other avenues of approaching Boaz appeared closed to them: Naomi may have been rebuffed if she approached Boaz on Ruth's behalf;[55] and they may not have been able to approach the town elders because they lacked male representation.[56]

In Naomi's mind, this only leaves one option: to press Boaz into action by arranging circumstances so that a marriage to Ruth is presented as an attractive option. By presenting Ruth as available on the threshing floor in the middle of the night, she is taking advantage of a situation that Boaz does not completely control.[57] Thus, although Naomi's scheme was fraught with risk, under the circumstances it enabled the desired goal of marriage between Boaz and Ruth to be realised.

Moreover, the favourable outcome of the scheme underscores its acceptability. Although Ruth's presence on the threshing floor was irregular, Boaz probably viewed it with some leniency owing to Ruth's liminal state. Certainly, Boaz does not chide Ruth for appearing on the threshing floor with a marriage proposal; instead, he praises her for what he views as an act of kindness (3:10), and devises a strategy for fulfilling her request (3:11-12). The eventual marriage of Ruth and Boaz, with their offspring becoming a forebear of king David is clear indication of YHWH's blessing on the union, as well as vindication of Naomi's scheme. Given such a favourable outcome, an implied reader would view the situation as one of two women under desperate circumstances, doing "what they have to do so that both may survive."[58] Taking into consideration the exceptional circumstances of their liminal, marginal, and underprivileged status, an implied reader is to commend Ruth for her

---

55 Sakenfeld, *Ruth*, 55.
56 Even if she was able to gain a hearing at the town gate, they would not have a strong legal basis for Boaz's intervention, because his kinship relation to Naomi and Ruth is sufficiently distant that he would be under no obligation to act. Cf. Bush, *Ruth*, 156.
57 Cf. LaCocque, *Ruth*, 86.
58 Pressler, *Joshua, Judges, Ruth*, 208.

resourcefulness, and Naomi for her initiative. Reality drives acceptability: desperate times call for desperate measures, and Naomi's initiative is a measure of her desperation.[59]

From an identity perspective, the two components of Naomi's identity are acting in concert in the Threshing Floor Scheme. Her social identity as mother-in-law has lain dormant, and initiative, as an aspect of her personal identity, has been suppressed by her overwhelming sense of bitterness and despair. When a connection to her kinship group is affirmed, however, her identity and role as mother-in-law is awakened, along with a revival of her individual initiative. Although her initiative eventually has beneficial effects for herself, its primary purpose is the long-term security of her daughter-in-law (3:1). Indeed, Naomi may already have had some security: whoever purchased the field would be responsible for her maintenance.[60] Furthermore, her initiative in seeking a marriage for her daughter-in-law is consistent with the level of intimacy of their relationship: Ruth is no longer treated as a daughter-in-law, but as a daughter, a fully-fledged family member. Thus, the initiative Naomi displays is consistent with her relating to Ruth on the level of mother-daughter: the social and personal components of her identity are acting harmoniously together.

2. Name

The revitalisation of Naomi's identity is complete by the end of the RN, as reflected in the reinstatement of her personal name. In complete contrast to her vehement protest at the use of her given name upon arrival in Bethlehem, her silent assent at its second usage by the womenfolk of the town reflects acceptance of her name's final suitability (4:17).[61] As she basks in the glory of her newborn grandson, she is no longer bitter; instead, she now has the capacity and willingness to be pleasant.[62] Rather than rejecting her personal name, she now openly welcomes it back. Naomi's restoration to life symbolised by the reinstatement of her personal name parallels the reversal found in the RN as a whole.[63]

---

59   Cf. Matthews, *Judges/Ruth*, 233.
60   Pressler, *Joshua, Judges, Ruth*, 286.
61   *Pace* Fewell and Gunn, *Compromising*, 80-82, who view her silence as a sign of equivocation.
62   Cf. Fischer, *Rut*, 257.
63   Additional instances of the reversal motif in chapter 4 can be found in, inter alios, Hubbard, *Ruth*, 269-79; Rauber, "Literary Values in the Bible: The Book of Ruth," 27-37.

Naomi's personal identity is thus revitalised due to the regaining of her social identities. Through Ruth's marriage to Boaz, he becomes her male patron, guardian, and legal representative. Her marginalised status is cast off, replaced by the social identities of Israelite, member of the clan of Elimelech, and member of the father's house of Boaz; she is once again a fully-fledged member of Israelite society. This is publicly recognised by the Bethlehem community, as represented by the womenfolk of the town, who call her Naomi again (4:17).[64] Her personal name, emblematic of her personal identity, is reinstated by the end of the narrative because her social status in the Bethlehem community has been re-established. The acceptance of her personal name is the culmination of a process that has led to the restoration of her kinship social identities.

As a result, Naomi sheds all the identities attached to her liminal status. She is now, finally, Naomi instead of Mara, integrated Israelite instead of marginalised repatriate. Even her social identities of widow and mother-in-law give way to her predominant identity as "mother" to Obed (4:17).[65] In short, she is fully reincorporated into Israelite society.

III. The Impact on the Identity of an Implied Reader

A. Naomi as Reinforcement

The portrait of Naomi reinforces the vital importance of the social component of identity and the Israelite social structure. Her social identities are such a core component of her identity that their abrogation leads to her rejection of her personal name. Of paramount practical importance is attachment to a father's house. The structure of ancient Israelite society is such that one who lacks a close connection to an adult male through this closest kinship group is rendered marginal and vulnerable.

Nonetheless, there is still recourse to assistance if an Israelite citizen lacks attachment to a father's house. For instance, legislation within the HB makes provision for the poor and underprivileged, with especial mention of the orphan, the immigrant alien, and the widow.[66] This suggests there was at least a rudimentary social welfare system in place, available to all

---

64 Cf. LaCocque, *Ruth*, 146, who designates them the "sociopsychological community" of Bethlehem, in contrast with the "legal community" formed by the men at the gate.
65 Due to the application of the levirate custom in this instance, Obed would be reckoned as Elimelech's heir (e.g., 4:10), and consequently, Naomi's son.
66 E.g., Exod 23:11; Lev 23:22; Deut 14:29; 16:11, 14; 24:17, 19-21; 26:12-13.

Israelite residents.[67] As the case of Naomi illustrates, if there was some connection to a clan, however tenuous, there was hope of assistance from a kinsman-redeemer.

Yet the desperate lengths Naomi takes highlights the inadequacy of the social support system if members of ancient Israelite society do not take up the responsibilities attached to their social identities. The danger and risk of sending Ruth to the threshing floor would have been avoided if a clansman had provided for the widows. Although any clansman could have undertaken the task, Mr So-and-So would have felt the greatest compulsion because of his closest kinship tie. Nevertheless, the role was one of familial responsibility, not duty; it was a choice, not a binding obligation. The honour attached to Boaz, who acted generously—beyond strict kinship obligations—reinforces the importance of חסד as a group norm. Acceptable behaviour for an Israelite is to be characterised by חסד. This other-person-centred identity descriptor is thus essentially social: it maintains the wellbeing of needy kin, and contributes to the integrity of the Israelite welfare system as a whole.

Lastly, Naomi serves to underscore the importance of perpetuating the family line as a value Israelites are to uphold *qua* a national group. While this was not Naomi's verbalised intention when sending Ruth to proposition Boaz (3:1), he quickly identifies it as a pressing concern. He sets in train a series of steps involving Elimelech's patrimony so that Elimelech's name would not be extinguished (4:10). In this way, Boaz's emphasis on the perpetuation of Elimelech's name upon his property would have been an accurate gauge of societal concerns, even if Naomi does not mention it explicitly.[68] While the task of keeping an ancestor's name alive was predominantly through each father's house, in exceptional circumstances it found application at the clan level (such as in the RN). Nonetheless, perpetuating the family line constitutes an identity descriptor that applies to all Israelites as a larger group.

---

67 For other elements of the social welfare system in ancient Israel, see Clements, "Poverty," 18-22.

68 One possible aim was to maintain a connection with a deceased progenitor to keep them safe from the terrors of Sheol; see Jeffrey H. Tigay, *Deuteronomy* (JPS Torah Commentary; Philadelphia: The Jewish Publication Society, 1996), 482-83. This occurs through communal memory, such as by the son taking on the patronymic of the deceased relative (e.g., Obed son of Elimelech), and hence keeping the name of the deceased amongst the living (see Deut 25:6; Ruth 4:5, 10; cf. Ps 109:13, 15).

B. Naomi as Challenge

The initiative displayed by Naomi presents a challenge to the personal component of an Israelite's identity. If the default mode of psychological functioning for an average Israelite was "dyadic" or "collectivist," the example of Naomi highlights the importance of autonomous thinking, especially under desperate circumstances. Even when Naomi is inert in her role as a mother-in-law, the resourcefulness of another—her daughter-in-law—is vital to the regaining of her identity, and the alleviation of their destitution. The decisive moment, however, is when Naomi grasps the initiative herself. The crucial nature of her scheme is underscored by considering what would have occurred if she remained inert: the two women most likely would have remained in their destitute state. Thus, initiative is presented as an important component of personal identity.

There is a further, closely connected challenge to Israelite identity in Naomi's Threshing Floor Scheme. The presence of Ruth on the threshing floor represented an overriding of a social or cultural norm: women do not belong on a post-harvest threshing floor at night.[69] Furthermore, that Ruth was at risk of sexual exploitation meant there was a concomitant risk of overriding ethical norms. The positive outcome to Naomi's scheme, however, sends the message that the revival of an Israelite clan prevails over cultural norms. Although the exceptional nature of Naomi's scheme seems to restrict the application of this principle, a restatement in more general terms broadens its applicability: achievement of larger kinship concerns may require overriding other established social or cultural norms. To achieve this end may require ingenuity and enterprise, elements of personal identity. Thus, there is a challenge to both social and personal components of identity. Since, under certain circumstances, an Israelite may need to elevate kinship concerns above wider social norms, then this could destabilise Israelite identity.

The final challenge to ancient Israelite identity is as males and females. Gender roles are an integral aspect of identity, with role casting beginning in childhood, and reinforced by social narratives.[70] Within a patriarchal society, the underlying gender hierarchy dictated that males held more power than females. Hence, within the societal structure there lay the potential for male abuse of power.[71] The RN is ostensibly placed in such a

---

69   Cf. Matthews, *Judges/Ruth*, 233.
70   See "The Social Identity Approach and Ancient Israelite Identity" in Chapter One.
71   When there are sex differences in power, there is a pan-cultural tendency for women to be disadvantaged in relation to men. Cf. Felicia Pratto, "Sexual Politics: The Gender Gap in the Bedroom, the Cupboard, and the Cabinet," in *Sex, Power, and Conflict: Evolutionary and Feminist Perspectives* (ed. David M. Buss and Neil M. Malamuth; New

historical setting. The beginning and end of the book is closely linked to the period of the Judges (1:1), and the beginning of the monarchy (4:17-22) respectively. Set in a period of increasing moral and political chaos,[72] the book of Judges is replete with stories of exploitation and abuse of women by men: Jephthah's daughter (Judg 11); the Levite's concubine (Judg 19); and the daughters of Shiloh (Judg 21).[73] Although not as endemic, the beginning of the monarchy also contains evidence of maltreatment of women: Bathsheba (2 Sam 11); and Tamar (2 Sam 13).[74] The RN sounds a dissonant note with its historical setting, and this contrast shapes the identity of both women and men.

Regarding women, the RN presents the case for continued ingenuity and initiative despite the milieu of lawlessness or oppression. If the *Zeitgeist* led to despondency or withdrawal as a protective mechanism, then Naomi presents a model to counter this. Although she isolates herself from society, and becomes passive in her social roles, the decisive point of her deliverance from destitution lay in her revived enterprise. Moreover, by taking the responsibility for the welfare of her daughter-in-law, she ultimately ensures the continuity of her family line. In this capacity, her actions are contiguous with those of the Matriarchs. Sarah, Rebecca, Rachel and Leah all actively ensured the birth of the next generation, and directed the proper line of inheritance.[75] Furthermore, Ruth's explicit link to Rachel and Leah (4:11), as well as to Tamar (4:12) underscores the importance of determination in the face of adversity in order to build up and preserve the people of Israel. Thus, to generalise, Naomi and Ruth function as exemplars to encourage or even empower Israelite women *qua* women in similar situations of defencelessness, isolation, or bereavement.[76]

Nonetheless, women are to display ingenuity within the bounds of the patriarchal system. Although the RN is primarily a women's story, driven by female actions and concerns,[77] it is still set in a man's world. Naomi is in desperate straits because she has been deprived of the direct support of male

---

York: Oxford University Press, 1996), 179-230; Michelle Z. Rosaldo and Louise Lamphere, "Introduction," in *Woman, Culture, and Society* (ed. Michelle Z. Rosaldo and Louise Lamphere; Stanford: Stanford University Press, 1974), 1-16.

72   See Judg 17:6; 18:1; 19:1; 21:25.

73   Mieke Bal, *Death and Dissymmetry: The Politics of Coherence in the Book of Judges* (Chicago: University of Chicago Press, 1988), 21-24, adds Samson's bride, who is burnt along with her father (Judg 15:6).

74   Cf. Linafelt and Beal, *Ruth & Esther*, 80-81.

75   Cf. Adele Berlin, "Big Theme, Little Book," *BRev* 12 (1996): 48.

76   Cf. Athalya Brenner, "Naomi and Ruth: Further Reflections," in *A Feminist Companion to Ruth* (ed. Athalya Brenner; Sheffield: Sheffield Academic, 1993), 144.

77   So, e.g., Brenner, "Naomi and Ruth: Further Reflections," 140-44; Pressler, *Joshua, Judges, Ruth*, 306-07.

kin; her only path to restoration is through a male. The two female protagonists display their awareness of this. Even when Naomi outlines her scheme to Ruth, she limits the role Ruth is to take: "He will tell you what you are to do" (3:4). Not only does Naomi know that Boaz would be a man of action (3:18), she also knows how the proposal would function best in a patriarchal society. Ruth is to make her availability for marriage known, but then the initiative is to pass to the male, who knows best how to manipulate the androcentric system in which he lives. Even when Ruth displays her own initiative in providing extra incentive for his acceptance (3:9), she is only strengthening the plan already set by Naomi, not deviating from it. In short, the two women do not seek a solution to their problem outside the patriarchal structure of their society. While they "work" the system to their advantage, they do not subvert it.[78]

This understanding of the RN is in contrast with that of some scholars, who instead maintain that the RN deconstructs gender. For instance, John Berquist notes that solutions are only achieved "when people transgress social conventions and take roles that society limits to the other gender."[79] In this way, the story's characters change the social reality of their narrative world, so that people can act beyond social-sexual role expectations. Berquist argues that the RN presents this deconstruction of gender boundaries as a lasting change, not just a temporary response to crisis, as evidenced in the role played by the women of the community naming the child.[80] This reading is implausible for two reasons. First, the naming of Obed by the women is not an overtly unconventional role.[81] The intertextual allusions to Gen 38:28-30, with the midwives being involved in the naming, reinforce this understanding. Second, the patrilineal genealogical conclusion to the RN undermines the permanence of the gender dedifferentiation. Rather, the narrative suggests a restoration to normal gender role functioning once a solution was found to the crisis.

Furthermore, women probably already held quite a degree of power within ancient Israelite society, which reduces the likelihood that the RN was used "as a rationale for social change."[82] As hinted at by the author of the book of Ruth, power was primarily at the household level (בית אמה;

---

78 Cf. Bauckham, "The Book of Ruth," 35.
79 Berquist, "Role," 35. For a recent subversive reading from a Bakhtinian perspective, see Nehama Aschkenasy, "Reading Ruth through a Bakhtinian Lens: The Carnivalesque in a Biblical Tale," *JBL* 126 (2007): 437-53.
80 Berquist, "Role," 36.
81 Cf. Victor H. Matthews and Don C. Benjamin, *Social World of Ancient Israel, 1250-587 BCE* (Peabody: Hendrickson, 1993), 79-80.
82 Berquist, "Role," 36. It is questionable whether women, as a subordinated class of people, could have used the RN in this way. This possibility will be assumed for the sake of argument in this present discussion.

1:8).[83] Evidence of female power can be found in areas such as textiles and food production, child-raising and household education.[84] Nonetheless, the overall picture in the HB is *not* one of gender uniformity; men and women fulfil different roles. Yet the picture of gender complementarity opens up the possibility for gender interdependence and co-operation.[85] In general, the authority of a woman may be deemed "unassigned power."[86] It may not be as explicit as the "assigned power" reserved for men within ancient Israelite society, but women still exerted a very real and significant influence. Sex differences in power, status, and control of resources nonetheless remained within ancient Israel, and consequently the need for societal reform. Yet the power held by women at the household level would have diminished the need to undermine gender roles in Israelite society.

Regarding men, the RN corrects unacceptable attitudes towards women, and an abuse of power deriving from the patriarchal structure of society. The RN addresses this problem in two ways. First, by offering a female perspective, it provides a means by which men can begin to understand, and even empathise with, the conditions of females. While male implied readers may be naturally predisposed to identify with Boaz or Mr. So-and-So in their respective plights owing to similarities in gender and the male concerns of progeny, land, and personal legacy, even male implied readers are intensely interested in the plight of Naomi and Ruth.

On a literary level, male empathy for Naomi is promoted through the perceptual point of view. While Ruth holds a reader's interest point of view, the perceptual point of view primarily resides with Naomi. Naomi is the central character in the RN, with the other characters standing in relation to her.[87] Since perceptual point of view generates empathy for a character, this is one device through which a male implied reader is led to adopt the conceptual point of view of the implied author concerning

---

83 See the discussion of the "mother's house" supra.
84 See, e.g., Claudia V. Camp, *Wisdom and the Feminine in the Book of Proverbs* (Sheffield: Almond, 1985), 81-82; Carol L. Meyers, "Everyday Life of Women in the Period of the Hebrew Bible," in *The Women's Bible Commentary* (ed. Carol A. Newsom and Sharon H. Ringe; Louisville: Westminster John Knox, 1998), 251-59.
85 Cf. Carol L. Meyers, "Returning Home: Ruth 1.8 and the Gendering of the Book of Ruth," in *A Feminist Companion to Ruth* (ed. A. Brenner; Sheffield: Sheffield Academic Press, 1993), 99.
86 Carole R. Fontaine, "The Sage in Family and Tribe," in *The Sage in Israel and the Ancient Near East* (ed. Leo G. Perdue and John G. Gammie; Winona Lake: Eisenbrauns, 1990), 161.
87 Berlin, *Poetics*, 83; cf. LaCocque, *Ruth*, 6.

women.⁸⁸ This might entail having an implied reader's existing norms supplanted by those presented in the RN. Thus, as a result of viewing the RN from Naomi's perceptual point of view, a male reader is more likely to modify unacceptable attitudes and behaviours towards women.

Second, the RN may correct misogynistic tendencies by highlighting the vital contribution of women to Israelite society. In the RN, women's primary contribution is to the continuance of the family line. Elimelech's line and post-mortem existence are only saved from extinction through Naomi and Ruth. If, as suggested in Chapter Two, Boaz was also without an heir, his marriage to Ruth also had the potential to maintain his legacy through the birth of sons in addition to Obed.⁸⁹ Ruth 4 in particular counteracts any tendencies towards male myopia. The narrative up to this point had focused on female concerns, culminating in the scene at the town gate. Yet while initiated by female concerns, the public legal manoeuvres are shaped by "patriarchal values, reflecting male interests and male perspectives."⁹⁰ Boaz may speak of Ruth's welfare in the privacy of the threshing floor, but his speech at the public world of the gate underlines the patriarchal character of the system: Elimelech's patrimony is presented as the major item on the agenda, an item to be redeemed or exchanged by men (4:7), in order to restore a man's name amongst his brothers (4:5, 10). Boaz even speaks of "acquiring" (קנה) Ruth as his wife, along with "acquiring" (קנה) the parcel of land (4:9-10). While the choice of this word is probably stylistic in this context,⁹¹ as Carolyn Pressler comments, "in this exchange Ruth is an object, not a subject, and if she is not chattel, she is subordinate."⁹² Nonetheless, amidst the male focus in this chapter, the implied author highlights the indispensable contribution Ruth makes. While the concentric structure of the blessing of the joyous crowd centres on Boaz's prosperity, it also specifies that this is wholly dependent upon the fecundity of Ruth (4:11-12).⁹³ The explicit comparison of Ruth with Rachel, Leah, and Tamar includes an allusion to their vital role in "building

---

88 Although perceptual point of view allows a reader to empathise with Naomi and her situation, an implied reader might not always sympathise with her. Cf. Wolde, *Ruth and Naomi*, 15: "[T]he first chapter of Ruth requires the reader to have a twofold attitude towards Naomi, of sympathy and antipathy at the same time."
89 The next son of their union would inherit his patrimony and continue his line, since Obed was reckoned to be Elimelech's. Even if Boaz already had an heir, the actions of the women served to perpetuate his name through his position as an ancestor of David (4:18-22).
90 Pressler, *Joshua, Judges, Ruth*, 302.
91 See the discussion in Chapter Two.
92 Pressler, *Joshua, Judges, Ruth*, 302.
93 Linafelt and Beal, *Ruth & Esther*, 74-75.

up the house of Israel."[94] Ruth's de-identification to "the woman" and "this young woman" only reinforces the importance of her reproductive function (4:11-12). In short, without the woman there is no blessing for the man.

Viewed as a whole then, the RN presents the case that female and male concerns can function co-operatively instead of independently. The female concern for security through husband and home can operate simultaneously with the male concern for legacy through land and heir.[95] Yet this may not be the understanding at first blush. On the one hand, the female interest in security predominates from chapter 1 (1:6-9; cf. 3:1), following the death of Naomi's husband and sons (1:3-5). The plot is driven by Naomi's emptiness and her search for wholeness, which is only achieved at the end of the narrative through Ruth's marriage to Boaz and the birth of a son. Subsequently, the womenfolk's congratulation of Naomi focuses on Obed's significance for her, leaving out any mention of his function as an heir for Elimelech (4:14-17). On the other hand, the male interest in inheritance and patrilineal descent dominates the scene at the town gate, while excluding any mention of female security interests. Furthermore, the concluding genealogy only seems to support this by tracing descent through men, and scripting the women out (4:17-22).[96] Thus, it seems that male and female concerns develop independently of each other.

A closer inspection, however, reveals three indications that the implied author promotes co-operation between the sexes. First, the proclamation of the womenfolk not only focuses on female concerns, but also male. While it centres on Obed's significance for the long-term welfare of Naomi, it also contains the wish that "his name be proclaimed in Israel" (4:14-15). This predominantly male interest for renown is here taken up by females, whose hope that the scope of Obed's fame ("in Israel") even exceeds that of the male crowd at the town gate for Elimelech (Bethlehem and Judah; 4:11). If widespread renown leads to greater perpetuation,[97] then this indicates the extent of the women's appreciation of male interests. Second, Obed, as the product of a male/female union, personifies the potential of gender co-operation. He is the son who fulfils the concerns of both

---

94   There may also be an allusion to Ruth's role as Naomi's surrogate, in the sense that Bilhah was for Rachel, and Zilpah was for Leah, when they bore sons by Jacob (Gen 30:3-13).
95   Cf. Bauckham, "The Book of Ruth," 39.
96   Cf. Bauckham, "The Book of Ruth," 31-32. In this respect, the Matthean genealogy serves as a counterpoint, with its inclusion of Tamar, Rahab, and Ruth (Matt 1:1-16).
97   Cf. NJPS, which, although it refers to YHWH as the subject, translates ויקרא שמו בישראל as: "May his name be *perpetuated* in Israel."

genders: he maintains the perpetuity of a patrilineal clan, *and* ensures the provision for a matriarch in her old age. Third, while Boaz only mentions male concerns at the town gate, this does not necessarily exclude his care for the well-being of Ruth and Naomi. Within the legal setting, it is simply the language of public discourse that he chooses to use. Indeed, it would be unnecessary and inappropriate for him to mention his personal concern for Ruth. Hence, Boaz only discloses what is required in and suitable for the male legal context, and which maximises the chances of success for his strategy. Ultimately, he also seeks the long-term security of Ruth and Naomi, as expressed in his gift of grain to Naomi after the events on the threshing floor.

To summarise, there are a number of challenges to Israelites as men and women deriving from the historical setting of the RN. Primarily this is through presenting acceptable and unacceptable attitudes and behaviours for members of Israelite society. Women are to continue to display initiative in pursuing kinship concerns within the bounds of the patriarchal structure of their society. Men are to value the significant contribution that women make to society, especially their vital role in the perpetuation of the Israelite kinship line. Furthermore, motivation is provided to play these gender roles because they are presented as mutually beneficial. While a gynocentric perspective primarily focuses on security, and an androcentric perspective primarily on perpetuity, the RN reveals that these two concerns dovetail in reality; they are complementary facets of the same goal.

IV. Summary and Conclusions

In this chapter, I examined how the loss of Naomi's primary social identities led to a rejection of her personal identity, as represented by her personal name. This was only regained upon the restoration of her social identities. Her restoration parallels her passage from a liminal state to a state of integration within Israelite society. Naomi's journey thus highlights the importance of attachment to social groups, and the crucial influence of social groups on personal identity. In this way, it buttresses the regnant corporate or collectivistic understanding of Israelite selfhood. Yet the means by which Naomi regains her personal identity provides a corrective to a sole focus on the social component of Israelite identity. For a decisive point in the restoration of her identity occurs when her initiative, an aspect of her personal identity, is rekindled. When the personal and social components of her identity finally act in conjunction, the synergistic effect precipitates the final restoration of her personal identity.

I also outlined how the portrait of Naomi in the RN can influence Israelite identity. Although it is a point well taken that the book of Ruth is not polemical in tone,[98] it nonetheless has the power to shape identity on multiple levels. These range from the centrality of all social kinship groups (father's house, clan, and Israelite nationality) as fundamental and indispensable components of Israelite identity, to the importance of an autonomic mode of thinking as an aspect of personal identity, to a challenge regarding the gender attitudes and behaviours of all Israelites. As a narrative, it can both reinforce and challenge the multiple inherent individual narratives that intertwine to form an individual's personal identity, and hence the behaviours consequent to this narrative understanding of the self. That the RN is not overtly disputative is advantageous in this regard; its gentle tone facilitates a surreptitious uptake of its message. Hence, its outward appearance belies the potential power of its influence. In the next chapter, I will consider how this narrative shaping of identity might have been pertinent in the Monarchic and Persian Periods.

---

98 Phyllis Trible, "Ruth, Book of," in *ABD* (ed. David N. Freedman; New York: Doubleday, 1992), 5:846.

A Provenance for the Book of Ruth

The previous three chapters investigated the relation between identity and ethics through an examination of the three main characters in the RN. Some implications for an implied reader of Ruth—situated in the late Monarchic to post-exilic period—were also discussed. Based on the emphases of the text arising from viewing the text through the lens of social identity theory, can this be refined further? That is, can we pinpoint a more specific historical and geographical provenance for the RN?

In this chapter, I explore two possible historical periods for the provenance of the RN: the Monarchic Period; and the Persian Period. In the first part of this chapter, I explore the possibility of a provenance for the RN in the Monarchic Period. Although the RN could have originated during the Josianic period, a degree of uncertainty remains since the social concerns of the RN do not completely match those of the Josianic period. Hence, in the second part of this chapter, I outline the social processes in the Persian Period, especially as described in Ezra-Nehemiah (henceforth EN). After demonstrating how the RN might have influenced identity within this social context, I will argue that Yehud in the early Persian Period is the most likely provenance for the RN.

I. The Monarchic Period

A. The Social Processes in the Monarchic Period

A number of interrelated social developments in the Monarchic Period form a potential backdrop to the message of the RN. Both external threat and internal developments led to the emergence of the Israelite state[1] at the end of the eleventh century B.C.E.[2] Based on an examination of the archaeological evidence concerning rural settlement patterns around this

---

1 Definitions of statehood generally focus on centralisation of administration and distribution of resources as the essential criterion. See Marshall D. Sahlins, *Tribesmen* (Englewood Cliffs: Prentice-Hall, 1968), 6; Elman R. Service, *Primitive Social Organization: An Evolutionary Perspective* (New York: Random House, 1962), 175.
2 For a summary, see Israel Finkelstein, "The Emergence of the Monarchy in Israel: The Environmental and Socio-Economic Aspects," *JSOT* 44 (1989): 43-74.

formative period, Avraham Faust suggests the primary factor for Israelite state formation was the strong Philistine threat, on a background of increasing socio-economic organisation.[3] In turn, external threat precipitated further ongoing urbanisation and social development. Two social changes are particularly germane to this discussion of the implied reader of the RN: the breakdown of kinship ties and responsibilities; and the development of gender hierarchy.

It is widely accepted that state formation and urbanisation processes lead to a weakening of kinship ties and a decline in the social significance of the family.[4] Applied to the context of ancient Israel, the smallest kinship groups (nuclear family to father's house) are emancipated from the larger kinship groups (clan and tribe), which are characteristic of rural life.[5] Hanoch Reviv suggests that although the father's house continued to be the economic and social base for the majority of the population after the emergence of the state, there was an increasing emphasis on the smaller nuclear family, especially in urban settings.[6] Archaeological findings dated to the Monarchic Period support this: larger-sized dwellings were found in the rural areas, while the houses in the cities were approximately half the size.[7] These smaller urban house structures are thought to only house a nuclear family, typically comprised of two parents and two to three unmarried children.[8]

Concurrently, external threat leads to group formation at the largest kinship level. In essence, the allegiance of each individual was transferred

---

[3] Avraham Faust, "Abandonment, Urbanization, Resettlement and the Formation of the Israelite State," *Near Eastern Archaeology* 66 (2003): 147-61. Cf. Oystein S. LaBianca and Randall W. Younker, "The Kingdoms of Ammon, Moab and Edom: The Archaeology of Society in Late Bronze/Iron Age Transjordan (ca. 1400-500 BCE)," in *The Archaeology of Society in the Holy Land* (ed. Thomas E. Levy; London: Facts on File, 1995), 399-415, who explain the rise of surrounding "tribal kingdoms" largely on the basis of the threat posed by Israel.

[4] E.g., Louis Wirth, "Urbanism as a Way of Life," *The American Journal of Sociology* 44 (1938): 1-24 (20-22); Betty Yorburg, "The Nuclear and the Extended Family: An Area of Conceptual Confusion," *Journal of Comparative Family Studies* 6 (1975): 5-14.

[5] Cf. Wirth, "Urbanism," 21.

[6] Hanoch Reviv, *The Society in the Kingdoms of Israel and Judah* (Jerusalem: Bialik Institute, 1993), 52 (Hebrew), as quoted in Avraham Faust, "Differences in Family Structure between Cities and Villages in Iron Age II," *Tel Aviv* 26 (1999): 244.

[7] Faust, "Family Structure," 233-43; Avraham Faust, "The Rural Community in Ancient Israel during Iron Age II," *BASOR* 317 (2000): 19.

[8] Avraham Faust and Shlomo Bunimovitz, "The Four Room House: Embodying Iron Age Israelite Society," *Near Eastern Archaeology* 66 (2003): 26; Yigal Shiloh, "The Population of Iron Age Palestine in the Light of a Sample Analysis of Urban Plans, Areas, and Population Density," *BASOR* 239 (1980): 25-35. Cf. Lawrence E. Stager, "The Archaeology of the Family in Ancient Israel," *BASOR* 260 (1985): 1-35.

to the kingdom of Israel, as people united in the common goal of seeking to repel the external threats. Later, division of the kingdom into twelve administrative districts across tribal boundaries would have continued this process (cf. 1 Kgs 4:7-19).⁹ Another factor leading to the breakdown of smaller kinship groups is the introduction of hired labour.¹⁰ During the monarchy, hired labour would have been required for construction of cities and other building projects, including the Temple and palace in Jerusalem.

Although gender hierarchy was present prior to the Monarchic Period, the degree of gender inequality is thought to have increased at this time in the urban areas. Carol Meyers describes the decline in the household as the dominant social unit, with the subsequent change in the locus of power to the public world of male control.¹¹ Aligned with the growing prominence of military, state, and religious bureaucracies is the rise in male power and prestige, since these institutions are typically male-controlled. In particular, warfare would have contributed to the reduced status of women in society at this time, owing to the anatomical and physiological differences favouring the selection of men for physical combat.¹² Urbanisation contributed to the decline of female status, since women became less productive wives of soldiers, bureaucrats, priests, craftsmen or shopkeepers, in comparison to their central economic role in agrarian households.¹³ If urban households were composed of nuclear, rather than extended, families, the woman's realm of authority would have also decreased.¹⁴

This gender hierarchy is reflected in the architecture of Monarchic Period. Every household throughout history contains "gendered space," certain loci predominantly used by one gender rather than the other to perform tasks.¹⁵ The proliferation of the so-called four-room house as the

---

9   For partial archaeological confirmation for these sites, see William G. Dever, *What Did the Biblical Writers Know and When Did They Know It?: What Archaeology Can Tell Us about the Reality of Ancient Israel* (Grand Rapids: Eerdmans, 2001), 138-44.

10 Since a hired worker provides for his kinship group, the amount earned restricts the size of the group. The smaller kinship group becomes economically independent, thereby weakening relations with larger kinship groups. Cf. Sidney M. Greenfield, "Industrialization and the Family in Sociological Theory," *The American Journal of Sociology* 67 (1961): 321-22.

11 Meyers, *Eve*, 189-90.

12 Marvin Harris, "The Evolution of Human Gender Hierarchies: A Trial Formulation," in *Sex and Gender Hierarchies* (ed. Barbara D. Miller; Cambridge: Cambridge University Press, 1993), 57-79 (61).

13 Meyers, "Everyday Life," 258.

14 Meyers, "Everyday Life," 258. See also the discussion in Chapter Four.

15 Susan Kent, *Analyzing Activity Areas: An Ethnoarchaeological Study of the Use of Space* (Albuquerque: University of New Mexico Press, 1984), 2; Tracy L. Sweely, "Gender, Space, People, and Power at Cerén, El Salvador," in *Manifesting Power: Gender and the*

dominant type of Israelite building at the inception of the Monarchic Period[16] suggests that a segregation of activities was taking place within its walls. One function posited by Moshe Weinfeld was to separate between pure and impure, such as the avoidance of women during menstruation.[17]

Thus, external threat not only contributed to state formation; the associated urbanisation contributed to internal social change.

B. The RN in the Monarchic Period

Within this milieu of the Monarchic Period, the RN could function as a countervoice to these major social shifts. From the perspective of social identity, the RN promotes group behaviour by emphasising closer identification with kinship groups, and hence the relative salience of social identity over personal identity. The RN also contains a message against the burgeoning gender stratification of the era. These concerns of the RN can be illustrated through the presentation of the protagonists.

C. Weakening Kinship Ties

The actions of Boaz, Ruth, and Naomi promote commitment to kinship groups, albeit at different levels. Boaz demonstrates the importance of commitment to the clan. It is only through his intervention that the widows are provided for, and the perpetuation of the name of a fellow-clansman is possible. The level of his commitment is deliberately contrasted with that of another clansman, whose personal identity is revealed to be more salient than his social identity. If the attitude and actions of Mr. So-and-So represent the great majority of the people in the time of the monarchy, then Boaz's contrary conduct would make an especially forceful impression.

Ruth demonstrates the importance of commitment to the smallest kinship group, the father's house. Although she was free to return to her mother's house in Moab, she chose to accompany her mother-in-law to Judah. The extraordinary nature of her decision is given emphasis by way of contrast with Orpah. Further evidence of her commitment to Naomi is

---

Interpretation of Power in Archaeology (ed. Tracy L. Sweely; London: Routledge, 1999), 155-71(64).

16 Faust and Bunimovitz, "Four Room," 22-31.
17 Ehud Netzer, "Domestic Architecture in the Iron Age," in *The Architecture of Ancient Israel from the Prehistoric to the Persian Periods* (ed. Aharon Kempinski and Ronny Reich; Jerusalem: Israel Exploration Society, 1992), 199, fn. 24.

found in her decision to marry within Elimelech's clan. The poignancy of the combination of the strength of Ruth's commitment, and the promotion of this group norm through a non-Israelite, lends this message especial power.

The experience of Naomi illustrates the importance of attachment to social groups as a whole, including the largest group. Her loss of ties with the smallest kinship group—the father's house—is her greatest loss, leaving her without a provider and protector. It is only when a member from her wider kinship circle intervenes that she is supplied with her basic needs. Yet the failure of the social welfare system in the case of Naomi and Ruth highlights the importance of each member of Israelite society contributing when others are in need. Hence, readers in the Monarchic Period are to take responsibility not only for the members of the smallest kinship groups, but also for those in their largest kinship group—Israel. Nonetheless, the RN also reinforces the expectation that greater responsibility falls on the closest kinship group members.

The presentation of *hesed* as a group norm is consonant with the promotion of commitment to kinship groups. A generous, beneficent attitude shown in acts of kindness beyond the call of duty is to be a central character trait of all members of Israel. From a social identity perspective, this is essentially a social-minded attitude, manifested in collectivist actions. Its widespread and general applicability ensures the perpetuation of kinship groups at all levels if it is accepted as a core group descriptor. Promotion of *hesed* as a group norm is especially germane in a period of increasing focus on personal identity.

Concurrently, the RN could acknowledge the individualistic *Zeitgeist* of the Monarchic Period. This is evidenced in the prominence given to the individual attribute of initiative, as seen in all the main characters, but chiefly in Ruth and Naomi. Nonetheless, initiative is not endorsed for personal gain, but for communal benefit. Thus, while there is recognition of the individualistic-leaning sentiment of the age, there is channelling of this attitude towards group goals. In short, the RN could have functioned as a social critique of the Monarchic Period through the presentation of the attitudes and actions of its protagonists.

D. Increased Gender Hierarchy

The RN could also function as a corrective to the increasing gender hierarchy of the Monarchic Period. This is particularly demonstrated through Ruth and Naomi. Within a tightly patriarchal society, Ruth and Naomi might have been thought to be powerless to change their situation.

Through their initiative, however, they were able to manipulate their circumstances for their ultimate benefit. In a society that is increasingly privileging male social roles and control, the RN could thus reinforce the fact that women can still exert real and effective influence.

Yet Ruth and Naomi are able to initiate change without subverting the patriarchal structure. In different ways they both exert their influence on a male leader within society, who in turn schemes to use channels found within the social structure. The ultimate outcome is the reinforcement of the patriarchal structure: a man's name and lineage is perpetuated, and the house of Israel is built up through the patrilineal monarchy.

E. A Historical Provenance for the RN

A more specific provenance for the RN in the Monarchic Period needs to take into consideration the particular social emphases of the text. The two most conspicuous are:

1. The salience of smaller kinship groups. This message is most pertinent at times of relative neglect, such as during a period of urbanisation. Moreover, a need to challenge the social structure is most keenly felt when there is a change or potential change to the structure. Thus, in broad terms there are two periods during the monarchy when these would have applied: at the initial formation of the monarchy; and when there was further expansion and/or consolidation. The concluding genealogy places the RN after the first period, so it can only apply during the second.[18] This produces the following possible eras: Solomonic; Hezekianic; and Josianic.

2. The acceptance of foreigners. The strongly group-forming dynamic triggered by foreign military threat generates an especially germane social background for this message.[19] A message of tolerance towards foreigners would be especially applicable within this milieu. Another particularly significant social undercurrent is friction between foreigners and incumbents, a situation which is typically triggered by a fresh or increased influx of outsiders. While either of these social conditions alone may be sufficient as the background for the RN, a more likely

---

18 This, of course, assumes that the genealogy does not post-date the narrative. On a structural level, the genealogy has internal links with the immediately preceding section of Ruth 4, as well as balancing the prologue of Ruth 1:1-6.

19 Regarding ethnocentrism and outgroup hostility, see "The Social Identity Approach" in Chapter One.

provenance would encompass both a time of robust nationalism produced by strong external threat, and a real or potential substantial influx of foreigners.

While the Solomonic era can be ruled out, both the Hezekianic and Josianic eras match this social picture, albeit on different levels. Although the biblical record suggests an increased interaction with foreigners in the Solomonic period (esp. 1 Kgs 9:10–10:29), there is a lack of a clear external threat.[20] Additionally, the interaction was primarily at an economic level, with an absence of large-scale immigration.[21] Archaeological evidence is suggestive of an increase in the population of Jerusalem in the century between Hezekiah and Josiah.[22] This accords with the transition to an urban society in the late eighth century B.C.E. in the rest of ancient Near East.[23] Occurring during a period in which there was a reduction in the population of Judah overall, this increased urbanisation is thought to be beyond a natural biological population increase; an influx of non-Jerusalemites was also involved.

Immigrants probably arrived from different regions during the time of Hezekiah and Josiah. Suggestions have included refugees from the north after the fall of northern kingdom, merchants and refugees who arrived from Philistia after the Assyrian invasion,[24] and resident aliens benefiting from the international commerce following the advent of the Pax Assyriaca.[25] The majority, however, probably came from rural regions of

---

20 Although there was some hostility between Israel and Edom and Damascus, they did not represent a real threat at a national level. Cf. J. Maxwell Miller and John H. Hayes, *A History of Ancient Israel and Judah* (2d ed.; Louisville: Westminster John Knox, 2006), 219.

21 While Solomon intermarried with foreigners (esp. 1 Kgs 11:1-8), there does not appear to be the migration of whole groups of people.

22 See, e.g., Magen Broshi, "The Expansion of Jerusalem in the Reigns of Hezekiah and Manasseh," *IEJ* 24 (1975): 21-26; Magen Broshi and Israel Finkelstein, "The Population of Palestine in Iron Age II," *BASOR* 287 (1992): 47-60; Amihay Mazar, *Archaeology of the Land of the Bible: 10,000-586 B.C.E* (New York: Doubleday, 1992), 417-24. For a recent contrary opinion, see Nadav Na'aman, "When and How Did Jerusalem Become a Great City? The Rise of Jerusalem as Judah's Premier City in the Eighth-Seventh Centuries B.C.E.," *BASOR* 347 (2007): 21-56.

23 Hartmut Kühne, "The Urbanization of Assyrian Provinces," in *Nuove fondazioni nel Vicino Oriente Antico: Realtà e ideologia* (ed. Stefania Mazzoni; Pisa: Giardini, 1994), 55-84

24 W. Boyd Barrick, *The King and the Cemeteries: Toward a New Understanding of Josiah's Reform* (Leiden: Brill, 2002), 147.

25 Cf. Avraham Faust and Ehud Weiss, "Judah, Philistia, and the Mediterranean World: Reconstructing the Economic System of the Seventh Century B.C.E," *BASOR* 338 (2005): 71-92.

Judah. Based on this reconstruction, both the Hezekianic and Josianic periods would match the first social emphasis of the RN.

F. A Hezekianic Provenance?

It is historically plausible that the RN originated during the rule of Hezekiah. The military threat posed by Assyria would have produced a powerful group-forming dynamic at the national level. In this context of rising ethnocentrism and the erection of more definite boundaries marking the Israelite ingroup, a message promoting acceptance of outsiders within their midst is relevant. The Assyrian empire under Sennacherib posed a clear and strong military threat during the time of Hezekiah. By contrast, there is no evidence of direct hostilities between Judah and Egypt until 609 B.C.E.[26] Thus, external threat as a group-forming dynamic seems to suggest a Hezekianic provenance.

Following in the wake of the Assyrian invasions during the Hezekianic period, there was probably a large influx of outsiders. Israel Finkelstein and Neil Silberman, for instance, argue that the sudden demographic increase in Judah in the late eighth century is predominantly attributed to a flow of refugees from the north after the fall of Israel to Assyria in 722 B.C.E.[27] Finkelstein and Silberman also add another "torrent of refugees" following the devastation of the Judahite Shephelah and the Beersheba Valley by Sennacherib in 701 B.C.E.[28] The prophet Micah's critique of the social changes brought to Jerusalem by the northern immigrants may provide evidence for their influence on society (Mic 3:9-10).[29]

However, a greater threat would have been presented by outsiders with more foreign ancestry. Any influx of northerners would have been viewed as a threat by the Judahite elite as well as the general populace. But at least members of the former northern kingdom would have spoken the same language or a dialect thereof, and the same holds for their religion. By contrast, the call for the acceptance of foreigners in the RN (Ruth *as a Moabite*) intimates a more specific interaction with foreigners, rather than Ephraimites. This points to a later provenance for the RN: a considerable

---

26 Mordechai Cogan and Hayim Tadmor, *II Kings* (AB 11; New York: Doubleday, 1988), 300.
27 Israel Finkelstein and Neil Asher Silberman, "Temple and Dynasty: Hezekiah, the Remaking of Judah and the Rise of the Pan-Israelite Ideology," *JSOT* 30 (2006): 259-85.
28 Finkelstein and Silberman, "Temple," 266, after Broshi, "The Expansion of Jerusalem," 21-26.
29 William M. Schniedewind, *How the Bible Became a Book: The Textualization of Ancient Israel* (Cambridge: Cambridge University Press, 2004), 94.

time after the repopulation of the former northern Israelite kingdom with foreigners is more likely.

G. A Josianic Provenance?

Within the Monarchic Period, an origin for the composition of the RN during the reign of Josiah better fits the historical and social realities. The report in 2 Kgs 17:24 indicates that the resettlement of the northern kingdom began soon after its fall, perhaps under Sargon II (722-705 B.C.E.). The HB also indicates further deportations under Esarhaddon (Ezra 4:2; 681-668 B.C.E.) and Ashurbanipal (Ezra 4:9-10; 668-626 B.C.E.), in total covering a span of around one hundred years.[30] By the Josianic period (639-609 B.C.E.), these waves of alien settlers would have produced an Assyrian-controlled territory with a significant proportion of non-Israelites.[31] As a result, it would be reasonable to assume that a century of intermingling would have resulted in an admixture of cultures, along with genetic stock.[32] Thus, any incorporation of people from the north during the Josianic period would have posed a relatively greater threat to the incumbent Judahite population than during Hezekianic period.

Furthermore, the biblical and historical evidence support a provenance for the RN during the Josianic reforms. His expansion to the north is indicated in 2 Kgs 23:15-20, which was part of his religious reforms. His destruction and desecration of the shrines of the high places at Bethel and other cities of Samaria signifies the extent of his northern ambitions (2 Kgs 23:15, 19-20). Josiah's interest in the north amounts to an attempted reunification of the former northern and southern kingdoms of Israel, and would have involved an incorporation of non-Judahites.

Although the extent of his unification is debated, his vision opened up the possibility of mass northern immigration. There is only equivocal archaeological evidence for the Josianic reforms, including his northern

---

30 Regarding the Assyrian deportation policy in general, see Bustenay Oded, *Mass Deportations and Deportees in the Neo-Assyrian Empire* (Wiesbaden: Reichert, 1979); for estimates of the numbers of deportations and deportees, see his table on page 20.

31 See Adam Zertal, "The Wedge-Shaped Decorated Bowl and the Origin of the Samaritans," *BASOR* 276 (1989): 82.

32 This would have been fostered by the Assyrian rulers and officials, since they treated both deportees and inhabitants of a conquered territory uniformly. As Oded, *Deportations*, 86, notes, the Assyrian attitude towards an individual was based on his political affiliation and territory of residence, instead of ethnic-national identity, and that "territorial unity rather [than] national purity determined the attitude of the Assyrian kings to [a] conquered population."

incursion.³³ Indeed, the relatively brief mention in the biblical record hints that it was only partially successful: while it is possible that his reforms may have reached further north, perhaps only the region up to Bethel was annexed.³⁴ What is certain is that any reunification only lasted a maximum of approximately twelve years until the death of Josiah.³⁵ Thus, a reasonable reading of the extant evidence is that the reality did not fully match Josiah's northern ambitions. Nonetheless, in view of Josiah's aim of a pan-Israelite state, the arrival of any northerners would have accentuated any nascent intolerance towards outsiders.

Moreover, just as the military threat posed by Assyria would have produced a powerful Israelite group-forming dynamic, Egypt would have had the same effect during the time of Josiah, especially during his reforms. External threat against Judah was a feature of the late seventh century B.C.E., and Judah was probably an Egyptian vassal throughout Josiah's reign.³⁶ While it would seem that the kingdom of Judah was left to its own devices at the beginning of Josiah's reign, tensions gradually rose as his rule progressed, culminating in his stand against Necho II.

In fact, Josiah's premature death by the hand of the Egyptians can be viewed as the climax of a series of measures he had taken to establish Judah as an independent kingdom. Many explanations have been proposed for Josiah's premature death at Meggido.³⁷ Yet whatever the exact reasons for Josiah's final act of resistance might have been, his internal policies had already put the state in direct conflict with Egypt—initially potential, then

---

33 For a discussion surrounding the "cult-cache" of "pillar" figurines found in Jerusalem, and its connection with Josiah's reforms, see William G. Dever, *Recent Archaeological Discoveries and Biblical Research* (Seattle: University of Washington Press, 1990), 159-60. For a discussion of the dating of the destruction of the sanctuary at Arad, see Ze'ev Herzog, Miriam Aharoni, and Anson F. Rainey, "Arad: An Ancient Israelite Fortress with a Temple to Yahweh," *BAR* 13 (1987): 35; Mazar, *Archaeology*, 496-98.

34 Cf. Gösta W. Ahlström, *The History of Ancient Palestine* (Minneapolis: Fortress, 1993), 765; Oded Lipschits, *The Fall and Rise of Jerusalem: Judah under Babylonian Rule* (Winona Lake: Eisenbrauns, 2005), 138; Graham S. Ogden, "The Northern Extent of Josiah's Reform," *ABR* 26 (1978): 26-34. Ahlström, *History*, 765, notes that Ezra 2:28-33 might be considered evidence for a territorial extension under Josiah, since it mentions Lod, Ono, and Hadid in the west, and Bethel and Ai in the north as places where the returnees from Babylonia settled.

35 This relatively short time-span and the nature of his activities are significant reasons for the dearth of archaeological data, such as the presence of Judahite material remains in the north.

36 Miller and Hayes, *History*, 450-53. Cf. 2 Kgs 23:28-35; 24:7.

37 See, inter alios, Steve Delamarter, "The Death of Josiah in Scripture and Tradition: Wrestling with the Problem of Evil?," *VT* 54 (2004): 29-60; Israel Finkelstein and Neil Asher Silberman, *The Bible Unearthed: Archaeology's New Vision of Ancient Israel and the Origin of Its Sacred Texts* (New York: Touchstone, 2001), 291.

real. Josiah's nationalistic measures would not have gone unnoticed by Egypt for too long. Adam Welch even suggests that Necho summoned Josiah to explain his suspicious conduct, and that what consequently occurred "was not so much a battle as a court-martial."[38] At the very least, the increasingly nationalistic and expansionist policies under Josiah would have raised the spectre of an Egyptian response in Judahite minds, given the adversative nature of Josiah's actions.

Yet it is difficult to separate Josiah's religious motivations from his political agenda. Negatively, his removal of foreign elements of worship is not only intended to purify the cult of syncretistic elements, and reparation for the sins committed by his forebears (esp. 2 Kgs 23:12-14; in 23:15-20 the sins of the former northern kingdom are also redressed), but also to remove foreign influence (e.g., 23:4-14). Positively, the observation of the Passover is not only an expression of a return to YHWH after decades of neglect (23:22), it is also an expression of Josiah's resolve to combat Egyptian rule. As such, the Passover is symbolic of the great conflict tradition with Egypt, and recalls the power of YHWH to rescue His people. It is clear how this message would resonate with the plight of Judah under Egyptian dominance. Seen in this light, the reforms and territorial expansion would not have been a unilateral initiative of Josiah; rather, as the monarch, he would have expressed the nationalistic and conservative aspirations of his people.

1. Josiah's Use of the Book of the Law for Nationalistic Purposes

Nonetheless, if there were still some doubters, the Book of the Law would have provided a powerful impetus for the nationalistic plans.[39] For instance, the centralising political tendencies of Deuteronomy can be used to strengthen Josiah's expansionist ambitions to the north, as well as to reinforce the hegemony of the Jerusalemite leadership and judiciary (esp. Deut 17:8–18:22) at the expense of clan-based leadership in the rural areas. The devaluation of kinship structures continues in the adversative stance, setting the present generation against the previous generation,[40] and the promotion of adherence to the law has the effect of linking Israelite

---

38   Adam C. Welch, "The Death of Josiah," *ZAW* 43 (1925): 257.
39   The critical consensus is that Deuteronomy was written just before or during Josiah's reign; see, e.g., Ernest W. Nicholson, *Deuteronomy and Tradition* (Philadelphia: Fortress, 1967), 1-17. For the purposes of this discussion, the date of composition of Deuteronomy is immaterial; the relevant point is that its contents were present by the time of Josiah, and amenable for usage to fan the patriotic fire.
40   Cf. Deut 11:2-7; 29:13-14[14-15].

identity more closely with allegiance to the covenant/law than with lineage.

This is part of the levelling urges of Deuteronomy, which could have been productively used by Josiah with the aim of imposing uniformity and unity at the national level. There is a move to diminish the distinctions of gender, class, and ethnicity that lead to factions within the nation.[41] It particularly lobbies women to become part of a national agenda, one which is divorced from patrilineage.[42] Even the king does not have immunity from these processes: his power is limited (Deut 17:16-17). The intended effect of this curbing of kingly excesses is to maintain his equality with his fellow citizens (17:20; cf. 17:15).

An anti-imperialist agenda has also been detected in the "Law of the King" (Deut 17:14-20). As Richard Lowery argues, the mention of horses, wives, taxes, and Egyptian bondage can be interpreted as manifestations of foreign alliances.[43] The danger of these associations is the annihilation of the kingdom of Judah. For Lowery, this is a veiled reference to Assyrian imperialism, which leads him to situate this text in the Hezekianic period. Ernest Nicholson, however, argues for a provenance in the last quarter of the seventh century B.C.E., and hence during the reign of Josiah.[44] For Nicholson, the prohibition of setting a foreign king on the Judahite throne is best understood on the background of a century of Assyrian hegemony, and the "catastrophic consequences" this had on both the northern and southern kingdoms.

By the late Monarchic Period, the Exodus tradition was probably already firmly established as a foundational Israelite narrative.[45] Hence, a reverse Exodus and a return to Egyptian bondage (לא תספון לשוב בדרך הזה עוד;[46] Deut 17:16c) would have been relevant in both the Hezekianic and

---

41 Halpern, "Jerusalem," 75.
42 Halpern, "Jerusalem," 75-76.
43 Richard H. Lowery, *The Reforming Kings* (JSOTSup 120; Sheffield: JSOT Press, 1991), 155-56.
44 Ernest W. Nicholson, "'Do Not Dare to Set a Foreigner Over You': The King in Deuteronomy and 'The Great King'," *ZAW* 118 (2006): 46-61.
45 The pervasiveness of the Exodus motif is evidenced in the allusions found in so-called D (e.g., Deut 1:27-30; 28:68), Deuteronomistic texts (e.g., Josh 3-4; 1 Sam 4-6), and prophetic texts often dated to the Monarchic Period (e.g., Isa 10-12; Jer 2:1-7; 16:14-15; 23:1-8; Amos 2:9-10; 3:1-2; Mic 6:1-5). See also Yair Hoffman, "The Exodus - Tradition and Reality: The Status of the Exodus Tradition in Ancient Israel," in *Jerusalem Studies in Egyptology* (ed. Irene Shirun-Grumach; Wiesbaden: Harrassowitz Verlag, 1998), 193-202.
46 This phrase recalls the idea of Israel's refusal to enter Canaan as an "anti-Exodus" (Deut 2:1); see Peter C. Craigie, *The Book of Deuteronomy* (NICOT; Grand Rapids: Eerdmans, 1976), 256.

Josianic periods. Nonetheless, the specific proscription against seeking an alliance or commerce with Egypt would have found an especially relevant application during the time of Josiah.

The promotion of David in the concluding genealogy of the RN is consistent with Josiah's nationalistic aim.[47] It is this sixteenth-generation lineal descendant of king David who once again revives the hope of a unified Israel, re-establishing the territory first given to God's people under Moses. Set in the transitional period between the entrance to the Promised Land, and settlement within Canaan, the RN describes how a single ruler can rise from the anarchy of a loose conglomeration of tribes with their rulers. Within this perspective, the RN celebrates the revival of the only God-ordained, and therefore legitimate dynasty in Israelite historiography. The presence of Moabite blood in the veins of David and his direct descendant Josiah then functions as prime motivation for tolerance towards outsiders, and demonstrates that nobility is more a matter of character than blood.[48]

In sum, the social emphases of the RN, and the many specific ways in which Deuteronomy could have been used by Josiah to reinforce and direct his nationalistic agenda, suggest a possible provenance for the RN in Judah during the time of Josiah's reforms.

H. Evaluation of a Provenance for the RN in the Josianic Period

Nonetheless, there is a degree of uncertainty for a Josianic provenance because of the prominence of the RN's message of tolerance towards outsiders. There are two main confounding factors. First, the relatively small influx of foreigners. As analysed supra, the threat from new waves of immigrants was more potential than real. Although Josiah's aim for a reunified kingdom might have been associated with a southern migration, historical reality indicates that his annexation of territory from the former northern kingdom was limited. Moreover, it is questionable whether any of the non-Ephraimite population would be motivated to resettle permanently in Judah, especially since they probably would have viewed

---

47 Marshall D. Johnson, *The Purpose of Biblical Genealogies with Special Reference to the Setting of the Genealogies of Jesus* (SNTSMS 8; Cambridge: Cambridge University Press, 1969), 81-82, notes that genealogies express the "theological and nationalistic concerns of a people."

48 Block, *Judges, Ruth*, 597. Both Sasson, *Ruth*, 251, and Block suggest a Josianic date for the RN. In contrast to the present discussion, Block suggests an author residing in the former northern kingdom. The social processes considered supra, however, all point to a provenance in Judah.

the desecration of their shrines and execution of their priests as an unsolicited and merciless intrusion into their affairs.[49]

Hence, the second factor inconsistent with the RN's concern for foreigners is the transient nature of their stay. Nadav Na'aman argues that any southward movement of refugees triggered by the Assyrian invasion was unlikely to be permanent.[50] Refugees must leave behind property and sources of livelihood, as well as their communal societies and their social standing within these. They arrive at their new location as aliens, dependent upon a local population that is unlikely to welcome them openly. The need for various commandments to protect the rights of sojourners or immigrants (גר) and provide for their physical needs through the law supports this understanding.[51] If this is a realistic historical reconstruction, as soon as conditions stabilised, many would return home; only a minority would remain in Judah.

This understanding of the temporary residence of sojourners from the north also applies to the Josianic period. While the influx of northerners during Josiah's reunification activity would have probably been smaller to begin with, it is feasible that many would have returned north again, especially with the progressively increasing Egyptian threat. From this perspective, Ruth's self-designation as a foreigner (נכריה) rather than an immigrant (גר; Ruth 2:10) is consistent with the temporary nature of their stay. As such, it is reflective of the intention of the majority of foreigners to return to their homeland in the Monarchic Period. Consequently, they retain an independent sense of identity, including a lack of any attachment to Judah's God, YHWH.[52]

I. Conclusion

Within the Monarchic Period, the RN could have functioned as a countervoice amidst the social change associated with the external threat, and the development of the monarchy with the attendant urbanisation. In a time of weakening kinship ties, the RN could have insisted that commitment to smaller kinship groups is still important. In a time of

---

49   Cf. Gary N. Knoppers, *Two Nations under God: The Deuteronomistic History of Solomon and the Dual Monarchies* (vol. 2; Atlanta: Scholars Press, 1993), 226.
50   Na'aman, "Jerusalem," 35-36.
51   E.g., Deut 1:16; 5:14; 14:21; 24:14, 17, 19-21; 26:12-13; 27:19.
52   Nonetheless, the RN's message of acceptance towards foreigners, and the presentation of the possibility of their integration into Israelite society is consistent with the hope in the HB that foreigners might be incorporated into the covenant community (e.g., Deut 29:21-23[22-24]; 1 Kgs 8:41-43; Isa 60:10; 61:5-6).

increasing gender disparity, it could have maintained that women can still exert a real influence within the patriarchal structure.

If a provenance for the RN was to be found during the monarchy, the social undercurrents of the RN would find closest correspondence with those in Judah during the Josianic period. Josiah's reforms with its associated nationalistic and expansionist drives would have formed an especially pertinent backdrop for the RN's focus on the salience of smaller kinship groups, and the acceptance of foreigners. However, the doubt arising from the relatively weak force of the foreign threat suggests the RN might find a tighter fit in another historical period. The degree of hesitation rises when placed against the prominence of the RN's message concerning foreigners.

II. The Persian Period

With this uncertainty surrounding the Monarchic Period, one era that compels exploration as a time of composition for the RN is the Persian Period. More specifically, the second part of this chapter will focus on the Persian Period as evident in EN for two reasons: (1) issues of identity were especially pressing at this time; and (2) many scholars date the composition of the RN to this period.[53] In this time of transition, the endorsement of the importance of smaller kinship groups is apposite. Moreover, in contrast to the Josianic period, there is a keen and persistent threat deriving from the non-Israelites within their midst.

A. The Nature of Identity in the Persian Period

The presence and composition of the Israelite community in the Archaemenid Period is a topic of much debate. Previously, most biblical historians were of the opinion that the land of Israel was left largely uninhabited following the conquest and exile of the population by Nebuchadnezzar in 586 B.C.E.[54] More recently, some scholars assert that the great majority of the inhabitants of Judah remained in the land during

---

53 Recent scholars include Korpel, *Structure*; LaCocque, *Ruth*.
54 Hans M. Barstad, *The Myth of the Empty Land: A Study in the History and Archaeology of Judah during the "Exilic" Period* (Oslo: Scandinavian University Press, 1996), 13. One current proponent of the total destruction of Judah is Ephraim Stern, *Archaeology of the Land of the Bible: The Assyrian, Babylonian, and Persian Periods, 732-332 BCE* (New York: Doubleday, 2001), esp. 303-11.

the "exilic period," with only a few going into captivity.[55] This "Myth of the Empty Land" is an offshoot of a thesis regarding "the mystical past" and the "myth of Israel,"[56] which views the HB as produced by Persian or Hellenistic Jews as a piece of propaganda for political and religious ends.[57] Consequently, any exiles who returned only had a minimal impact on the life, culture, and identity of those who remained in the land. In short, the distinction between pre-exilic and post-exilic Judah is regarded as fictional rather than historical.

Most scholars now, however, agree that the "Myth of the Empty Land" is unnecessary. Based on the biblical and archaeological evidence, continuous inhabitation of the land is the correct understanding. The biblical texts state that not all the Israelites were deported; the poorest of the population remained to work the land (2 Kgs 24:14; 25:12; Jer 40:7). That is, passages such as these make the invention of the emptiness of the land redundant.[58] Although some are sceptical of the historical veracity of the biblical accounts, the archaeological findings point in the same direction. The data indicate that the Babylonian destruction centred on Jerusalem and the surrounding towns of Judah, while sparing the area of Benjamin.[59] This negates the statement of Hans Barstad that the majority of the inhabitants remained in Judah, "where life went on after 586 B.C.E. pretty much the same way it did before the arrival of Nebuchadnezzar's armies."[60] His statement may be correct regarding life in the territory of Benjamin, but not Judah. Rather, the current evidence points to significant destruction in Judah, especially in Jerusalem and surrounding areas, with the vast bulk of deportees to Babylon deriving from these locations.

This interpretation of the exile maintains the historicity of the returnees as the centre of influence for cultural and spiritual life, and for establishing identity in the Persian Period. There is a tension between continuity and discontinuity in the biblical texts concerning the exilic and post-exilic periods, with the latter motif predominating. Discontinuity and

---

55 E.g., Barstad, *Myth*, 42, 78.
56 E.g., Thomas L. Thompson, *The Mythic Past: Biblical Archaeology and the Myth of Israel* (New York: Basic Books, 1999).
57 E.g., Robert P. Carroll, "The Myth of the Empty Land," *Semeia* 59 (1992): 79-93; Philip R. Davies, "Exile? What Exile? Whose Exile?," in *Leading Captivity Captive: The Exile as History and Ideology* (ed. Lester L. Grabbe; JSOTSup 278; Sheffield: Sheffield Academic, 1998), 135-37.
58 For a presentation of the evidence from other biblical texts, see Bustenay Oded, "Where Is the 'Myth of the Empty Land' To Be Found? History versus Myth," in *Judah and the Judeans in the Neo-Babylonian Period* (ed. Oded Lipschits and Joseph Blenkinsopp; Winona Lake: Eisenbrauns, 2003), 55-74.
59 Lipschits, *Fall and Rise*, 270-71.
60 Barstad, *Myth*, 79.

reinvention are particularly evidenced in passages depicting the exile and return as one of death and resurrection (Ezek 37:1-14) and the return from Babylon as a second Exodus (e.g., Ezra 1:5, 6, 7, 8, 11;[61] Ezek 11:16-17; 20:41-42; 36:24; 37:21-22).[62] This emphasis on discontinuity points to the greater influence of the returnees on the Israelite community in Yehud. Continuity would be the overriding experience of those who remained in the land, but it would irrelevant for those who experienced life in Babylon.

Thus, the HB records that the Exile had a decisive impact on Israelite identity. The external markers of national identity—Temple and city—had been destroyed, and Davidic rule suspended, if not abandoned altogether.[63] Exile in a foreign land presented the deportees with an opportunity to reassess the issues central to their identity, both individually and corporately. As represented in the book of Ezekiel, they had to wrestle with issues including the presence of YHWH without the Temple, the essence of worship, the importance of obedience to God's Law, and their role as Israelites within a universal setting.[64] Without the external markers of their identity, they were forced to form new boundaries between themselves and outsiders.

The return of the Israelites to their homeland heralded another challenge to their identity. In many ways, it was a chance to return to the core components of their identity prior to the Exile. This is evidenced in the priority invested in rebuilding the Temple and the walls of the Jerusalem, as well as the primacy of the Law. A consequence of their return to Israel, however, is that they are in a liminal state, a state of transition and adjustment from being Israelites in a foreign country, to being Israelites back on home territory. The main description of the attempt of the returned Israelites to reconstruct their identity is found in Ezra-Nehemiah, "a tale of transition between exilic and post-exilic identity."[65]

---

61 See, e.g., Mark A. Throntveit, *Ezra-Nehemiah* (Interpretation; Louisville: John Knox Press, 1992), 15-18; H. G. M. Williamson, *Ezra, Nehemiah* (Waco: Word, 1985), 15-19.

62 As many scholars note, Ezekiel is presented as a prophet like Moses in the book of Ezekiel; e.g., Henry McKeating, "Ezekiel the 'Prophet Like Moses'?," *JSOT* 61 (1994): 97-109, and most recently Rebecca G. S. Idestrom, "Echoes of the Book of Exodus in Ezekiel," *JSOT* 33 (2009): 489-510.

63 Cf. John Bright, *A History of Israel* (4th ed.; Louisville: Westminster John Knox, 2000), 343.

64 See, e.g., Walter Brueggemann, *Hopeful Imagination: Prophetic Voices in Exile* (Philadelphia: Fortress, 1986), 50-87; Ralph W. Klein, *Israel in Exile: A Theological Interpretation* (Philadelphia: Fortress, 1979), 69-96; John F. Kutsko, *Between Heaven and Earth: Divine Presence and Absence in the Book of Ezekiel* (Biblical and Judaic Studies 7; Winona Lake: Eisenbrauns, 2000).

65 H. Zlotnick-Sivan, "The Silent Women of Yehud: Notes on Ezra 9-10," *JJS* 51 (2000): 17.

To demonstrate the transitional nature of identity within Israel at this time, I will discuss one example from each end of the identity spectrum: the identity of an Israelite; and an individual role of a protagonist in the EN narrative.

B. The Liminality of the People of God

There is evidence of liminality regarding the identity of the people of God in the Persian Period. Sara Japhet comments that in EN there is only one Israelite community in Yehud, "the returned exiles" (שבי הגולה; Ezra 2:1; Neh 7:6).[66] This community included the Judeans, Benjaminites, priests, and Levites (Ezra 1:5), as listed in Ezra 2 and Nehemiah 7. Indeed, the repetition of the list serves to "stress the nature of the reconstituted community."[67] The equation of the returnees with Israel is particularly seen in Ezra 9-10.[68] In addition to the designation of the people of God as "the returned exiles" they are also referred to as "the exiles" (הגולה; 9:4; 10:6), "children of the exile" (בני הגולה; 10:7, 16; cf. 4:1; 6:19, 20; 8:35), or "the assembly of exiles" (קהל הגולה; 10:8), which is the same group as "Israel" (10:2, 10), "all Israel" (10:7), or "the children of Israel" (בני ישראל; 10:2, 10). Israel is defined by the ethno-religious term "the people of the Exile."[69]

This self-understanding of Israelite identity is in contradistinction to "the people of the land" (עם הארץ).[70] There were at least three different groups within the land of Israel who could have claimed identity as Israel:[71] (1) the group of "returned exiles"; (2) the community who remained in Judah after the Babylonian deportation; and (3) either inhabitants of northern Israel who remained after the Assyrian invasion or foreigners who

---

66 Sara Japhet, "People and Land in the Restoration Period," in *From the Rivers of Babylon to the Highlands of Judah: Collected Studies on the Restoration Period* (Winona Lake: Eisenbrauns, 2006), 108 (originally published in 1983).

67 Tamara C. Eskenazi, "The Structure of Ezra-Nehemiah and the Integrity of the Book," *JBL* 107 (1988): 648.

68 Japhet, "People," 107-08.

69 According to Bill T. Arnold, "The Use of Aramaic in the Hebrew Bible: Another Look at Bilingualism in Ezra and Daniel," *JNSL* 22 (1996): 1-16, this is only the view of the Jewish author of EN, writing as an "insider." The external point of view of the Aramaic outsider, as reflected in the Aramaic narrative found in Ezra 4:8–6:18, is predominantly in geopolitical terms: "the Judeans," or "the people of Judah." Cf. Joshua Berman, "The Narratorial Voice of the Scribes of Samaria: Ezra iv 8-vi 18 Reconsidered," *VT* 56 (2006): 313-26.

70 The expression עם הארץ has a general and fluid meaning in the HB, one which varies according to the context. See Japhet, "People," 96-116; Ernest W. Nicholson, "The Meaning of the Expression עם הארץ in the Old Testament," *JSS* 10 (1965): 59-66.

71 Japhet, "People," 97-99.

were settled in the land by the Assyrians (2 Kgs 17:24; cf. Ezra 4:2, 10). In response to this mixture of people, EN sought to answer the pressing question: "Who is Israel?"[72] The answer is clear: only the Babylonian returnees. While this is consistent with the exilic prophets,[73] this self-identification is in direct contrast with the prophets of the early Restoration period, who equated Israel with "the people of the land." In Hag 2:4, the phrase refers to the citizenry of Israel as distinct from the leaders Zerubbabel and Joshua, with the pre-exilic connotation of "assembly of the people."[74] In Haggai there is no mention of returnees, or indeed, the exile. Similarly, in Zech 7:5 "the people of the land" refers to the citizenry of Israel as a whole, in this instance as distinct from the priests.[75] Yet there is also no mention of a community of returnees in Zechariah, and no identification of this group with "Israel."

While the author of EN might be importing a later contention regarding Israelite identity into the early Restoration period, its presence in the narrative context of EN suggests that it was still a disputed issue in the middle Restoration period. That is, Israelite identity was still in a state of transition. Even those who might claim to worship the same God are consigned to the category of "people(s) of the land" (Ezra 4:1-4). Thus, those who might identify themselves as Israelites by descent or religion are not part of Israel.

C. The Liminality of the Role of the Scribe

The second manifestation of the liminality of identity in the time of EN is the description of Ezra as scribe/priest. The occupation of a scribe is not an innovation of the Persian Period; the royal court of Judah employed "scribes"/"secretaries" (ספר; e.g., 2 Sam 8:17; 20:25; 2 Kgs 12:11; 18:18, 37; 19:2) and "recorders" (מזכיר; e.g., 2 Sam 8:16; 20:24; 1 Kgs 4:3; 2 Kgs 18:18, 37). Scribes were not generally associated with teaching the law in the HB, yet this is found in EN.[76] Ezra is first designated a "scribe" (ספר) in Ezra 7:6, one who is "skilled in the law of Moses" (מהיר בתורת משה). Part of his task

---

72 Japhet, "People," 100.
73 E.g., Ezek 11:15-21; 33:23-29; Jer 24:1-10.
74 Carol L. Meyers and Eric M. Meyers, *Haggai, Zechariah 1-8* (AB 25B; New York: Doubleday, 1987), 51. The phrase is in parallel with "the remnant of the people" (שארית העם; 2:2), which in the context of the book of Haggai probably refers to those who remained in the land and were witnesses to both Temples. See Japhet, "People," 104-06.
75 Meyers and Meyers, *Haggai, Zechariah 1-8*, 387.
76 His official Persian title is "scribe of the law of God of heaven" (7:12, 21), perhaps a "secretary of state for Jewish affairs"; Williamson, *Ezra, Nehemiah*, 100.

is then spelt out in 7:10, which describes Ezra as being devoted to studying the law of YHWH, and to observing and teaching its statutes and judgements in Israel. The subsequent narrative, especially Nehemiah 8, reinforces this aspect of his task.[77]

The teaching role is more conventionally associated with the priesthood, Ezra's second designation. His impeccable priestly pedigree is highlighted in Ezra 7:1-5: he is descended from Aaron, from the Zadokite line, although he is not a high priest himself. The teaching function of the priest is well attested in the HB, at least by the late-Monarchic Period onwards. In Jeremiah, the law (תורה) is associated with the priest, just as counsel is associated with the wise, and the word with the prophet (Jer 18:18; cf. Ezek 7:26). In texts dated to the Persian Period, the priest is explicitly linked with teaching ("teaching priest"; כהן מורה) and the law (2 Chron 15:3; cf. Mal 2:7).[78]

The liminality of identity in the Restoration period is reinforced by the fact that EN is the only place in the HB where the functions of priest and scribe are combined.[79] Ezra is a scribe whose work focuses on the book of the Torah, whose primary priestly task is associated with teaching; he is a priest who is "first and foremost a scribe."[80] Despite establishing his credentials as a priest,[81] the EN narrative only mentions one priestly task: the consecration of the Temple vessels and the commissioning of the bearers (Ezra 8:24-30). For the rest of the narrative he is a student and teacher of the law, identifying him as a scribe or as a priest who primarily teaches.[82] His priestly pedigree conveys the message that Ezra's function with respect to the law is contiguous with that of the pre-exilic priesthood,[83] and, moreover, ensures his acceptance prior to establishing his

---

77 In this chapter, which describes Ezra joining the people to celebrate the seventh month, the emphasis is on his role as "the scribe" (mentioned four times; 8:1, 4, 9, 13). His other titles occur only once each (הכהן; 2; הכהן הספר; 9).
78 It could be argued that Deuteronomy laid the groundwork for this shift in the role of the priest by placing all Israel, including its authorities, under the authority of YHWH. See Martha Himmelfarb, *A Kingdom of Priests: Ancestry and Merit in Ancient Judaism* (Philadelphia: University of Pennsylvania Press, 2006), 11-14.
79 Cf. Tamara C. Eskenazi, *In an Age of Prose: A Literary Approach to Ezra-Nehemiah* (Atlanta: Scholars Press, 1988), 75.
80 Eskenazi, *Prose*, 75.
81 Throntveit, *Ezra-Nehemiah*, 40-41, describes four ways the narrative emphasises the importance of Ezra as descended from the priestly line that provided Israel's high priests.
82 Cf. Lester L. Grabbe, "A Priest is without Honor in His Own Prophet: Priests and Other Religious Specialists in the Latter Prophets," in *The Priests in the Prophets: The Portrayal of Priests, Prophets, and Other Religious Specialists in the Latter Prophets* (ed. Alice Ogden Bellis; JSOTSup 408; New York: T&T Clark, 2004), 79-97, esp. 92.
83 Joseph Blenkinsopp, *Ezra-Nehemiah* (OTL; Philadelphia: Westminster, 1988), 136.

primary role of teaching the law.[84] Thus, in Ezra's role there are two innovations: not only is he a scribe who teaches, he is also a scribe-priest. If the vocation of priests involves a state of "permanent liminality," then breaking new ground would come more naturally to them.[85]

To summarise, these two examples of change—in identifying the Israelite community and the role of a scribe—point to the state of flux in the Restoration period. While pre-exilic traditions were influential, the milieu of the time fostered re-invention or reconstruction. This was almost by necessity for two reasons.[86] First, the majority of returnees did not have first-hand experience of life in Israel. Second, the restoration of their identity took place in a local context that was now different politically. The presence of other groups located in Yehud meant that reconstruction of identity took place in interaction with, and sometimes in opposition to these groups.

D. The Influence of the RN on Identity in the Persian Period

Having established the Restoration period as one of transition, as well as mentioning some factors contributing to this change, in the following section I will consider the impact that the RN might have had on identity. Once again, this will be outlined according to the two main components of identity: personal and social.

E. Personal Component

On an individual level, there are two particularly apposite messages from the RN for a reader located in the Persian Period. First, is the crucial importance of initiative as a character trait.[87] Although Ruth and Naomi return to Judah in a desperate and destitute state, through their initiative

---

84   This is consistent with the general movement of EN: there is now an alternate foundation for the community of God. While the Temple remains important as an identity marker, the Torah is now of prime importance. See, most recently, Jacob L. Wright, "Writing the Restoration: Compositional Agenda and the Role of Ezra in Nehemiah 8," *Journal of Hebrew Scriptures* 7 (2007): 19-29.
85   Richard D. Nelson, *Raising Up a Faithful Priest: Community and Priesthood in Biblical Theology* (Louisville: Westminster John Knox, 1993), 83-85, suggests that since priests live on the boundary of sacred and profane, their lifestyle mirrors this status. The overlap of professions is similar to the overlap of priest and prophet in Jeremiah and Ezekiel.
86   Esler, "Ezra-Nehemiah," 417.
87   In am indebted to Carolyn Leeb for some ideas found in the following two paragraphs (personal communication, dated 22/8/07).

and resourcefulness they are able to not only survive, but ultimately thrive. Georg Braulik finds the Exodus tradition evoked in Ruth 1, painting "Naomi's sojournship in Moab and her return to Bethlehem in the colours of the sojourn in Egypt and of the Exodus."[88] Equating their experience with the Exodus from Egypt, a returnee from Babylon would identify with Naomi on a general level. On an emotional level, a reader in the Restoration period may be feeling emotions similar to those of Naomi when she returned: downcast and destitute. They would identify with Naomi's desperate situation as an אלמנה, because they would feel "feminised": powerless and struggling under Persian domination.[89] At least during the early Restoration period, they may also draw a parallel between her de-identified status as one without any connection to a social group, and their own situation as a group of people without any external symbols of their identity.

Yet the RN presents a model for a way in which those in desperate situations can combine their meagre resources to overcome their destitution. Ruth is the foremost character displaying initiative, but as discussed in Chapter Four, the decisive point in the narrative is when Naomi finally also takes some initiative. It may therefore be significant that the author of the RN withholds the label אלמנה for Naomi, although it would have been a suitable descriptor upon her return from Moab. For although she is without a connection to a בית אב, and seemingly without any hope of attachment to one, the creative combination of Naomi's productive resources and Ruth's reproductive resources ensures they achieve security and provision in a new household.[90] Similarly, although the lot of a reader in the Restoration period may seem dismal, hope is provided through the exercise of initiative, using whatever scanty resources may be available.

The second message from the RN is that acting beyond conventional roles may be required. This is a practical outworking of initiative as a personal character trait, and is seen in each of the main characters, as discussed in the previous three chapters. In breaking from the normal societal mould, the characters in the RN illustrate how a post-exilic reader can behave in supraconventional ways. Thus, the RN can function

---

88 Georg Braulik, "The Book of Ruth as Intra-Biblical Critique of the Deuteronomic Law," *AcT* 19 (1999): 11.

89 Feminist theorists use a number of terms to describe the perceived male domination, such as "oppression," "patriarchy," and "subjection." The basic notion is that power is exercised in an unjust and oppressive manner; see, e.g., Catharine A. MacKinnon, *Feminism Unmodified: Discourses on Life and Law* (Cambridge, Mass.: Harvard University Press, 1987), 123.

90 Cf. Leeb, "Widow," 161.

paradigmatically: while the specific behaviour of the characters may be neither suitable nor applicable for each reader, they can still follow the same underlying principle. And the Restoration period, as a time of flux, would be a more accepting context for this type of behaviour.

F. Social Component

The following discussion of the social component of identity will focus on two kinship groups: the father's house; and "Israel." Since both groups underwent significant changes in Restoration era, I will first outline these changes, and then based on this understanding I will proceed to suggest some influences of the RN on identity in the Persian Period.

1. Kin: Fathers' House

a. The Father's House in the Persian Period

The exile led to a great upheaval in kinship structure, with the returnees settling in urban areas and forming a new kinship unit: the fathers' house. The decimation of kinship groups as a result of the deportations to and returns from Babylon necessitated the formation of the בית אבות. David Clines draws a direct parallel between the בית אבות and the pre-exilic בית אב.[91] However, two factors militate against a straight correspondence between the two terms. First, the number of members comprising each group exceeds the numbers found in the pre-exilic period.[92] Although this new social grouping maintained affinities with the בית אב ("father's house"), it was closer in size to the pre-exilic משפחה ("clan"). Second, the prevalence of בית אבות ("fathers' house") in texts associated with a post-exilic provenance suggests either that it originated or was most prevalent in this period.[93]

There is a further important difference between these two kinship groups. The familial lineage of a בית אבות was not as strong as a בית אב;

---

91 David J. A. Clines, *Ezra, Nehemiah, Esther* (NCBC; Grand Rapids: Eerdmans, 1984), 39-40.
92 Daniel L. Smith, *The Religion of the Landless: The Social Context of the Babylonian Exile* (Bloomington: Meyer Stone Books, 1989), 102.
93 It occurs sixty-five times in EN and Chronicles, and only six times in the Deuteronomic history; John J. Collins, "Marriage, Divorce, and Family in Second Temple Judaism," in *Families in Ancient Israel* (ed. Leo G. Perdue, et al.; Louisville: Westminster John Knox, 1997), 105.

rather, as a survival mechanism, this social construct most likely contained fictional elements. Joel Weinberg explains: "The *bêt'ābôt* of the Archaemenid era is an agnatic band which came into existence in the peculiar situation of the exile and repatriation, and which unified a number of families that were related (either genuinely or fictionally)."[94] In connection to this, the recounting of the amalgamation of the father's houses of Jeush and Beriah in 1 Chronicles 23:11 is highly suggestive.[95] Despite the divergences, the usage of the nomenclature of the smaller group was probably intentional. As an expression of social solidarity, not only did the fathers' houses incorporate non-kinship groups, it also reinforced old kinship ties.[96]

The בית אבות had a number of functions. Minimally, it identified the members of "Israel." Those who could trace their ancestry to a ראש האבות established their membership within Israel. Conversely, those who could not prove that "their fathers' houses and ancestry were from Israel" (בית אבותם וזרעם אם מישראל הם; Ezra 2:59; Neh 7:61) were excluded. As such, the genealogical lists in EN function to safeguard the purity of the nation, a unique function in the context of the HB.[97] In particular, the lists served to distinguish Israel from the עם הארץ. Yet, as Marshall Johnson adds, undergirding the notion of legitimacy and ethnic purity "is the desire to express the continuity of the people of God, ... the identity of the new Israel with the old Israel of the monarchy."[98]

Membership of a בית אבות entailed a range of benefits. The attachment of the name of the בית אבות onto the full names of its members adds to their sense of solidarity with the kinship group.[99] Other benefits included the operation of a kinsman-redeemer, and the inheritance of patrimony.[100] Weinberg asserts that the fathers' houses were based on communal ownership of land,[101] but the outcry of the poor in Neh 5:2 suggests that a

---

94 Joel P. Weinberg, *The Citizen-Temple Community* (trans. Daniel L. Smith-Christopher; Sheffield: JSOT Press, 1992), 61. Cf. Smith, *Landless*, 115.
95 Smith, *Landless*, 115.
96 Reinforcement of kinship ties is reflected in the genealogies found in EN.
97 Johnson, *Genealogies*, 43.
98 Johnson, *Genealogies*, 43-44. In this way, it is similar to the "census" list of Numbers 26, which serves to identify the people of the Exodus with the patriarchs listed in Genesis 46.
99 Weinberg, *Community*, 57.
100 Weinberg, *Community*, 57.
101 Weinberg, *Community*, 61. He further states that the fathers' house was "the basic structural unit of the citizen-Temple community of the sixth to fourth centuries BCE." For critiques of Weinberg's "citizen-Temple community" model, see Charles E. Carter, *The Emergence of Yehud in the Persian Period: A Social and Demographic Study* (Sheffield: Sheffield Academic, 1999), 294-307; H. G. M. Williamson, "Judah and the Jew," in *Studies in Persian History: Essays in Memory of David M. Lewis* (ed. Maria

section of the population had no right to a patrimonial estate. Indeed, there is no indication of the solidarity of a fathers' house apart from (an alleged) common ancestry. It is plausible, however, that the majority of members of fathers' houses were involved in the farming of subdivided common land, and that this economic co-operation would have functioned as an effective unifying factor, producing a degree of stability in the בית אבות as a social unit.[102]

Only those listed by fathers' houses (Ezra 2:2-20; Neh 7:8-24) are the returnees, while those listed by location (Ezra 2:21-35; Neh 7:25-38) remained in the land during the exile, but were subsequently granted membership into Israel by the returnees (cf. Ezra 6:21).[103] Support for this understanding is found in the distribution of the towns: of the twenty towns, the majority are found within the border of Benjamin (twelve), three each in the region south of Jerusalem and in the Ono-Lod Valley, and two in the Jordan Valley.[104] This is consistent with the current archaeological data, which indicate that the Babylonian deportations centred around Jerusalem.

Hence, the division in the list also reflects a mixed understanding of the family in the Restoration period. The social orientation of some members of community was based on the fathers' house, while other members reckoned themselves "by households grouped according to locality."[105] According to Williamson, there is a shift in identification to "place of residence (i.e., a collection of households rather than the בית אב)" in the late pre-exilic period.[106] While this is a plausible reconstruction, it is more likely that the father's house continued as the basic social unit. His argument rests partly on an understanding of the sedentarising and urbanising influences of the Monarchic Period.[107] These influences cannot be denied, but their overall importance should not be overemphasised. For instance, Oded

---

    Brosius and Amelie Kuhrt; Leiden: Nederlands Instituut voor het Nabije Oosten, 1998), 145-63.

102 Cf. Weinberg, *Community*, 57.

103 Japhet, "People," 111; Weinberg, *Community*, 132; H. G. M. Williamson, "The Family in Persian Period Judah: Some Textual Reflections," in *Symbiosis, Symbolism, and the Power of the Past: Canaan, Ancient Israel, and Their Neighbors from the Late Bronze Age through Roman Palaestina: Proceedings of the Centennial Symposium W. F. Albright Institute of Archaeological Research and American Schools of Oriental Research Jerusalem, May 29-31, 2000* (ed. William G. Dever and Seymour Gitin; Winona Lake: Eisenbrauns, 2003), 479. *Pace* Blenkinsopp, *Ezra-Nehemiah*, 85, who states that the division "does not seem to have any significance."

104 Lipschits, *Fall and Rise*, 157.

105 Williamson, "Family," 479.

106 Williamson, "Family," 475.

107 Williamson, "Family," 474-75.

Lipschits concludes from the archaeological evidence: "[D]uring the Persian Period, ... there was a marked attenuation of urban life in Judah.... This phenomenon contrasts with the continuation of rural settlements in Judah."[108] Hence, the majority of the population remained agrarian and involved in subsistence agriculture.[109] Moreover, while the importance of the larger kinship groupings of tribe and clan probably diminished, the significance of the father's house remained.[110]

Therefore, the overall picture is that the returnees understood themselves as members of fathers' houses and predominantly settled in Jerusalem, while "the remainees" continued the kinship structure of father's houses in the rural regions.

b. The Influence of the RN on the Fathers' House in the Persian Period

Amidst the angst and uncertainty surrounding the formation of a new kinship group, the RN reveals that it is possible to flourish within a new family structure. The RN begins with a typical father's house—a father, mother, and two sons—to which two daughters-in-law are soon added. By the end of the narrative, the father's house includes Boaz and Ruth, a foreign wife who produces Obed, who is subsequently looked after by a grandmother-in-law. LaCocque describes Obed's birth as the outcome of a series of substitutions,

> not only in the person of his biological mother but also of his father, who took the place of So-and-so and also substituted himself for the deceased Elimelek. Boaz generates a son instead of Mahlon. Naomi is the 'mother' of Obed. Ruth is better than ten sons in Naomi's eyes. Obed, rather than his father Boaz, is the *gōʾēl* of his grandmother (4:15).[111]

If fathers' houses in the Restoration period are composed of real kinship bonds, along with fictional ties substituting for real, then the RN demonstrates that this combination can be harmonious and successful. For

---

108 Oded Lipschits, "Archaemenid Imperial Policy and the Status of Jerusalem," in *Judah and the Judeans in the Persian Period* (ed. Oded Lipschits and Manfred Oeming; Winona Lake: Eisenbrauns, 2006), 28. Cf. Carter, *Emergence*, 137-66.

109 Lipschits, "Imperial Policy," 30, notes that maintaining rural settlements in the hill country of Judah was in the interests of the Archaemenids, who probably collected the agricultural produce as tax.

110 Archaeological evidence indicates that the typical four-roomed house continued throughout the monarchy. See Larry G. Herr, "Archaeological Sources for the History of Palestine: The Iron Age II Period: Emerging Nations," *BA* 60 (1997): 114-83, esp. 126. Faust, "Rural," 19-20, posits that the larger building sizes and the internal division of rooms in the rural areas supported the housing of an extended family, or father's house.

111 LaCocque, *Ruth*, 146-47.

the reasons outlined supra, this message is more pertinent for the returnees than those who remained in the land.

Survival can only be assured, however, if all members treat each other as genuine kin. If, as suggested previously, the deliberate use of the terminology "father's house" is to conjure up the intimacy of the bonds and build stronger relationships with those who are not genetically related, then the RN demonstrates the inherent roles and responsibilities. Even if members are only related by invention, they are still to treat one another as close family. This understanding of invented bonds for identity in the Restoration period complements the observations of Ronald Clements concerning wisdom literature in the post-exilic period. In particular, he points out the prominence of the teaching in Proverbs concerning conduct towards a "neighbour" (רֵעַ): a neighbour is anyone who is in need, and in adversity, the role of a "good neighbour can be as supportive as a brother."[112] This is precisely the attitude that all members of a fathers' house in the Restoration period are to have. In reality, a person may only be a neighbour without any blood ties, but she is to be treated as kin.[113]

The primary responsibility of looking after kin is especially acute when a section of the population is deprived. The ideal outcome of fully functioning fathers' houses is that each member is adequately provided for; the large number of members helps ensure that the wealthier can assist those in need. Yet the situation presented in Neh 5 indicates that there was a breakdown of the social support network associated with a fathers' house. Perhaps owing to a lack of provision from fellow kin, those facing starvation resorted to pledging either their children or their land to buy grain (Neh 5:2-3),[114] while others fell into debt in order to pay the king's tax (5:4). Under such circumstances, the message of the RN concerning the importance of upholding kinship responsibilities is especially appropriate.

Alternatively, Joseph Blenkinsopp proposes that the breakdown was between "the long-term residents of the province and the more wealthy

---

112 Ronald E. Clements, "The Good Neighbour in the Book of Proverbs," in *Of Prophets' Visions and the Wisdom of Sages: Essays in Honour of R. Norman Whybray on his Seventieth Birthday* (ed. Heather A. McKay and David J. A. Clines; JSOTSup 162; Sheffield: JSOT Press, 1993), 216.

113 Clements, "Good Neighbour," 216-17, understands this elevation of responsibilities of "the good neighbour" as resulting from a reduction in the size of the kinship group, and when the "extended family" was no longer "a primary reference for economic, moral and spiritual support." "Neighbourliness" then becomes more important than "the protection and support of even a person's most immediate kin." This diverges from the presentation in EN, where there is an encouragement of support within the "fathers' house" by invoking traditional kinship ties and obligations.

114 For a discussion of different interpretations of Neh 5:2, see Clines, *Ezra, Nehemiah, Esther*, 166; Williamson, *Ezra, Nehemiah*, 232, 37.

Babylonian *olim*."[115] The protest against the "Jews" (היהודים; 5:1) was against the privileged stratum of the population, "probably those who had returned from the Babylonian diaspora with their leaders" (Ezra 1:4-6; 2:68-69; 7:16; Zech 6:9-14).[116] Although Blenkinsopp's reconstruction is questionable,[117] his demarcation of the population in Yehud is still germane. This is especially the case given the continual threat of famine in the fifth and sixth centuries B.C.E.,[118] along with the additional financial burden of the royal land tax.[119] Within this context, not only some members of a fathers' house, but complete fathers' houses may at times require kinship support from other fathers' houses. Since a central thrust of the RN is to encourage behaviour beyond the strict requirements of kinship bonds, its application in the Restoration period would be the following: if the Jerusalemites are in desperate straits, those in rural Yehud should assist, and vice versa.

Nehemiah's response to the economic crisis is also instructive vis-à-vis appropriate behaviour in relation to the law. While it is disputed whether the actions of "the nobles and officials" (את החרים ואת הסגנים; Neh 5:7) were strictly illegal, it is clear that the conduct of the leaders is viewed as inappropriate.[120] The majority of commentators understand the actions of the wealthy Jewish brothers as transgressing the law forbidding the charging of interest on loans.[121] Clines, however, argues that they are demanding pledges without interest, and consequently, "Nehemiah cannot charge the moneylenders … with breaking the law, but can only argue

---

115 Blenkinsopp, *Ezra-Nehemiah*, 258.
116 Blenkinsopp, *Ezra-Nehemiah*, 256.
117 In its current literary context, this episode is connected to the rebuilding of the Jerusalem wall. Since those involved in its reconstruction derive from both groups (Neh 3:1-32), it would be expected that both would be effected to some degree. Furthermore, there is a lack of archaeological or other findings to suggest that Jerusalem was a large, wealthy urban centre during the Persian Period. See Lipschits, *Fall and Rise*, 214-16; Stern, *Land of the Bible*, 434-36; Lipschits, "Imperial Policy," 31.
118 Cf. Hag 1:5-6, 10-11; 2:15-16; Mal 3:9-12; Joel 1-2.
119 There was also the added burden of supporting the Temple and cult, but it is questionable whether this was followed at the time (cf. Mal 3:8-10), a doubt reinforced by its non-mention in EN. A Temple tax is pledged by the people after the completion of the wall (Neh 10:32-33).
120 Cf. Williamson, *Ezra, Nehemiah*, 233.
121 E.g., F. Charles Fensham, *The Books of Ezra and Nehemiah* (Grand Rapids: Eerdmans, 1982), 195; Matthew Levering, *Ezra and Nehemiah* (Grand Rapids: Brazos Press, 2007), 156.

that what they are doing is 'not good'" (לא טוב; 5:9).[122] On textual[123] and contextual[124] grounds, this reading is more plausible.

Whichever view is accepted, the relevant point for this discussion is that the episode is predicated on an understanding of appropriate behaviour that goes beyond what is prescribed by law. If the majority view is accepted, a strict application of the law would only require cessation of the interest-taking; the loaning of money on pledge, and debt-slavery were permitted.[125] Yet not only is there a cancellation of debt, there is also the return of all property. Consequent to the economic crisis, an emergency jubilee is proclaimed[126] without waiting for the set time (Neh 5:11-13; cf. Lev 25:8-22). The point of the episode is, then, that the law only sets the minimal standard of behaviour toward the poor, and this is not suitable for the current predicament.

If Clines' view is accepted, it adds another layer of understanding to the law. Not only is the law concerned with behaviour, but also with the motivation for behaviour. It is not acceptable for some of the community to become prosperous "masters," while others become mired in their destitution as "slaves," since the all members of the community are to be viewed as kin. The demand for social justice is based on their status as "brothers" (Neh 5:1, 5, 7, 8, 10; cf. Lev 25:25, 35-36, 39, 46-48).[127] Moreover, there are additional motivations for their actions: fear of God; and upholding his reputation amongst the nations (Neh 5:9, 15; cf. Lev 25:36, 43). The employment of Lev 25 in this section of Nehemiah further buttresses the argument that Neh 5 presents a hermeneutic in which the law is to be applied in accordance with its perceived intentions rather than its specifics, and proper behaviour is marked by right motivation.

The RN would reinforce this understanding of the law. As many scholars suggest, the RN promotes the spirit rather than the letter of Israelite law as it functioned in the father's house and clan. Baruch Levine is representative: "[The author of the book of Ruth] created a story in which the ultimate purposes of the several interlocking legal institutions, all expressive of collective, clan responsibility, were amazingly fulfilled; but

---

122 Clines, *Ezra, Nehemiah, Esther*, 168. Cf. Loring W. Batten, *A Critical and Exegetical Commentary on the Books of Ezra and Nehemiah* (ICC; Edinburgh: T & T Clark, 1913), 241.
123 This involves taking the מ in ומאת as enclitic. See Rendsburg, "Eblaite," 33-41, esp. 40; Wallace, "*WM-* in Nehemiah 5:11," 31.
124 The charges against the rich make no mention of interest being charged in Neh 5:2-5. Cf. Williamson, *Ezra, Nehemiah*, 238.
125 See Exod 21:2-11; 22:24-26[25-27]; Lev 25; Deut 15:1-18; 23:20-21[19-20]; 24:10-13.
126 Blenkinsopp, *Ezra-Nehemiah*, 259.
127 Cf. Jacob M. Myers, *Ezra, Nehemiah* (AB 14; New York: Doubleday, 1965), 131.

their fulfilment came in a manner that exceeded the strict limits of legal applicability." The author manipulated legalities, so transposing "*laws* into *legal themes.*"[128] In the RN there is a general appropriation of the law; application is not restricted to the specific circumstances outlined in the law.

More specifically, the RN presents *hesed* as a group norm, which can be understood as the virtue of excess. As the underlying attitude for applying the Torah, it encourages behaviour that would support the poor in Israelite society, although it is not required by a strict application of the law. In particular, the actions of Boaz *qua* גאל would further encourage adherence to the stipulations leading to social equality and provision for the needy in Lev 25 by depicting one concrete illustration from that chapter. This way of applying the law in EN, however, only applies to fellow Israelite "brothers," members of fathers' houses. A harsher hermeneutic for the law as applied to "foreigners" is discussed infra.

2. Kin: Israelite

a. Israel as an Ethnic Group in the Persian Period

The second kinship group for consideration is "Israel." As described in EN, the presence of other groups within the land led to the self-identification of Israel as an ethnic group.[129] The anthropological insight that ethnicity is a relational rather than biological phenomenon is germane to this discussion.[130] A consequence of its relational nature, according to Jonathan Hall, is that it is "the result of a series of conscious and socially embedded choices, which attach significance to certain criteria from a universal set

---

128 Baruch A. Levine, "In Praise of the Israelite *Mišpaḥâ*: Legal Themes in the Book of Ruth," in *The Quest for the Kingdom of God: Studies in Honor of George E. Mendenhall* (ed. Herbert B. Huffmon, Frank A. Spina, and Alberto R. W. Green; Winona Lake: Eisenbrauns, 1983), 97-98 (emphasis original). Some scholars even posit that the author of the RN wove his story around the laws in Deuteronomy 22-25, functioning as a commentary upon them; Michael D. Goulder, "Ruth: A Homily on Deuteronomy 22-25?," in *Of Prophets, Visions and Wisdom of Sages: Essays in Honour of R Norman Whybray on his Seventieth Birthday* (ed. Heather A. McKay and David J. A. Clines; JSOTSup 162; Sheffield: Almond, 1993), 307-19, and most recently Joshua Berman, "Ancient Hermeneutics and the Legal Structure of the Book of Ruth," *ZAW* 119 (2007): 22-38. Cf. Braulik, "Critique," 1-20.

129 For the rationale behind designating Israel as an ethnic group in the Persian Period, see "The Social Identity Approach and Ancient Israelite Identity" in Chapter One.

130 Cf. Esler, "Ezra-Nehemiah," 413-26; Anselm C. Hagedorn, "Looking at Foreigners in Biblical and Greek Prophecy," *VT* 57 (2007): 432-48.

while ignoring others."¹³¹ There are two important aspects of this understanding. First, an ethnic group identifies itself by the perceived or imagined dissimilarities—such as history, religion, physical appearance and language—that seem to exist between itself and others.¹³² These signs of cultural difference maintain the boundaries that separate a social group from outgroups, and structure interactions across those boundaries.¹³³ Second, there is a downplaying of similarities; in fact, the process of defining ethnicity may also involve the conscious denial or disguising of resemblance.¹³⁴ This involves the systematic forgetting of shared features, or felt similarities between groups. The emergence of ethnicity is usually in the context of conquest, migration, or the acquisition of resources by one group at the expense of others.¹³⁵

These anthropological and social psychological insights provide a helpful matrix for understanding processes in the Restoration period. As established previously, in EN the definition of an Israelite is "a returned exile." There are hints that this shared history was not always strictly followed, such as the integration into the Temple community of those who had not been in exile but who separated themselves from the nations of the land (Ezra 6:21), as well as the legitimisation of those in Benjamin as part of the returnees although they were probably never exiled (Ezra 2; Neh 7).¹³⁶ Nonetheless, the redefinition of these outliers as returnees testifies to the strength of EN's understanding of "Israel." In addition to placing stress on return from Babylon as a marker of dissimilarity, the many similarities between this group and the other groups present in the land, such as physical appearance and language, would have necessitated a denial of the resemblance. The exclusion of those who claimed to worship the same God, although explicitly based on political grounds (Ezra 4:1-3; cf. 1:2-4), may also have been motivated by spiritual concerns.¹³⁷ Indeed, Japhet

---

131 Jonathan M. Hall, *Ethnic Identity in Greek Antiquity* (Cambridge: Cambridge University Press, 1997), 20-21.
132 Jonathan M. Hall, *Hellenicity: Between Ethnicity and Culture* (Chicago: The University of Chicago Press, 2002), 9.
133 Fredrik Barth, *Ethnic Groups and Boundaries: The Social Organization of Culture Difference* (Boston: Little, Brown, 1969), 18-20.
134 Hagedorn, "Nahum," 230.
135 Barth, *Ethnic Groups*, 21. For a recent application of the development of Israelite ethnicity in opposition to another group, see Franz V. Greifenhagen, *Egypt on the Pentateuch's Ideological Map: Constructing Biblical Israel's Identity* (JSOTSup 361; London: Sheffield Academic Press, 2002).
136 Japhet, "People," 111.
137 The HB mentions non-Israelites who had been imported by the Assyrians into the territory of the former northern kingdom (cf. 2 Kgs 17), and had adopted the local worship practices. The presence of a group from the north who continued to sacrifice at

suggests that the danger posed by their religious similarity might have motivated the sharp demarcation.[138] If the outsiders' claim can be accepted at face value,[139] then even religion, a central component of Israelite identity in EN, is not sufficient for membership in "Israel."

b. Core Identity Markers for Israel

This leads to the question of what constitutes the core markers of identity for Israel in the Restoration period. The two core markers as presented in EN will be discussed under the themes of Temple and Torah, both of which exhibit continuity with the pre-exilic period. Yet there are also lines of development from the pre-exilic period, which can be traced to the experience of the exiles in Babylon. In this section, I will discuss the importance of the Temple and Torah as components of Israelite identity, followed by the contribution of the RN within the context of the Restoration period.

While the Temple remained a core identity marker for Israel in EN, there is a development in its significance in comparison to the pre-exilic period. In many ways, the Temple is presented as a central component of identity in EN. For instance, Tamara Eskenazi identifies the Temple as being pivotal to the overall movement of the book.[140] Furthermore, the importance of the Temple as an identity marker is underlined by its continuity with the past. These include the parallels between the Solomonic Temple and the Second Temple,[141] the priests and Temple personnel,[142] and the cultic practices they oversee.[143] Overall, then, Melody Knowles correctly describes the returned community as "a *worshipping*

---

    the site of the old Temple during the exile (Jer 41:5) increases the likelihood that their self-description was genuine.

138 Japhet, "People," 113.

139 Williamson, *Ezra, Nehemiah*, 49: "We have no reason to doubt their self-description." Nonetheless, it is possible that their claim only included part of the truth: they worshipped YHWH as well as other deities (cf. 2 Kgs 17:24-41). The syncretism of this group as a basis for rejection is suggested by Blenkinsopp, *Ezra-Nehemiah*, 107; Myers, *Ezra, Nehemiah*, 35-36.

140 Eskenazi, *Prose*, 38-39.

141 H. G. M. Williamson, *Ezra and Nehemiah* (OTG; Sheffield: JSOT Press, 1987), 82-84.

142 E.g., Ezra 2:36-58; 6:18; Neh 12:24, 45-46.

143 The cultic practices include the dedication ceremony, which evokes the one from Solomon's time (e.g., 3:3-6, 10-11; 6:19-20; 8:35; Neh 8:13-18; 10:29-39; 13:10-14).

community, a community that places Jerusalem and its Temple at the center of its worship life."[144]

Nonetheless, there is also a significant development in the Temple as a core Israelite identity marker in the post-exilic period: the importance lies not in the Temple *per se*, but in what it represents. The initial shift in understanding probably occurred as a result of the absence of the Temple, with worship recommencing prior to its reconstruction.[145] The returnees presented sacrifices on the altar at the site of the former Temple, and celebrated the Festival of Tabernacles before laying the foundations of the Temple (Ezra 3:1-6). Worship probably then continued *sans* Temple for some twenty-four years until the Temple was finally completed (6:15). When reconstruction commenced, the whole congregation supported the task of rebuilding. This was in contrast to historical precedent, in which pious monarchs had been primarily responsible for the building and restoration of the Temple.[146] An Israelite king was not involved in the restoration of the Temple; instead, a foreign king supports and provides for its reconstruction (Ezra 1).[147] Indeed, overall, the fortunes of the Davidic house do not seem to be a high priority in EN.

This egalitarian trajectory in relation to the Temple is highlighted in EN in two interrelated ways. First, holiness, as a typical marker of priestly identity, now spreads to characterise the whole of the people of God. This concept is conveyed through the unity of the Temple with the wall of Jerusalem: the building of the wall is an extension of the building the Temple.[148] Thus, sanctification is the first step in the building of the walls (Neh 3:1); those usually assigned to the Temple gates are now appointed to guard the walls (Neh 7:1; 13:22), and upon its completion the city as a whole is declared holy (עיר הקדש; Neh 11:1, 18). Second, the enlargement of the Temple on an architectural level has an impact on those present in the city on a spiritual level. The entire community gather as one (כל העם כאיש אחד; Neh 8:1), rededicating themselves to rigorous observance of the Torah (Neh 8:1–10:40). The dedication ceremony is marked by the purification of the walls, along with the entire community (Neh 12:27-30).

---

144 Melody D. Knowles, "Pilgrimage Imagery in the Returns in Ezra," *JBL* 123 (2004): 73 (emphasis original). Cf. William J. Dumbrell, "The Purpose of the Books of Chronicles," *JETS* 27 (1984): 261.

145 Cf. Esler, "Ezra-Nehemiah," 420.

146 These Israelite monarchs include: Solomon (1 Kgs 6; 2 Chron 3); Hezekiah (2 Kgs 18; 2 Chron 29-31); and Josiah (2 Kgs 22-23; 2 Chron 34-35). For further details, see William Riley, *King and Cultus in Chronicles: Worship and the Reinterpretation of History* (Sheffield: JSOT Press, 1993), 37-156.

147 If an important function of a monarch is to authorise and sustain its cultus, then the Persian kings fulfilled this role *de facto*; Williamson, *Ezra, Nehemiah*, 88.

148 Eskenazi, *Prose*, 37-126.

Therefore, while the Temple remains an important identity marker for Israel, it is not the Temple itself that is drawn upon, but its signification of the worship of YHWH by a sanctified people.

Second, EN restores obedience to the Torah as a core identity marker, and elevates its significance relative to the Temple. According to HB texts describing the last days of the southern kingdom, the overwhelming emphasis of the people in Judah was on the Temple at the expense of the Torah. The Judahite kings and the people were relying on the trappings of the Temple while disregarding the requirements of the law (esp. Jer 7:1-20). This contravened YHWH's primary requirement for his people to respond to him with obedience to his commandments, such as expressed in Deuteronomy (esp. 5:1; 6; 30:16; cf. Exod 19:5). Instead, the Judahites had emphasised external religious observances, such as sacrifices (e.g., 1 Sam 15:22; Jer 7:21-26; Hos 6:6). A reversal of this emphasis is found in EN: adherence to the Torah replaces Temple and sacrifice in pre-eminence.

This reversal of emphasis is demonstrated in three main ways. First, the location of the reading of the Torah highlights its importance vis-à-vis the Temple. Although there is debate concerning the exact location of the plaza in front of the Water Gate (Neh 8:1), the central point of the location is clear: the reading of the Torah did not take place in the Temple.[149] H. L. Ellison elaborates on the significance of this shift in location: "In the choice of site we have Ezra's deliberate proclamation that the Torah was greater than the Temple and its sacrifices, indeed that the Torah as such was above anything it might contain."[150]

Second, from a literary perspective, the placement of the reading of the Torah parallels the presentation of sacrifices in Ezra 3. The list of returnees in Ezra 2 leads to the building of the altar and worship, while the list in Nehemiah 7 leads to the reading of the Torah. As Eskenazi postulates, this may be "an early version of a view that later becomes normative, that is, that the study of Torah replaces the offering of sacrifices."[151] Further evidence for this view is found in the rarity and speed of reporting of sacrifices in Ezra-Nehemiah, especially after Nehemiah 8.[152]

---

149 This is in contrast to 1 Esdras 9:38, which locates the reading of the Torah in front of the Temple gate ("the broad place of the holy porch toward the east"). As Fensham, *Ezra and Nehemiah*, 216, notes, it is unlikely to have taken place in the Temple because only men were allowed in the Temple precincts. Cf. Myers, *Ezra, Nehemiah*, 153.
150 Henry L. Ellison, *From Babylon to Bethlehem: The Jewish People from the Exile to the Messiah* (Exeter: Paternoster, 1976), 47.
151 Eskenazi, "Structure," 650.
152 Eskenazi, "Structure," 650.

Third, those who comprise Israel are now identified as the rest of the people, the priests, the Levites, the gatekeepers, the singers, the Temple servants, and

כל הנבדל מעמי הארצות אל תורת האלהים

"All who had separated from the peoples of the lands *to follow the Torah of God*" (Neh 10:29[28]). Hence, proselytes also seem to be included, which is the counterpart in Nehemiah of Ezra 6:21:

כל הנבדל מטמאת גוי הארץ אלהם לדרש ליהוה

"All who had separated from the uncleanness of the nations of the lands to worship YHWH."[153]

Similar to Deuteronomy, the Israelite community pledge themselves to following the general (Neh 10:29-30) and specific stipulations (10:31-40) of "God's law" (cf. Deut 8:6; 28:15).[154] Although adherence to the Torah becomes the primary focus for identification in EN, the Temple nonetheless continues as an identity marker. As Jacob Wright points out, along with scribes and prayer, the Torah is "the means for the community as a whole to participate in the sanctity of the Altar, priests and sacrifices."[155]

Consequently, there is a particular understanding of the Torah in EN. It is made available to everyone; the understanding and application of the text is not limited to only priests or scribes. Even Ezra is absorbed into the community: "[A]s a true teacher, he makes himself ultimately dispensable."[156] This egalitarian nature of the Torah is consistent with the presentation of the Israelite community in EN, with the rebuilding of the Temple and the wall accomplished by the people.

EN highlights the importance of adherence to the Torah, along with a particular hermeneutic. The case of the ruling against mixed marriages will function as the parade example of this hermeneutic, which essentially utilises the Torah as a boundary marker for Israelite identity.

On first inspection, EN appears to present a hard-line stance against intermarriage with foreign women based on the Torah.[157] This is the way

---

153 Passover observance functions as an identity marker that forms a boundary between Israel and non-Israel. See Peter H. W. Lau, "Gentile Incorporation into Israel in Ezra–Nehemiah?," *Bib* 90 (2009): 356-73.
154 See David J. A. Clines, "Nehemiah 10 as an Example of Early Jewish Biblical Exegesis," *JSOT* 21 (1981): 111.
155 Wright, "Writing," 28.
156 Eskenazi, *Prose*, 138.
157 The problem of marriage to foreign women in EN has spawned a host of studies examining the situation from different perspectives. For a summary, see A. Philip Brown, II, "The Problem of Mixed Marriages in Ezra 9-10," *BSac* 162 (2005): 437-58. See also Tamara C. Eskenazi, "The Missions of Ezra and Nehemiah," in *Judah and the Judeans in*

the problem is presented to Ezra by the officers, who frame their accusation with citations from the Torah, viz. Deut 7:3 and Lev 19:19 (Ezra 9:1-2). When Ezra accepts Shecaniah's suggestion to expel the "foreign wives," this blanket expulsion is asserted to be "done in accordance with the Torah" (כתורה יעשה; Ezra 10:3).

As noted by many scholars, however, marriage with foreigners is not completely prohibited in the Torah. Israelites are forbidden to intermarry with the "seven nations" who inhabit the land of Canaan (Exod 34:11-16; Deut 7:1-4), but this is not the case with regard to non-inhabitants of Canaan (Deut 21:10-14). The problem was not with intermarriage with foreigners *per se*, but the dangers inherent in making a covenant with foreigners and the subsequent negative influence on Israelite religion (e.g., Deut 7:3-6). The uncompromising stance of EN against mixed marriages can thus be understood to derive from a certain hermeneutic: interpretation of the Torah with a view to pragmatic application.[158] Deuteronomy 7 and Lev 19 are adduced to lend weight to the decision to maintain the genetic purity of the people of God. However, no strict adherence to the original context or intention of the law is attempted.

This prohibition of exogamous marriage on genealogical grounds is based on an innovative purity strategy in EN.[159] Since Israel is a "holy seed," any intermingling of this seed through intermarriage with the peoples of the lands is a sacrilege (מעל; Ezra 9:1, 2; cf. 9:4; 10:2, 6, 10; Neh 13:27). Indeed, the intermingling of "holy seed" with unconsecrated seed amounts to profanation, the atonement for which could only be made by divorcing the foreign wives and bringing a guilt offering (אשם; Ezra 10:19; cf. Lev 5:14-16).[160]

The biblical foundation for this ban based on genealogy derives from expansive exegesis of the Torah.[161] As Christine Hayes notes, this concern

---

the Persian Period (ed. Oded Lipschits and Manfred Oeming; Winona Lake: Eisenbrauns, 2006), 509-29.

158 Cf. Sara Japhet, "Law and 'The Law' in Ezra-Nehemiah," in *From the Rivers of Babylon to the Highlands of Judah: Collected Studies on the Restoration Period* (Winona Lake: Eisenbrauns, 2006), 147 (originally published 1985).

159 For the purity ideology in EN as a whole, see Rainer Albertz, "Purity Strategies and Political Interests in the Policy of Nehemiah," in *Confronting the Past: Archaeological and Historical Essays on Ancient Israel in Honor of William G. Dever* (ed. Seymour Gitin, J. Edward Wright, and J. P. Dessel; Winona Lake: Eisenbrauns, 2006), 199-206; Saul M. Olyan, "Purity Ideology in Ezra-Nehemiah as a Tool to Reconstruct the Community," *JSJ* 35 (2004): 1-16.

160 Cf. Jacob Milgrom, *Leviticus 1-16* (AB 3; New York: Doubleday, 1992), 359.

161 See Michael Fishbane, *Biblical Interpretation in Ancient Israel* (Oxford: Clarendon, 1975), 121-23; Milgrom, *Leviticus 1-16*, 359-60.

for genealogical purity is not new to EN.¹⁶² In addition to general marriage prohibitions for priests (Lev 21:7), there is a stricter prohibition for the high priest: he can only marry an Israelite virgin (בתולה מעמיו; Lev 21:14-15). Ezekiel extends this restriction to the whole priesthood (Ezek 44:22). The innovation in EN is that this is extended to the laity—all Israelites.¹⁶³ Once again, this involvement of the whole community is consistent with the extension of holiness in EN.¹⁶⁴

Closer inspection of EN reveals that in addition to a genealogical basis for banning exogamous marriage there is a religious basis. While the expulsion of foreign wives does not distinguish between the people of the land and proselytes (Ezra 6:21; Neh 10:29[28]), there are hints in EN that a basis for the dissolution of mixed marriages was religious, not genetic. When the officers present the problem to Ezra, they compare the people of the land with the eight foreign nations on the basis of their abhorrent practices (תועבתיהם; 9:1). Here there is a clear textual allusion to Deut 7:1-4, which describes how intermarriage with the foreign nations would lead to apostasy for the people of God.¹⁶⁵ Ezra's subsequent prayer continues the allusion to Deut 7, highlighting the basis of the problem as the abhorrent practices of the foreigners, not in their foreignness *per se* (9:11-14).¹⁶⁶

This is consistent with the portrayal of "foreign wives" in the rest of the HB, with their propensity to lead the people of God astray (e.g., Gen 24; 28:1-9; 1 Kgs 11:1-8). This understanding is present in Neh 13:26,

---

162 Christine E. Hayes, *Gentile Impurities and Jewish Identities: Intermarriage and Conversion from the Bible to the Talmud* (New York: Oxford University Press, 2002), 27.

163 Cf. Michael L. Satlow, *Jewish Marriage in Antiquity* (Princeton: Princeton University Press, 2001), 138, who views Ezra's attack on mixed marriages as part of his ideological agenda to "reconstitute Israel as a holy nation, a nation of priests."

164 Foreign wives and their children are expelled from the community in EN. Formerly, the patrilinear structure of inheritance of landed property was closely allied to the determination of a son's lineage through his father. In EN, however, ancestry is determined by both parents, so that any alien ancestry results in "a child's classification as an alien and, therefore, exclusion from the community"; Saul M. Olyan, *Rites and Rank: Hierarchy in Biblical Representations of Cult* (Princeton: Princeton University Press, 2000), 89.

165 The list of nations that are mentioned are an amalgamation of the lists found in Deut 7:1-3 and 23:4-9[3-8]. Fishbane, *Interpretation*, 116-17, observes that the exegetical extension of Deut 7:1-3 is effected by means of "an adaptation and interpolation of feature" from Deut 23:4-9[3-8].

166 For a recent discussion of the relation between penitential prayers (including Ezra 9:6-14; Neh 1:5-11; 9:6-37; Dan 9:4b-19) and communal laments, see Dalit Rom-Shiloni, "Socio-Ideological *Setting* or *Settings* for Penitential Prayers?," in *Seeking the Favor of God. Volume 1: The Origins of Penitential Prayer in Second Temple Judaism* (ed. Mark J. Boda, Daniel K. Falk, and Rodney A. Werline; Atlanta: Society of Biblical Literature, 2006), 51-68.

which asserts that "foreign wives also caused him to sin" (גם אותו החטיאו הנשים הנכריות). It does not state that marriage to the foreign women was sinful in itself, but that they caused him to sin (החטיאו; *hiphil*). Bringing this understanding back to its usage in Ezra 10 then, the "foreign women" here are more specifically those who would lead, and indeed may have already led, Israelite men astray by following their gods. The repetition of this outlandish designation for the women (10:2, 10-11, 14, 17-18, 44) would then function to underscore their threat to the community of returnees.

This understanding of the rationale for banning exogamous marriage is also consistent with Nehemiah's actions in Neh 13. The description of the offspring of mixed marriages suggests that at least part of the ban was on the basis of maintaining their ethnic identity (13:24). However, the importance of speaking Hebrew, the language of Judah (דבר יהודית) is more pertinently related to being able to understand the Torah.[167] The singling out of the language of Ashdod, most likely a non-Semitic language,[168] lends further weight to this argument because the children would not be able to understand Hebrew.[169] In contrast, the Ammonite and Moabite languages are closely related to Hebrew, so much so that they may be understood as dialects.[170] Thus, the importance of language is again tied to following the Torah as a way of life, and hence, the religion of YHWH as an identity marker is more important than the language *per se*.[171]

---

167 Cf. Williamson, *Ezra, Nehemiah*, 397: "For a religion in which Scripture plays a central part, grasp of language is vital; one may compare the importance of Arabic for Islam."

168 It was probably a relic of the Philistine language. Cf. R. A. Stewart Macalister, *The Philistines: Their History and Civilization* (Oxford: Oxford University Press, 1914), 66-67. Myers, *Ezra, Nehemiah*, 216-17, suggests that the Ashdodite language was closer to Aramaic. Cf. Ingo Kottsieper, "'And They Did Not Care to Speak Yehudit': On Linguistic Change in Judah during the Late Persian Era," in *Judah and the Judeans in the Fourth Century B.C.E.* (ed. Oded Lipschits, Gary N. Knoppers, and Rainer Albertz; Winona Lake: Eisenbrauns, 2007), 95-124. However, it seems unlikely that Nehemiah would have become so angry if the children only spoke Aramaic because of its similarity to Hebrew. Hence, only a markedly different language would be consistent with the narrative.

169 Clines, *Ezra, Nehemiah, Esther*, 246. Edward Ullendorff, "C'est de l'hebreu pour moi!," *JSS* 13 (1968): 125-35, suggests that Ashdodite is "a model of a non-Semitic and totally incomprehensible language." This seems unlikely considering the naming of specific ethnic women (Ashdodite, Ammonite, and Moabite) in Nehemiah 13:23.

170 For a recent discussion see Anson F. Rainey, "Whence Came the Israelites and Their Language?," *IEJ* 57 (2007): 41-64, esp. 52-57.

171 *Pace* Ina Willi-Plein, "Problems of Intermarriage in Postexilic Times," in *Shai: Studies in the Bible, Its Exegesis and Language Presented to Sara Japhet* (ed. Moshe Bar-Asher, et al.; Jerusalem: The Bialik Institute, 2007), 177-89, esp. 186-89.

The tension deriving from the presence of these two grounds for the dissolution of exogamous marriages—genealogical and religious—is another indicator of the liminal state of Israelite identity in the Restoration period. The dilemma facing the returned exiles was deciding whether Israelite identity had a religious or genetic basis. Within a context of uncertainty concerning, and hence threat to identity, only a genealogical basis would have formed an impenetrable boundary between Israel and foreigners.[172] The choice of genealogy may have also been influenced by political factors: the edict of Artaxerxes provides Ezra with a mandate to establish a religious community (Ezra 7:11-26).[173]

As a primary identity marker, the Torah is drawn upon for guidance. Yet this raises two problems: finding the relevant legislation; and applying it to a concrete situation. By comparing the return from Exile with the Exodus from Egypt, the leaders of the returning community parallel the Mosaic restrictions on mixed marriages in Deut 7:1-5 with the current situation in Yehud.[174] By combining this with legislation from Lev 19, the leaders produce an interpretation and application based solely on genealogical purity. The possibility that a "foreign wife" can be a follower of YHWH is not entertained; to be a non-Israelite is to be involved in false worship.[175]

Yet although the concern for genealogy dominates in EN, the religious component does not completely disappear. After all, the goal and climax of EN is the presentation of a holy community, joyfully worshipping YHWH (Neh 12:27-43). In this sense, the ultimate aim of genealogical purity can be understood to be religious purity.[176]

Overall, then, in EN there is a downplaying of the overall importance of overt external institutions—Temple and monarchy—as foundational for

---

[172] If an essentially religious basis for entry into the Israelite community was chosen, this would have produced a permeable boundary between Israel and outsiders. Cf. Hayes, *Gentile Impurities*, 27.

[173] Williamson, *Ezra, Nehemiah*, 160.

[174] Cf. Fishbane, *Interpretation*, 116; Japhet, "People," 112-13.

[175] Although a genealogical basis for exclusion was chosen by the leaders in EN, there are hints that the implied author's viewpoint is that foreigners devoted to YHWH could gain membership into Israel (Ezra 6:21; Neh 10:29[28]). See Lau, "Gentile Incorporation into Israel in Ezra–Nehemiah?," esp. 369-73.

[176] *Pace* Hayes, *Gentile Impurities*, who adds the category "genealogical impurity" to "ritual" and "moral" impurity. Since, using her categorisation, moral purity would be the goal of genealogical purity, it would be better to understand genealogical purity as a subset of moral purity. Cf. Jonathan Klawans, *Impurity and Sin in Ancient Judaism* (Oxford: Oxford University Press, 2000).

Israelite identity.[177] This change can be traced back to the exile: neither the Temple nor the monarchy was constitutive of their ethnic identity in Babylon. Furthermore, YHWH's presence had left the Temple to reside with his people beyond the borders of Israel.[178] The relative lack of emphasis on the Davidic monarchy can be explained by its apparent failure and subsequent downfall, as most clearly spelt out in the book of Ezekiel.[179] Yet hope for a restored and modified Davidic ruler in Ezekiel[180] can also be detected in EN, as will be examined in the next section.

Furthermore, the Torah functioned as a boundary marker for Israelite identity in EN.[181] The Torah was used to clearly delineate the Israelite ingroup as those who followed its precepts. These measures were required to maintain the community's integrity and to avoid the dilution of its identity with "the people of the land." This usage of the Torah is underlined in the last chapter of EN, which narrates four instances of foreigners being expelled from the Temple (Neh 13:1-3; 4-9; 23-27; 28-29).

c. The Influence of the RN on Israelite Identity in the Persian Period

Within this historico-social setting, the RN would have shaped Israelite identity with regards to three main institutions: the Temple; the Davidic monarchy; and the Torah.

The RN would have encouraged the decentring of the Temple as a core Israelite identity marker in the Persian Period. There is no mention of the Temple and cult in the RN, as would be expected given the historical context in which the narrative is set. The quiet presence of YHWH, continuing to work through the lives of ordinary Israelites, is consonant with the understanding of God's presence with his people in the absence of a physical sanctuary. The egalitarian tone of the RN is also consistent with the focus of EN: God's presence is recognised through the lives of everyday

---

177 The omission of circumcision as a prerequisite for participation in the Passover, in preference to devotion to YHWH (Ezra 6:21), reflects this tendency on an individual level.
178 E.g., Ezek 11:16. This represented a major paradigm shift in the understanding of those who were exiled: YHWH was no longer a regional god confined to the Temple; he was now recognised as omnipresent.
179 E.g., Ezek 17; 19; 22:6; 34:1-16; 45:8-9. For a discussion of the Judahite kings in Ezekiel and their failings, see Iain M. Duguid, *Ezekiel and the Leaders of Israel* (Leiden: Brill, 1994), 10-57.
180 E.g., Ezek 34:23-24; 37:22-25.
181 This is similar to the way the wall around Jerusalem separated its inhabitants from outsiders.

Israelites, not just the leaders (prophets, kings, etc.). Hence, the ability of the people of God to maintain their identity in the absence of the Temple as an external identity marker would support the relative shift in emphasis from Temple to Torah in the Restoration period.

The RN would have also been instructive regarding another overt identity marker: the Davidic monarchy. On the one hand, the setting of the RN in the pre-Monarchic Period once again testifies to the resilience of Israelite identity *sans* monarchy. On the other hand, the RN re-establishes the Davidic hope. Although the viewpoint from the broader context of the book of Judges may suggest otherwise (Judg 17:6; 18:1; 19:1; 21:25), at least at the clan level, Israel can function and maintain its identity without a king. This may be understood as a general move away from the central importance of a ruling class, and can be detected in other biblical texts often dated to the post-exilic period. For instance, John Berquist assigns the formulation of four biblical "short stories" to colonial Yehud: the book of Ruth, the book of Jonah, the book of Esther, and the book of Daniel. Berquist comments: "[N]one of these stories places any emphasis on the local governors, the priests, and the sages—the very forces of social maintenance."[182] In this way, the RN would have reinforced the egalitarian impulse of the Persian Period.

Similarly, regarding kingship in Deuteronomy, another book whose final shape is often dated to the Persian Period, many have noted that, in contrast to other ancient near Eastern monarchies, there is a limit to the accumulation of royal power above other Israelites (Deut 17:14-20).[183] Patricia Dutcher-Walls, writing within a social-scientific framework, states that deuteronomic kingship eschews an "exclusionary power strategy"; rather, it is a post of authority "within a corporate power strategy," always emphasising "a corporate solidarity of society as an integrated whole."[184] Joshua Berman notes that this strong sense of citizenry is manifest throughout Deuteronomy.[185] Hence, while Deuteronomy does not remove

---

[182] Jon L. Berquist, *Judaism in Persia's Shadow: A Social and Historical Approach* (Minneapolis: Fortress, 1995), 231.

[183] E.g., Craigie, *Deuteronomy*, 254-56; Tigay, *Deuteronomy*, 166. For specific comparative studies, see, e.g., John Day, *King and Messiah in Israel and the Ancient Near East: Proceedings of the Oxford Old Testament Seminar* (JSOTSup 270; Sheffield: Sheffield Academic, 1998); Bernard M. Levinson, "The Reconceptualization of Kingship in Deuteronomy and the Deuteronomistic History's Transformation of Torah," *VT* 51 (2001): 511-34.

[184] Patricia Dutcher-Walls, "The Circumscription of the King: Deuteronomy 17:16-17 in Its Ancient Social Context," *JBL* 121 (2002): 607-08.

[185] Joshua Berman, "Constitution, Class, and the Book of Deuteronomy," *Hebraic Political Studies* 1 (2006): 526-27.

the notion of kingship, it does shift a significant degree of power to the people of Israel as a whole.

If, as many scholars assert, EN presents the "theocratic" perspective,[186] "urging the importance of faithfulness to God, the law, and its institutions"[187] as well as the possibility of national existence under foreign rule and the advantages of a position of political quietism,[188] then the RN would reinforce this stance. In a historical context when Israel is under the power of a foreign king, the RN presents the case for continued devotion to YHWH, and the importance of remaining faithful to social roles and responsibilities as identity markers. YHWH's sovereign control of history, as manifest in interaction with human choice in the RN, is still operative in the Restoration period, revealed in his manipulation of the Persian kings for his purposes (e.g., Ezra 1:1-2; 7:6, 27-28; 9:9; Neh 2:8).

On the other hand, the RN would restore royalist hope to Israelite consciousness. It would remind the Israelite community living in the Persian Period that they are heirs of the Davidic promise, and thus ignite aspirations that the Davidic monarchy might be re-established again. In contrast to the late Monarchic Period, however, the RN presents the monarchy as a firmly and resolutely kinship-based institution: the king will issue from David's house. In contrast to the northern kingdom, monarchic rule is not to be seized but inherited. If EN represents the exclusive voice of the ruling urban élite as embodied in Ezra, Nehemiah, the priests, and governors under Persia, then the RN is a reminder that the kinship groups of the rural hinterland can still make an important contribution to the life and identity of Israel.

The "law of the king" (Deut 17:14-20) would reinforce this hope. Its anti-imperialist sentiment would find particular resonance in the context of Persian domination. As Lowery observes, this sentiment is found primarily in verses 14-17, which warns against the domination of the Israelite throne by a foreign power, with foreign alliances leading to the loss of land and a reverse Exodus.[189] Although Lowery dates this passage to the Hezekianic period and therefore describes it as "a veiled reference to Assyrian

---

186 That is, that the Davidic dynasty has failed, and thus has no further significance apart from the roles of David and Solomon in establishing the Temple and cult, which are now regarded as the true expressions of God's rule; see, e.g., James D. Newsome, Jr., "Toward a New Understanding of the Chronicler and His Purposes," *JBL* 94 (1975): 214, and more recently, Gabriele Boccaccini, *Roots of Rabbinic Judaism: An Intellectual History, from Ezekiel to Daniel* (Grand Rapids: Eerdmans, 2002).

187 Williamson, *Ezra, Nehemiah*, li.

188 Cf. Sara Japhet, "Sheshbazzar and Zerubbabel—Against the Background of the Historical and Religious Tendencies of Ezra-Nehemiah," *ZAW* 94 (1982): 71-80.

189 Lowery, *Reforming*, 153-57.

imperialism,"[190] the same general stance is applicable to the Persian rule. If the newly reconstituted Israel is to remain in the land, they are to seek headship "from amongst their brothers,"[191] while avoiding foreign alliances, especially with the Archaemenid kings.

But what form of self-rule was Israel seeking in the Persian Period? It would be difficult to envisage them calling for an independent state under the rule of a priest or governor. Evidence from the end of the prayer in Neh 9 suggests that Israel still held out a hope for a Davidic king. Although Israel is back in the land, they still suffer under the hand of a foreign king (9:36-37). So in the prayer Israel calls on God to deliver them.[192] The most straightforward understanding is that Israel wants a return to a kingdom: a nation under the rule of their own monarch. Yet even those who identify an openness to the future, a hope that former prophecies would be fulfilled,[193] decline to advance a royalist hope in EN. Its presence, however, is hinted at in the prayer itself (Neh 9:35), as well as in the claim for "greater Israel." The list of occupied towns in Neh 11:25-35 is universally understood to be non-historical, with those around Beersheba known to be under Edomite-Arab control at the time of Nehemiah.[194] Von Rad suggests that the similarity of the list in Neh 11 with that found in Josh 15 is intended to present post-exilic Israel idealistically, as a province approximating the extent of Judah in Josiah's day.[195] J. G. McConville finds further possible evidence for this aspiration to Israelite sovereignty in the phrase "the men who willingly offered" (Neh 11:2). If this is a deliberate reference to Judg 5:2 ("the people offered themselves willingly"), then the occupation of Jerusalem under Nehemiah "becomes a cryptic allusion to a battle involving all Israel (in principle) for sovereignty over its own territory."[196] Therefore, although muted in the overall perspective of EN, the hope for a future Davidic dynasty is still present. Consequently, it

---

190 Lowery, *Reforming*, 155.

191 Further resonance for this passage in the Persian Period derives from its description of the place of the law. The king is to be subordinate to the law, within a programme for the nation of Israel in which the law is the supreme authority. Cf. McBride, "Polity," 229-44. This is consistent with the presentation of the law in EN, especially obedience to it as a core identity marker.

192 Williamson, *Ezra, Nehemiah*, 317.

193 K. Koch, "Ezra and the Origins of Judaism," *JSS* 19 (1974): 173-97; J. G. McConville, "Ezra-Nehemiah and the Fulfilment of Prophecy," *VT* 36 (1986): 205-24; Williamson, *Ezra, Nehemiah*, li-lii.

194 Blenkinsopp, *Ezra-Nehemiah*, 329.

195 Gerhard von Rad, *Das Geschichtsbild des chronistischen Werkes* (BWANT 54; Stuttgart: Kohlhammer, 1930), 21-25. Followed by Williamson, *Ezra, Nehemiah*, 350.

196 McConville, "Ezra-Nehemiah and the Fulfilment of Prophecy," 223.

remained a small but significant component of Israelite identity in the Restoration period.

Support for this Davidic hope is found in the Psalter. Although a number of the psalms may have originated in a pre-exilic or exilic context, the Psalter in its final form probably functioned in a liturgical setting in the Persian Period.[197] While the main emphasis in the Psalter is on the kingship of YHWH, it does not remove hope in the Davidic monarchy. As David Howard affirms: "[T]he point in the Psalter is not that the Davidic Covenant itself has failed; ... [r]ather, YHWH's *people* have failed, and thus the Davidic Covenant has of necessity taken a back seat historically (and in the Psalter) for a time."[198] The divine kingship of YHWH, as expressed in Israel through the human Davidic kingship,[199] thus awaits expression at God's chosen time.

Finally, the RN would have influenced the application of the Torah as a marker of Israelite identity. The Israelites were a fledgling community under threat in the Restoration period. In response, the community chose to use the Torah as an instrument of prohibition and restriction in EN. Although religious purity was the ultimate aim, it was equated with genealogical purity and hence, was, effectively, ethnocentric. The RN offers a corrective. The presentation of Ruth, a proselyte who follows the requirements of the Torah, demonstrates that not only can outsiders become members of Israel, they can also make crucial contributions to it. As such, it foregrounds religion over descent: a foreigner can become an Israelite through dedication to the Torah. If the scribal profession produced a meritocracy as part of the *Zeitgeist* of EN, the RN would confirm this in relation to the acceptance of outsiders. Thus, in addition to its exclusionary function, the Torah can function as means of reconciliation and inclusion. The RN does not contradict EN; rather, it modifies the concept of "holy seed" to include those who are willing to dedicate themselves to YHWH, his people, and the Torah.

---

197 See the discussion in Hans-Joachim Kraus, *Psalms 1-59: A Commentary* (trans. Hilton C. Oswald; Minneapolis: Augsburg, 1988), 62-68. The extended historical retrospective in Nehemiah 9 has evoked comparison with a number of psalms, in particular Psalm 106. See, e.g., Blenkinsopp, *Ezra-Nehemiah*, 301-06; F. Charles Fensham, "Neh. 9 and Pss. 105, 106, 135 and 136: Post-exilic Historical Traditions in Poetic Form," *JNSL* 9 (1981): 35-51.

198 David M. Howard, *The Structure of Psalms 93-100* (Winona Lake: Eisenbrauns, 1997), 205 (emphasis original).

199 Howard, *Structure*, 207.

III. Summary and Conclusion

In this chapter I have demonstrated that although a provenance for the RN could have been found in the Monarchic Period, the social emphases of the RN find its greatest resonance in the Persian Period.

The RN would have had a major impact on identity in the Persian Period. I first explored its influence on personal identity, particularly the crucial importance of initiative and its expression in supraconventional actions. This is especially required in a time of need and destitution, which is common to both the RN and at regular intervals within the Persian Period. The RN would have also influenced two kinship groups: the father's house and Israel. I discussed the place of the newly-formed "fathers' houses" as an identity marker, in addition to its function as a survival mechanism. The RN was found to be instructive for members of this group in relation to the generous application of the law. Finally, I pointed to the upheaval of Israelite identity associated with the exile and return, and the subsequent eschewal of external identity markers. The RN would have supported the decentring of the Temple, while offering a reminder of the Davidic monarchy as an important component of Israelite identity. The RN would have also presented an alternate, more inclusive use of the Torah in relation to outsiders. In all these elements of identity, the openness of the Persian Period would have increased the effectiveness of the RN.

These emphases drawn from the RN are more pointed for a returnee from Babylon to Yehud. Initiative and ingenuity would be required as they seek to rebuild their homes and lives in a new location. The need for a clear understanding of the behavioural identity markers for a member of a fathers' house would be more acute for an urban returnee than for a rural dweller who remained in a father's house. While a wider application of the law, and its use as a tool for the acceptance of non-Israelites might apply to both rural and urban dwellers, the message concerning external Israelite identity markers is particularly apposite for a returnee. After all, those who stayed in the countryside had already survived for decades without a Temple. And a reminder about the Davidic covenant may be more suitable for one who voluntarily returned under the mandate of a Persian king, with his largesse in their bags.

On the basis of these findings, one may posit a more specific origin for the composition of the RN. Since the issues of identity drawn from the RN dovetail nicely with those in the atmosphere of the Restoration period, it seems reasonable to suggest they share the same historical provenance. Based on this inference, and given that the burden of the RN weighs more heavily on an urban returnee, it is then only a short deductive step to conclude that the RN reflects the voice of the rural hinterland. If EN focuses upon or even glorifies the urban Jerusalem ruling class, then the RN aims to redress the imbalance. In response to the question, "Can anything good come out of the country?"[200] the RN insists: the greatest Israelite king came from the Ephrathite clan of the town of Bethlehem.

---

200 Borrowed from John 1:46, where it is said of Jesus, "Can anything good come out of Nazareth?"

Summary and Conclusions

Summary

The key concern of this study, introduced at the start, was the marginalisation of narrative ethics, and the need for its inclusion in a construction of HB ethics. To this end, the concept of identity was employed as a lens through which to understand and derive ethics. The preceding chapters sought to demonstrate how the application of social identity theory (SIT) highlights the social emphases of a biblical text, and consequently assists in understanding its original ethical message. The RN functions to shape or reinforce the identity of an ancient Israelite implied reader, and his attitudes and behaviour as a result.

Chapter One established the methodological assumptions undergirding this study. Narratives have the potential to shape personal identity because identity is narrative in form. Identity, in turn, has a strong influence on behaviour. Consequently, narrative can influence behaviour by changing the way a person understands her identity. Since ancient Israelite society is generally held to be predominantly collectivist in orientation, the chapter outlined the modified form of SIT applied to this study. Within SIT, group norms are identity descriptors, and hence an aspect of identity. Since SIT also incorporates an understanding of individuality, I sketched a portrait of an ancient Israelite with two main components of identity: personal and social. The chapter then situated the implied reader in the late Monarchic to the Persian Period.

Chapter Two first focused on establishing a connection between identity and ethics in the male protagonist Boaz. His actions predominantly derive from the social component of his identity. Nonetheless, I found that although his actions had a strong communal motivation, they ultimately reinforced his personal identity. I also argued that Boaz's proposal to the nearer kinsman in 4:5 implies an inextricable connection between the right of redemption and the levirate duty. Understood in this way, the refusal of Mr. So-and-So to accept these responsibilities contrasts with Boaz's willing response. The RN thus presents Boaz as virtuous from an identity perspective: in acting for the welfare of Ruth and Naomi, he was willing to place the social component of his identity before his personal component.

Although Boaz has been criticised for his lack of initiative in not securing long-term provision for Naomi and Ruth, I suggested a more nuanced explanation from an identity perspective. It is not that Boaz was unwilling, but rather he was unable to act because a combination of the personal and social components of his identity had placed him in a bind. I concluded the chapter by noting that Boaz's actions go beyond the strict requirements of the law, and would thus be unsettling for an implied reader.

In Chapter Three I examined the transformation of Ruth's identity. The central change is from a Moabite outsider to an integral member of Israelite society. Her incorporation into Israelite society is achieved through her interaction with Naomi and Boaz. This chapter revealed that the exercise of her personal characteristics were crucial to her transformation. I analysed Ruth's interactions with Naomi and Boaz, and showed that in her initiative she did not overstep the social and legal boundaries of her time. From an identity perspective, Ruth's actions can be understood as the personal component of her identity acting in accord with the social component.

The chapter then considered the impact of Ruth upon an implied reader. While most scholars note that the character of Ruth in the RN would function to reinforce Israelite identity, I suggested instead that she would provide a challenge by maintaining elements of her "foreignness." In addition, the basis for membership into the people of God would be challenged, and hence the essence of an Israelite. The acceptance of Ruth into Israelite society challenged the notion that entrance was based solely on descent; rather, decision and personal character are also important.

Chapter Four demonstrated the importance of a connection to a social group through the presentation of Naomi. The loss of her crucial social identities led to a rejection of her personal identity. The shedding of her temporary name and the reinstatement of her given name only occurred through her reattachment to a kinship group, and hence a restoration of her social identities. Nonetheless, the crucial turning point in her restoration was when she acted resourcefully, primarily through her Threshing Floor Scheme. I contended the implied author presents the Scheme as both appropriate and necessary under Naomi and Ruth's desperate circumstances. From the perspective of identity, I noted Naomi's action could be understood as the personal and social components of her identity acting together.

The fourth chapter then considered the impact of Naomi upon an implied reader. While Naomi illustrates the vital importance of the social component of identity and the Israelite social structure, she also highlights the inadequacy of the social support system. This raised the issue of the nature of the familial role, and I proposed that ultimately it was one of responsibility, not duty. Naomi also serves to underscore the importance of perpetuating the family line as an Israelite group norm. The chapter also considered the challenge Naomi presented to Israelite identity deriving from her initiative, both on a personal and social level. I suggested an additional challenge was at the level of gender, with a pertinent message for both women and men.

In Chapter Five I sought to pinpoint a specific provenance for the RN within either the Monarchic or Persian periods, based on the emphases arising from viewing the RN from a social identity perspective. I suggested if an origin for the composition of the RN were to be found in the Monarchic Period, the Josianic era would be the most likely. However, I argued the social undercurrents of the Persian Period correspond most closely to those found in the RN. I established the liminality characterising this period, and then discussed the influence of the RN on both the personal and social components of identity in the Persian Period. Regarding personal identity, the two related messages were the importance of initiative and the possible need for acting beyond conventional roles. The influence of the RN on social identity focused on two kinship groups: the fathers' house and Israel. I suggested the RN demonstrates that the combination of real and fictional kinship bonds in a fathers' house can be successful, although survival can only be assured if all members treat one another as genuine kin.

I then looked at Israelite identity in the Restoration period and summarised the two core components as Temple and Torah, both of which exhibit continuity with and development from the pre-exilic period. It was argued that adherence to the Torah becomes the focus of identification in EN, with a relative downplaying of external identity markers including Temple and monarchy. Within this context, the RN supports the decentring of the Temple as a core identity marker. I evaluated the possible influence of the RN upon the monarchy, and concluded that the royalist hope remained a small but significant element of Israelite identity. I also suggested that the RN presents a corrective to the ethnocentric use of the Torah in the Restoration period. Finally, I proposed that the RN is more apposite for a returnee than one who remained in the land, and subsequently suggested that the RN reflects the voice of the rural hinterland in contradistinction to the Jerusalem ruling class.

Conclusions

A burden of this study was to demonstrate that ethics springs from elements of identity. However, I also found the reverse relation holds: behaviour can shape identity. On a personal level, this was seen especially in Naomi and Ruth. The actions of both these characters led to a change in their identities. While some of their actions can be understood as role-playing based on personal and social components of their identities, their actions extend beyond conventional roles and shape their future identity. Once they had developed their identities, these provided a foundation for ethics. In this sense, personal identity is not static, but has the potential for ongoing formation.

In contrast, an important aspect of social identity remains stable. This study reinforced the persistence of the status of the law, as outlining the fundamental norms for the people of God, throughout the time of the HB. Although, according to the witness of the HB, the law was originally given at the establishment of the nation of Israel, it maintained its authority throughout the historical period described in the HB. In this study, the relevant laws were shown to influence the behaviour of the protagonists of the RN in the narrative setting of the time of the Judges, as well as an implied reader of the RN in the Persian Period. Similarly, as a core identity marker in EN, the law is both authoritative and applicable in the post-exilic period. As such, God's requirements for his people as reflected in the law remain an unchanging element of their social identity throughout the HB.

Nonetheless, while the law remains constant, there is flexibility in its application to concrete situations. In the RN, there was a generous interpretation of the law according to the principle of חסד. This was especially seen in the actions of Boaz. A strict application of the legal circumstances described in the law would have meant that he was not obligated to act as the levir. Yet Boaz's actions in the RN illustrate how narrative can broaden the scope of the law by acting consistently with the moral principle underlying the law. This is one manifestation of Wenham's observation regarding law and narrative: the law outlines God's basic ethical requirements, while narrative describes the ideal of godly behaviour.[1]

The episode in Neh 5 reinforces this understanding, albeit in a different way. In this case, it was shown that although the law permitted the loaning of money on pledge and debt-slavery, it was not suitable for the current predicament. What was required instead was a charitable response to the destitution of the "brothers," with the immediate return of

---

1   Wenham, "Gap," 17-29; Wenham, *Story*, esp. 73-107.

all property. Hence, the application of the law in Neh 5 reveals that it is not appropriate to follow the details of the law in some circumstances. What is required is a consideration of the moral logic underlying the law; righteous behaviour may involve acting in accordance with the law's perceived intentions rather than its specific stipulations.

In contrast, there is a strict application of the law concerning exogamous marriage in EN. When confronted with this situation, the post-exilic Israelite community chose to use the law in a restrictive sense. Although the ultimate goal was religious purity, the law was used to exclude foreigners from the community of Israel on genealogical grounds. This essentially ethnocentric application was contrary to the inner logic of the law, as the implied author suggests, for there was still an inclusion of foreigners on the basis of religion in the narrative account. The incorporation of gentiles who were willing to separate themselves from "the peoples of the lands" to join with the community of Israel to worship YHWH exclusively (Ezra 6:21; Neh 10:29[28]) hints that membership was granted not only on the basis of genealogy, but also on the basis of devotion to YHWH. In this way, the implied author calls for an interpretation of the law beyond its specifics to its underlying motivation.

This study also has broader implications for understanding the nature of ancient Israelite identity. A foundational premise of SIT, that social identity is generally more salient than personal identity in self-conception, fits well with the regnant understanding of ancient Israelite identity as being predominantly corporate in nature. As shown in this study, however, the RN also promotes the value of autonomous thinking, and hence underlines the significance of personal identity within a collectivist society. As such, it joins the chorus of individualist-leaning HB texts (e.g., Deut 24:16; 29:16-21; Jer 31:29-30; Ezek 18) in qualifying and complementing the corporate ideals found in the majority of the HB.

In conclusion, this study demonstrates that narrative can influence ethics by shaping identity, as understood within the historico-social matrix of an implied or actual reader. This study is offered in the hope that it will stimulate further investigation into the message of biblical texts from the perspective of identity, the impact of other HB texts upon the formation of identity, and that it will reinforce the validity of narrative in the development of an "Ethics of the HB."

Bibliography

Adler, Nancy J. "Re-Entry: Managing Cross-Cultural Transitions." *Group & Organization Studies* 6 (1981): 341-56.
Aharoni, Y. *Arad Inscriptions*. Jerusalem: Israel Exploration Society, 1981.
Ahlström, Gösta W. *The History of Ancient Palestine*. Minneapolis: Fortress, 1993.
Albertz, Rainer. "Purity Strategies and Political Interests in the Policy of Nehemiah." In *Confronting the Past: Archaeological and Historical Essays on Ancient Israel in Honor of William G. Dever*. Edited by Seymour Gitin, J. Edward Wright and J. P. Dessel, 199-206. Winona Lake: Eisenbrauns, 2006.
Allport, Floyd H. *Social Psychology*. Boston: Houghton Mifflin, 1924.
Allport, Gordon W. *The Nature of Prejudice*. Cambridge, Mass.: Addison-Wesley, 1954.
Alter, Robert. *The Art of Biblical Narrative*. New York: Basic Books, 1981.
Andersen, Francis I. "Israelite Kinship Terminology and Social Structure." *BT* 20 (1969): 29-39.
———. "Yahweh, the Kind and Sensitive God." In *God Who is Rich in Mercy: Essays Presented to Dr. D. B. Knox*. Edited by Peter T. O' Brien and David G. Peterson, 41-88. Sydney: Lancer, 1986.
Anderson, Benedict R. O' G. *Imagined Communities: Reflections on the Origin and Spread of Nationalism*. London: Verso, 1983.
Arendt, Hannah. *The Human Condition*. Chicago: University of Chicago Press, 1958.
Arnold, Bill T. "The Use of Aramaic in the Hebrew Bible: Another Look at Bilingualism in Ezra and Daniel." *JNSL* 22 (1996): 1-16.
Aschkenasy, Nehama. "Reading Ruth through a Bakhtinian Lens: The Carnivalesque in a Biblical Tale." *JBL* 126 (2007): 437-53.
———. *Woman at the Window: Biblical Tales of Oppression and Escape*. Detroit: Wayne State University Press, 1998.

Baker, David L. "To Glean or Not to Glean..." *ExpTim* 117 (2006): 406-10.
Bal, Mieke. *Death and Dissymmetry: The Politics of Coherence in the Book of Judges*. Chicago: University of Chicago Press, 1988.
Baldwin, Joyce G. "Ruth." In *The New Bible Commentary: Revised*. Edited by Donald Guthrie and J. Alec Motyer, 277-83. London: InterVarsity, 1970.
Barbieri, William A. "Ethics and the Narrated Life." *The Journal of Religion* 78 (1998): 361-86.
Barker, Paul A. *The Triumph of Grace in Deuteronomy: Faithless Israel, Faithful Yahweh in Deuteronomy*. Carlisle: Paternoster, 2004.

Barrick, W. Boyd. *The King and the Cemeteries: Toward a New Understanding of Josiah's Reform.* Leiden: Brill, 2002.
Barstad, Hans M. *The Myth of the Empty Land: A Study in the History and Archaeology of Judah during the "Exilic" Period.* Oslo: Scandinavian University Press, 1996.
Barth, Fredrik. *Ethnic Groups and Boundaries: The Social Organization of Culture Difference.* Boston: Little, Brown, 1969.
Barton, John. *Ethics and the Old Testament.* 2d ed. London: SCM, 1998.
———. *Understanding Old Testament Ethics: Approaches and Explanations.* Louisville: Westminster John Knox, 2003.
Batten, Loring W. *A Critical and Exegetical Commentary on the Books of Ezra and Nehemiah.* ICC. Edinburgh: T & T Clark, 1913.
Bauckham, Richard. "The Book of Ruth and the Possibility of a Feminist Canonical Hermeneutic." *BibInt* 5 (1997): 29-45.
Baylis, Charles P. "Naomi in the Book of Ruth in Light of the Mosaic Covenant." *BSac* 161 (2004): 413-31.
Beattie, D. R. G. "Kethibh and Qere in Ruth IV 5." *VT* 21 (1971): 490-94.
———. "Ruth III." *JSOT* 5 (1978): 39-48.
Bechtel, Lyn M. "Shame as a Sanction of Social Control in Biblical Israel: Judicial, Political, and Social Shaming." *JSOT* 49 (1991): 47-76.
Bendor, Shunya. *The Social Structure of Ancient Israel: The Institution of the Family (beit 'ab) from the Settlement to the End of the Monarchy.* Jerusalem Biblical Studies 7. Jerusalem: Simor, 1996.
Berger, Peter L. *Invitation to Sociology: A Humanistic Perspective.* Harmondsworth: Penguin, 1963.
Berlin, Adele. "Big Theme, Little Book." *BRev* 12 (1996): 40-43, 47-48.
———. *Poetics and Interpretation of Biblical Narrative.* Sheffield: Almond Press, 1983.
———. "Ruth." In *HarperCollins Bible Commentary.* Edited by James L. Mays, 240-44. San Francisco: Harper & Row, 2000.
Berman, Joshua. "Ancient Hermeneutics and the Legal Structure of the Book of Ruth." *ZAW* 119 (2007): 22-38.
———. "Constitution, Class, and the Book of Deuteronomy." *Hebraic Political Studies* 1 (2006): 523-48.
———. "The Narratorial Voice of the Scribes of Samaria: Ezra iv 8-vi 18 Reconsidered." *VT* 56 (2006): 313-26.
Bernstein, Moshe J. "Two Multivalent Readings in the Ruth Narrative." *JSOT* 50 (1991): 15-26.
Berquist, Jon L. *Judaism in Persia's Shadow: A Social and Historical Approach.* Minneapolis: Fortress, 1995.
———. "Role Differentiation in the Book of Ruth." *JSOT* 57 (1993): 23-37.

Berry, John W. "Acculturation as Varieties of Adaptation." In *Acculturation: Theory, Models, and Some New Findings*. Edited by Amado M. Padilla, 9-25. Boulder: Westview, 1980.

———. "Acculturation: Living Successfully in Two Cultures." *International Journal of Intercultural Relations* 29 (2005): 697-712.

———. "A Psychology of Immigration." *Journal of Social Issues* 57 (2001): 615-31.

Bertman, Stephen. "Symmetrical Design in the Book of Ruth." *JBL* 84 (1965): 165-68.

Black, James. "Ruth in the Dark: Folktale, Law and Creative Ambiguity in the Old Testament." *Literature and Theology* 5 (1991): 20-36.

Blenkinsopp, Joseph. *Ezra-Nehemiah*. OTL. Philadelphia: Westminster, 1988.

Block, Daniel I. *Judges, Ruth*. NAC 6. Nashville: Broadman & Holman, 1999.

Boccaccini, Gabriele. *Roots of Rabbinic Judaism: An Intellectual History, from Ezekiel to Daniel*. Grand Rapids: Eerdmans, 2002.

Boling, Robert G. *Judges*. AB 6A. Garden City: Doubleday, 1975.

Booth, Wayne C. *The Company We Keep: An Ethics of Fiction*. Los Angeles: University of California Press, 1988.

———. *The Rhetoric of Fiction*. Chicago: University of Chicago Press, 1961.

Bos, Johanna W. H. "Out of the Shadows: Genesis 38; Judges 4:17-22; Ruth 3." *Semeia* 42 (1988): 37-67.

Bosman, Jan P. "Social Identity in Nahum: A Theological-Ethical Enquiry." D.Th. diss., University of Stellenbosch, 2005.

Braulik, Georg. "The Book of Ruth as Intra-Biblical Critique of the Deuteronomic Law." *AcT* 19 (1999): 1-20.

Brenner, Athalya. "Naomi and Ruth." *VT* 33 (1983): 385-97.

———. "Naomi and Ruth: Further Reflections." In *A Feminist Companion to Ruth*. Edited by Athalya Brenner, 140-44. Sheffield: Sheffield Academic Press, 1993.

———, ed. *A Feminist Companion to Ruth*. Sheffield: Sheffield Academic Press, 1993.

———, ed. *Ruth and Esther: A Feminist Companion to the Bible*. Sheffield: Sheffield Academic Press, 1999.

Brett, Mark G. "Nationalism and the Hebrew Bible." In *The Bible in Ethics*. Edited by John W. Rogerson, Margaret Davies and M. Daniel Carroll, 136-63. Sheffield: Sheffield Academic Press, 1995.

Brewer, Marilynn B., and Ya-Ru Chen. "Where (Who) Are Collectives in Collectivism? Toward Conceptual Clarification of Individualism and Collectivism." *Psychological Review* 114 (2007): 133-51.

Brewer, Marilynn B., and Wendi Gardner. "Who Is This 'We'? Levels of Collective Identity and Self Representations." *Journal of Personality & Social Psychology* 71 (1996): 83-93.

Brewer, Marilynn B., and Masaki Yuki. "Culture and Social Identity." In *Handbook of Cultural Psychology*. Edited by Shinobu Kitayama and Dov Cohen, 307-22. New York: Guilford Press, 2007.

Brichto, Herbert C. "Kin, Cult, Land, and Afterlife - A Biblical Complex." *HUCA* 44 (1973): 1-54.
Bright, John. *A History of Israel*. 4th ed. Louisville: Westminster John Knox, 2000.
Broshi, Magen. "The Expansion of Jerusalem in the Reigns of Hezekiah and Manasseh." *IEJ* 24 (1975): 21-26.
Broshi, Magen, and Israel Finkelstein. "The Population of Palestine in Iron Age II." *BASOR* 287 (1992): 47-60.
Brown, A. Philip, II. "The Problem of Mixed Marriages in Ezra 9-10." *BSac* 162 (2005): 437-58.
Brown, Rupert. *Group Processes: Dynamics within and between Groups*. Oxford: Basil Blackwell, 1988.
Brueggemann, Walter. *Hopeful Imagination: Prophetic Voices in Exile*. Philadelphia: Fortress, 1986.
Bruner, Jerome. "Life as Narrative." *Social Research* 54 (1987): 11-32.
Buhl, Frants. "Some Observations on the Social Institutions of the Israelites." *AJT* 1 (1897): 728-40.
Burrows, Millar. "The Marriage of Boaz and Ruth." *JBL* 59 (1940): 445-54.
Bush, Frederic W. *Ruth, Esther*. WBC 9. Dallas: Word Books, 1996.
Byrne, Donn E. *The Attraction Paradigm*. New York: Academic, 1971.

Camp, Claudia V. *Wisdom and the Feminine in the Book of Proverbs*. Sheffield: Almond, 1985.
Campbell, Anne, Louisa Shirley, and Lisa Caygill. "Sex-Typed Preferences in Three Domains: Do Two-Year-Olds Need Cognitive Variables?" *British Journal of Psychology* 93 (2002): 203-17.
Campbell, Edward F. "Naomi, Boaz, and Ruth, *hesed* ".and Change)חסד(*Austin Seminary Bulletin* 105 (1990): 64-74.
———. *Ruth*. AB 7. Garden City: Doubleday, 1975.
Carasik, Michael. "Ruth 2,7: Why the Overseer Was Embarrassed." *ZAW* 107 (1995): 493-94.
Carmichael, Calum M. "'Treading' in the Book of Ruth." *ZAW* 92 (1980): 248-66.
Carroll, Noël. *Beyond Aesthetics: Philosophical Essays*. Cambridge: Cambridge University Press, 2001.
Carroll, Robert P. "The Myth of the Empty Land." *Semeia* 59 (1992): 79-93.
Carter, Charles E. "A Discipline in Transition: The Contributions of the Social Sciences to the Study of the Hebrew Bible." In *Community, Identity, and Ideology: Social Science Approaches to the Hebrew Bible*. Edited by Charles E. Carter and Carol L. Meyers, 3-36. Winona Lake: Eisenbrauns, 1996.
———. *The Emergence of Yehud in the Persian Period: A Social and Demographic Study*. Sheffield: Sheffield Academic Press, 1999.
Chatman, Seymour. *Story and Discourse: Narrative Structure in Fiction and Film*. Ithaca: Cornell University Press, 1978.

Childs, Brevard S. *Introduction to the Old Testament as Scripture*. Philadelphia: Fortress, 1979.
Chirichigno, Gregory C. *Debt-Slavery in Israel and the Ancient Near East*. JSOTSup 141. Sheffield: JSOT Press, 1993.
Clark, Gordon R. *The Word Hesed in the Hebrew Bible*. JSOTSup 157. Sheffield: Sheffield Academic Press, 1993.
Clements, Ronald E. "The Good Neighbour in the Book of Proverbs." In *Of Prophets' Visions and the Wisdom of Sages: Essays in Honour of R. Norman Whybray on his Seventieth Birthday*. Edited by Heather A. McKay and David J. A. Clines, 209-28. JSOTSup 162. Sheffield: JSOT Press, 1993.
———. "Poverty and the Kingdom of God - An Old Testament View." In *The Kingdom of God and Human Society: Essays by Members of the Scripture, Theology and Society Group*. Edited by Robin Barbour, 13-27. Edinburgh: T&T Clark, 1993.
Clines, David J. A. *Ezra, Nehemiah, Esther*. NCBC. Grand Rapids: Eerdmans, 1984.
———. "Nehemiah 10 as an Example of Early Jewish Biblical Exegesis." *JSOT* 21 (1981): 111-17.
Cogan, Mordechai, and Hayim Tadmor. *II Kings*. AB 11. New York: Doubleday, 1988.
Cohen, Shaye J. D. "Crossing the Boundary and Becoming a Jew." *HTR* 82 (1989): 13-33.
Collins, John J. "Marriage, Divorce, and Family in Second Temple Judaism." In *Families in Ancient Israel*. Edited by Leo G. Perdue, Joseph Blenkinsopp, John J. Collins and Carol Meyers, 104-62. Louisville: Westminster John Knox, 1997.
———. "Review of Shane Kirkpatrick, *Competing for Honor: A Social-Scientific Reading of Daniel 1-6*." Review of Biblical Literature [http://www.bookreviews.org] (2008).
Cover, Robert N. "Foreword: *Nomos* and Narrative." *Harvard Law Review* 97 (1986): 4-68.
Cox, J. Ben. "The Role of Communication, Technology, and Cultural Identity in Repatriation Adjustment." *International Journal of Intercultural Relations* 28 (2004): 201-19.
Craigie, Peter C. *The Book of Deuteronomy*. NICOT. Grand Rapids: Eerdmans, 1976.
Crites, Stephen. "The Narrative Quality of Experience." *JAAR* 39 (1971): 291-311.
Crocker, Jennifer, and Riia Luthanen. "Collective Self-Esteem and Ingroup Bias." *Journal of Personality and Social Psychology* 58 (1990): 60-67.
Crook, Zeba A. "Structure versus Agency in Studies of the Biblical Social World: Engaging with Louise Lawrence." *JSNT* 29 (2007): 251-75.

Darwall, Stephen L. *Philosophical Ethics*. Boulder: Westview, 1998.
Daube, David. *Ancient Jewish Law: Three Inaugural Lectures*. Leiden: Brill, 1981.

David, M. "The Date of the Book of Ruth." *OtSt* 1 (1942): 55-63.
Davies, Eryl W. "Inheritance Rights and the Hebrew Levirate Marriage: Part 2." *VT* 31 (1981): 257-68.
———. "Ruth IV 5 and the Duties of the Go'el." *VT* 33 (1983): 231-34.
Davies, Philip R. "Exile? What Exile? Whose Exile?" In *Leading Captivity Captive: The Exile as History and Ideology*. Edited by Lester L. Grabbe, 128-38. JSOTSup 278. Sheffield: Sheffield Academic Press, 1998.
Day, John. *King and Messiah in Israel and the Ancient Near East: Proceedings of the Oxford Old Testament Seminar*. JSOTSup 270. Sheffield: Sheffield Academic Press, 1998.
Dearman, J. Andrew, ed. *Studies in the Mesha Inscription and Moab*. Atlanta: Scholars Press, 1989.
Delamarter, Steve. "The Death of Josiah in Scripture and Tradition: Wrestling with the Problem of Evil?" *VT* 54 (2004): 29-60.
Dennett, Daniel. "The Self as a Center of Narrative Gravity." In *Self and Consciousness: Multiple Perspectives*. Edited by Frank S. Kessel, Pamela M. Cole and Dale L. Johnson, Reprinted at http://ase.tufts.edu/cogstud/papers/selfctr.htm. Hillsdale: Erlbaum, 1992.
Dever, William G. *Recent Archaeological Discoveries and Biblical Research*. Seattle: University of Washington Press, 1990.
———. *What Did the Biblical Writers Know and When Did They Know It?: What Archaeology Can Tell Us about the Reality of Ancient Israel*. Grand Rapids: Eerdmans, 2001.
Dommershausen, Werner. "Leitwortstil in der Ruthrolle." In *Theologie im Wandel*. Edited by Johannes Neumann and Joseph Ratzinger, 394-407. Munich-Freiburg: Wewel, 1967.
Donaldson, Laura E. "The Sign of Orpah: Reading Ruth through Native Eyes." In *Ruth and Esther: A Feminist Companion to the Bible (Second Series)*. Edited by Athalya Brenner, 130-44. Sheffield: Sheffield Academic Press, 1999.
Doosje, Bertjan, and Naomi Ellemers. "Stereotyping under Threat: The Role of Group Identification." In *The Social Psychology of Stereotyping and Group Life*. Edited by Russell Spears, Penelope J. Oakes, Naomi Ellemers and S. Alexander Haslam, 257-72. Oxford: Blackwell, 1997.
Douglas, Mary T. *Purity and Danger: An Analysis of Concepts of Pollution and Taboo*. London: Routledge & K. Paul, 1966.
Driver, S. R. *A Critical and Exegetical Commentary on Deuteronomy*. 3d ed., ICC. Edinburgh: T&T Clark, 1901.
Dube, Musa W. "Divining Ruth for International Relations." In *Other Ways of Reading: African Women and the Bible*. Edited by Musa W. Dube, 179-98. Atlanta: Society of Biblical Literature, 2001.
Duguid, Iain M. *Ezekiel and the Leaders of Israel*. Leiden: Brill, 1994.
Dumbrell, William J. "The Purpose of the Books of Chronicles." *JETS* 27 (1984): 257-66.

Dunn, Judy, and Claire Hughes. "'I Got Some Swords and You're Dead!': Violent Fantasy, Antisocial Behavior, Friendship, and Moral Sensibility in Young Children." *Child Development* 72 (2001): 491-505.
Dutcher-Walls, Patricia. "The Circumscription of the King: Deuteronomy 17:16-17 in Its Ancient Social Context." *JBL* 121 (2002): 601-16.

Eagly, Alice H. *Sex Differences in Social Behavior: A Social-Role Interpretation*. Hillsdale, N. J.: Lawrence Erlbaum Associates, 1987.
Eichrodt, Walther. *Theology of the Old Testament*. Translated by John A. Baker. 2 vols. Philadelphia: Westminster, 1966.
Elliott, John H. *Social-Scientific Criticism of the New Testament*. London: SPCK, 1993.
———. *What is Social-Scientific Criticism?* Minneapolis: Fortress, 1993.
Ellison, Henry L. *From Babylon to Bethlehem: The Jewish People from the Exile to the Messiah*. Exeter: Paternoster, 1976.
Eriksen, Thomas H. *Ethnicity and Nationalism: Anthropological Perspectives*. London: Pluto Press, 1993.
Erikson, Erik H. *Childhood and Society*. London: Imago, 1950.
Eskenazi, Tamara C. *In an Age of Prose: A Literary Approach to Ezra-Nehemiah*. Atlanta: Scholars Press, 1988.
———. "The Missions of Ezra and Nehemiah." In *Judah and the Judeans in the Persian Period*, edited by Oded Lipschits and Manfred Oeming, 509-29. Winona Lake: Eisenbrauns, 2006.
———. "The Structure of Ezra-Nehemiah and the Integrity of the Book." *JBL* 107 (1988): 641-56.
Esler, Philip F. "2 Samuel–David and the Ammonite War: A Narrative and Social-Scientific Interpretation of 2 Samuel 10-12." In *Ancient Israel: The Old Testament in Its Social Context*. Edited by Philip F. Esler, 191-207. London: SCM, 2005.
———. *Ancient Israel: The Old Testament in Its Social Context*. London: SCM, 2005.
———. *Conflict and Identity in Romans: The Social Setting of Paul's Letter*. Minneapolis: Fortress, 2003.
———. "Ezra-Nehemiah as a Narrative of (Re-Invented) Israelite Identity." *BibInt* 11 (2003): 413-26.
———. *The First Christians in Their Social Worlds: Social-Scientific Approaches to New Testament Interpretation*. London: Routledge, 1994.
———. *Galatians*. London: Routledge, 1998.
———. "Jesus and the Reduction of Intergroup Conflict: The Parable of the Good Samaritan in the Light of Social Identity Theory." *BibInt* 8 (2000): 325-57.
———. "Social-Scientific Models in Biblical Interpretation." In *Ancient Israel: The Old Testament in Its Social Context*. Edited by Philip F. Esler, 3-14. London: SCM, 2005.

Esler, Philip F., and Anselm C. Hagedorn. "Social-Scientific Analysis of the Old Testament." In *Ancient Israel: The Old Testament in Its Social Context*. Edited by Philip F. Esler, 15-32. London: SCM, 2005.
Ethier, Kathleen, and Kay Deaux. "Hispanics in Ivy: Assessing Identity and Perceived Threat." *Sex Roles* 22 (1990): 427-40.
———. "Negotiating Social Identity When Contexts Change: Maintaining Identification and Responding to Threat." *Journal of Personality and Social Psychology* 67 (1994): 243-51.
Exum, J. Cheryl. *Song of Songs*. OTL. Louisville: Westminster John Knox, 2005.

Faust, Avraham. "Abandonment, Urbanization, Resettlement and the Formation of the Israelite State." *Near Eastern Archaeology* 66 (2003): 147-61.
———. "Differences in Family Structure between Cities and Villages in Iron Age II." *Tel Aviv* 26 (1999): 233-52.
———. "The Rural Community in Ancient Israel during Iron Age II." *BASOR* 317 (2000): 17-39.
Faust, Avraham, and Shlomo Bunimovitz. "The Four Room House: Embodying Iron Age Israelite Society." *Near Eastern Archaeology* 66 (2003): 22-31.
Faust, Avraham, and Ehud Weiss. "Judah, Philistia, and the Mediterranean World: Reconstructing the Economic System of the Seventh Century B.C.E." *BASOR* 338 (2005): 71-92.
Fensham, F. Charles. *The Books of Ezra and Nehemiah*. Grand Rapids: Eerdmans, 1982.
———. "Neh. 9 and Pss. 105, 106, 135 and 136: Post-exilic Historical Traditions in Poetic Form." *JNSL* 9 (1981): 35-51.
———. "Widow, Orphan, and the Poor in Ancient Near Eastern Legal and Wisdom Literature." *JNES* 21 (1962): 129-39.
Fewell, Danna N., and David M. Gunn. "Boaz, Pillar of Society: Measures of Worth in the Book of Ruth." *JSOT* 45 (1989): 45-59.
———. *Compromising Redemption: Relating Characters in the Book of Ruth*. Louisville: Westminster John Knox, 1990.
———. "'A Son is Born to Naomi!': Literary Allusions and Interpretation in the Book of Ruth." *JSOT* 40 (1988): 99-108.
Finkelstein, Israel. "The Emergence of the Monarchy in Israel: The Environmental and Socio-Economic Aspects." *JSOT* 44 (1989): 43-74.
Finkelstein, Israel, and Neil Asher Silberman. *The Bible Unearthed: Archaeology's New Vision of Ancient Israel and the Origin of Its Sacred Texts*. New York: Touchstone, 2001.
———. "Temple and Dynasty: Hezekiah, the Remaking of Judah and the Rise of the Pan-Israelite Ideology." *JSOT* 30 (2006): 259-85.
Fisch, Harold. "Ruth and the Structure of Covenant History." *VT* 32 (1982): 425-37.

Fischer, Irmtraud. "The Book of Ruth: A 'Feminist' Commentary on the Torah?" In *Ruth and Esther: A Feminist Companion to the Bible (Second Series)*. Edited by Athalya Brenner, 24-49. Sheffield: Sheffield Academic Press, 1999.

———. *Rut*. HTKAT. Freiburg: Herder, 2001.

Fishbane, Michael. *Biblical Interpretation in Ancient Israel*. Oxford: Clarendon, 1975.

Fontaine, Carole R. "The Sage in Family and Tribe." In *The Sage in Israel and the Ancient Near East*. Edited by Leo G. Perdue and John G. Gammie, 155-64. Winona Lake: Eisenbrauns, 1990.

Frevel, Christian. *Das Buch Ruth*. Neuer Stuttgarter Kommentar: Altes Testament 6. Stuttgart: Theologischer Verlag, 1992.

Friedmann, Daniel. *To Kill and Take Possession: Law, Morality, and Society in Biblical Stories*. Peabody: Hendrickson, 2002.

Galpaz-Feller, Pnina. "The Widow in the Bible and in Ancient Egypt." *ZAW* 120 (2008): 231-53.

Gellner, Ernest. *Nations and Nationalism*. Ithaca: Cornell University Press, 1983.

Gennep, Arnold van. *Les rites de passage*. Paris: Nourry, 1909.

Gerleman, Gillis. *Ruth. Das Hohelied*. BKAT 18. Neukirchen-Vluyn: Neukirchener Verlag, 1965.

Geus, C. H. J. de. *The Tribes of Israel: An Investigation into Some of the Presuppositions of Martin Noth's Amphictyony Hypothesis*. Studia Semitica Neerlandica 18. Assen: Van Gorcum, 1976.

Ginzberg, Louis. *The Legends of the Jews*. Translated by Henrietta Szold, Paul Radin and Boaz Cohen. 7 vols. Vol. 4. Philadelphia: Jewish Publication Society of America, 1928.

Glanzman, George S. "The Origin and Date of the Book of Ruth." *CBQ* 21 (1959): 201-07.

Glueck, Nelson. *Hesed in the Bible*. Translated by Alfred Gottschalk. Cincinnati: Hebrew Union College Press, 1967.

Goodblatt, David M. *Elements of Ancient Jewish Nationalism*. Cambridge: Cambridge University Press, 2006.

Gordis, Robert. "Love, Marriage, and Business in the Book of Ruth: A Chapter in Hebrew Customary Law." In *A Light unto My Path*. Edited by Howard N. Bream, Ralph D. Heim and Carey A. Moore, 241-64. Philadelphia: Temple University Press, 1974.

———. "Personal Names in Ruth - A Note on Biblical Etymologies." *Judaism* 35 (1986): 298-99.

Gorospe, Athena E. *Narrative and Identity: An Ethical Reading of Exodus 4*. Biblical Interpretation Series 86. Leiden: Brill, 2007.

Goslinga, C. J. *Joshua, Judges, Ruth*. Translated by Ray Togtman. Bible Student's Commentary. Grand Rapids: Zondervan, 1986.

Gottwald, Norman K. *The Hebrew Bible: A Socio-Literary Introduction*. Philadelphia: Fortress, 1985.
———. *The Tribes of Yahweh: A Sociology of the Religion of Liberated Israel, 1250-1050 BCE*. Maryknoll: Orbis, 1979.
Goulder, Michael D. "Ruth: A Homily on Deuteronomy 22-25?" In *Of Prophets, Visions and Wisdom of Sages: Essays in Honour of R Norman Whybray on his Seventieth Birthday*. Edited by Heather A. McKay and David J. A. Clines, 307-19. JSOTSup 162. Sheffield: Almond, 1993.
Gow, Murray D. *The Book of Ruth: Its Structure, Theme and Purpose*. Leicester: Apollos, 1992.
Grabbe, Lester L. "A Priest is without Honor in His Own Prophet: Priests and Other Religious Specialists in the Latter Prophets." In *The Priests in the Prophets: The Portrayal of Priests, Prophets, and Other Religious Specialists in the Latter Prophets*. Edited by Alice Ogden Bellis, 79-97. New York: T&T Clark, 2004.
Gray, John. *Joshua, Judges, Ruth*. NCBC. Grand Rapids: Eerdmans, 1986.
Greenfield, Sidney M. "Industrialization and the Family in Sociological Theory." *The American Journal of Sociology* 67 (1961): 312-22.
Greifenhagen, Franz V. *Egypt on the Pentateuch's Ideological Map: Constructing Biblical Israel's Identity*. JSOTSup 361. London: Sheffield Academic Press, 2002.
Grosby, Steven E. *Biblical Ideas of Nationality: Ancient and Modern*. Winona Lake: Eisenbrauns, 2002.
Grossman, Jonathan. "'Gleaning among the Ears'—'Gathering among the Sheaves': Characterizing the Image of the Supervising Boy (Ruth 2)." *JBL* 126 (2007): 703-16.
Guttmann, Michael. "The Term 'Foreigner' (נכרי) Historically Considered." *HUCA* 3 (1926): 1-20.

Hagedorn, Anselm C. *Between Moses and Plato: Individual and Society in Deuteronomy and Ancient Greek Law*. FRLANT 204. Göttingen: Vandenhoeck & Ruprecht, 2004.
———. "Looking at Foreigners in Biblical and Greek Prophecy." *VT* 57 (2007): 432-48.
———. "Nahum—Ethnicity and Stereotypes: Anthropological Insights into Nahum's Literary History." In *Ancient Israel: The Old Testament in Its Social Context*. Edited by Philip F. Esler, 223-39. London: SCM, 2005.
Hall, Jonathan M. *Ethnic Identity in Greek Antiquity*. Cambridge: Cambridge University Press, 1997.
———. *Hellenicity: Between Ethnicity and Culture*. Chicago: The University of Chicago Press, 2002.
Halpern, Baruch. "Jerusalem and the Lineages in the Seventh Century BCE: Kinship and the Rise of Individual Moral Liability." In *Law and Ideology in Mo-*

narchic Israel. Edited by Baruch Halpern and Deborah W. Hobson, 11-107. Sheffield: JSOT Press, 1991.

Hals, Ronald M. *The Theology of the Book of Ruth*. Philadelphia: Fortress, 1969.

Harm, Harry J. "The Function of Double Entendre in Ruth Three." *JOTT* 7 (1995): 19-27.

Harris, J. Gordon, Cheryl A. Brown, and Michael S. Moore. *Joshua, Judges, Ruth*. NIBCOT 5. Peabody: Hendrickson, 2000.

Harris, Marvin. "The Evolution of Human Gender Hierarchies: A Trial Formulation." In *Sex and Gender Hierarchies*. Edited by Barbara D. Miller, 57-79. Cambridge: Cambridge University Press, 1993.

Harvey, Dorothea. "Book of Ruth." In *Interpreter's Dictionary of the Bible*. Edited by George A. Buttrick, 131-34. Nashville: Abingdon, 1962.

Hauerwas, Stanley. *The Peaceable Kingdom: A Primer in Christian Ethics*. Notre Dame: University of Notre Dame, 1984.

———. *Truthfulness and Tragedy: Further Investigations in Christian Ethics*. Notre Dame: University of Notre Dame Press, 1977.

———. *Vision and Virtue*. Notre Dame: University of Notre Dame, 1974.

———. "Vision, Stories, and Character." In *The Hauerwas Reader*. Edited by John Berkman and Michael Cartwright. Durham: Duke University Press, 2001.

Hayes, Christine E. *Gentile Impurities and Jewish Identities: Intermarriage and Conversion from the Bible to the Talmud*. New York: Oxford University Press, 2002.

Herr, Larry G. "Archaeological Sources for the History of Palestine: The Iron Age II Period: Emerging Nations." *BA* 60 (1997): 114-83.

Herzog, Ze'ev, Miriam Aharoni, and Anson F. Rainey. "Arad: An Ancient Israelite Fortress with a Temple to Yahweh." *BAR* 13 (1987): 16-35.

Hiebert, Paula S. "Whence Shall Help Come to Me? The Biblical Widow." In *Gender and Difference*. Edited by Peggy L. Day, 125-41. Minneapolis: Fortress, 1989.

Himmelfarb, Martha. *A Kingdom of Priests: Ancestry and Merit in Ancient Judaism*. Philadelphia: University of Pennsylvania Press, 2006.

Hinkle, Steve, and Rupert Brown. "Intergroup Comparisons and Social Identity: Some Links and Lacunae." In *Social Identity Theory: Constructive and Critical Advances*. Edited by Dominic Abrams and Michael A. Hogg, 48-70. London: Harvester Wheatsheaf, 1990.

Hoffman, Yair. "The Exodus - Tradition and Reality: The Status of the Exodus Tradition in Ancient Israel." In *Jerusalem Studies in Egyptology*. Edited by Irene Shirun-Grumach, 193-202. Wiesbaden: Harrassowitz Verlag, 1998.

Hogg, Michael A. "Social Identity and the Sovereignty of the Group." In *Individual Self, Relational Self, Collective Self*. Edited by Marilynn B. Brewer and Constantine Sedikides, 123-43. Philadelphia: Psychology Press, 2001.

———. "Subjective Uncertainty Reduction through Self-Categorization: A Motivational Theory of Social Identity Processes." *European Review of Social Psychology* 11 (2000): 223-55.

Hogg, Michael A., and Dominic Abrams. *Social Identifications: A Social Psychology of Intergroup Relations and Group Processes*. London: Routledge, 1988.

Hogg, Michael A., David K. Sherman, Joel Dierselhuis, Angela T. Maitner, and Graham Moffitt. "Uncertainty, Entitativity, and Group Identification." *Journal of Experimental Social Psychology* 43 (2007): 135-42.

Hogg, Michael A., and Joanne R. Smith. "Attitudes in Social Context: A Social Identity Perspective." *European Review of Social Psychology* 18 (2007): 89-131.

Holladay, Carl R. "Contemporary Methods of Reading the Bible." In *NIB*, 125-49. Nashville: Abingdon, 1994.

Holmberg, Bengt. "The Methods of Historical Reconstruction in the Scholarly 'Recovery' of Corinthian Christianity." In *Christianity at Corinth: The Quest for the Pauline Church*. Edited by Edward Adams and David G. Horrell, 255-71. Louisville: Westminster John Knox, 2004.

Honig, Bonnie. "Ruth, the Model Emigrée: Mourning and the Symbolic Politics of Immigration." In *Ruth and Esther: A Feminist Companion to the Bible (Second Series)*, edited by Athalya Brenner, 50-74. Sheffield: Sheffield Academic Press, 1999.

Horrell, David G. "Models and Methods in Social-Scientific Interpretation: A Response to Philip Esler." *JSNT* 78 (2000): 83-105.

Howard, Cecil G. "The Returning Overseas Executive: Cultural Shock in Reverse." *Human Resource Management* 13 (1974): 22-26.

Howard, David M. *The Structure of Psalms 93-100*. Winona Lake: Eisenbrauns, 1997.

Hubbard, Robert L. *The Book of Ruth*. NICOT. Grand Rapids: Eerdmans, 1988.

Hurvitz, Avi. "Can Biblical Texts be Dated Linguistically? Chronological Perspectives in the Historical Study of Biblical Hebrew." In *Congress Volume: Oslo 1998*. Edited by André Lemaire and Magne Sæbø, 143-60. VTSup 80. Leiden: Brill, 2000.

———. "The Date of the Prose-Tale of Job Linguistically Reconsidered." *HTR* 67 (1974): 17-34.

———. *A Linguistic Study of the Relationship between the Priestly Source and the Book of Ezekiel*. CahRB 20. Paris: Gabalda, 1982.

Hutchinson, John, and Anthony D. Smith. "Introduction." In *Ethnicity*. Edited by John Hutchinson and Anthony D. Smith, 3-14. Oxford: Oxford University Press, 1996.

Hydén, Lars-Christer. "Illness and Narrative." *Sociology of Health and Illness* 19 (1997): 48-69.

Idestrom, Rebecca G. S. "Echoes of the Book of Exodus in Ezekiel." *JSOT* 33 (2009): 489-510.
Iser, Wolfgang. *The Act of Reading: A Theory of Aesthetic Response*. Baltimore: Johns Hopkins University Press, 1978.

Janzen, Waldemar. *Old Testament Ethics: A Paradigmatic Approach*. Louisville: Westminster John Knox, 1994.
Japhet, Sara. "Law and 'The Law' in Ezra-Nehemiah." In *From the Rivers of Babylon to the Highlands of Judah: Collected Studies on the Restoration Period*, 137-51. Winona Lake: Eisenbrauns, 2006.
———. "People and Land in the Restoration Period." In *From the Rivers of Babylon to the Highlands of Judah: Collected Studies on the Restoration Period*, 96-116. Winona Lake: Eisenbrauns, 2006.
———. "The Relationship between the Legal Corpora in the Pentateuch in Light of Manumission Laws." In *Studies in Bible 1986*. Edited by Sara Japhet, 63-89. Jerusalem: Magnes Press, 1986.
———. "Sheshbazzar and Zerubbabel—Against the Background of the Historical and Religious Tendencies of Ezra-Nehemiah." *ZAW* 94 (1982): 66-98.
Jepsen, A. "Amah und Schiphchah." *VT* 8 (1958): 293-97.
Johnson, Marshall D. *The Purpose of Biblical Genealogies with Special Reference to the Setting of the Genealogies of Jesus*. SNTSMS 8. Cambridge: Cambridge University Press, 1969.
Jonker, Louis. "Reforming History: The Hermeneutical Significance of the Books of Chronicles." *VT* 57 (2007): 21-44.
———. "Who Constitutes Society? Yehud's Self-understanding in the Late Persian Era as Reflected in the Books of Chronicles." *JBL* 127 (2008): 703-24.
Joüon, Paul. *Ruth: Commentaire philologique et exégétique*. Rome: Pontifical Biblical Institute, 1924.

Kaiser, Walter C. *Preaching and Teaching From the Old Testament: A Guide for the Church*. Grand Rapids: Baker Academic, 2003.
———. *Toward an Exegetical Theology*. Grand Rapids: Baker Book House, 1981.
———. *Toward Old Testament Ethics*. Grand Rapids: Academic, 1983.
Kaminsky, Joel S. *Corporate Responsibility in the Hebrew Bible*. JSOTSup 196. Sheffield: Sheffield Academic Press, 1995.
Kates, Judith A., and Gail T. Reimer, eds. *Reading Ruth: Contemporary Women Reclaim a Sacred Story*. New York: Ballantine, 1994.
Keel, Othmar. *The Song of Songs*. CC. Minneapolis: Fortress Press, 1994.
Keil, Carl F., and Franz Delitzsch. *Biblical commentary on the Old Testament*. Translated by James Martin. Edinburgh: T&T Clark, 1872.
Keita, Schadrac, and Janet W. Dyk. "The Scene at the Threshing Floor: Suggestive Readings and Intercultural Considerations on Ruth 3." *BT* 57 (2006): 17-32.

Kent, Susan. *Analyzing Activity Areas: An Ethnoarchaeological Study of the Use of Space.* Albuquerque: University of New Mexico Press, 1984.

Kirkpatrick, Shane. *Competing for Honor: A Social-Scientific Reading of Daniel 1–6.* Biblical Interpretation Series 74. Leiden: Brill, 2005.

Klawans, Jonathan. *Impurity and Sin in Ancient Judaism.* Oxford: Oxford University Press, 2000.

Klein, Ralph W. *Israel in Exile: A Theological Interpretation.* Philadelphia: Fortress, 1979.

Kleinman, Arthur. *The Illness Narratives: Suffering, Healing, and the Human Condition.* New York: Basic Books, 1988.

Knight, Douglas A., and Carol L. Meyers, eds. *Ethics and Politics in the Hebrew Bible*, Semeia 66. Atlanta: Scholars Press, 1994.

Knoppers, Gary N. *Two Nations under God: The Deuteronomistic History of Solomon and the Dual Monarchies.* Vol. 2. Atlanta: Scholars Press, 1993.

Knowles, Melody D. "Pilgrimage Imagery in the Returns in Ezra." *JBL* 123 (2004): 57-74.

Koch, K. "Ezra and the Origins of Judaism." *JSS* 19 (1974): 173-97.

Korpel, Marjo C. A. *The Structure of the Book of Ruth.* Pericope 2. Assen: Van Gorcum, 2001.

Kottsieper, Ingo. "'And They Did Not Care to Speak Yehudit': On Linguistic Change in Judah during the Late Persian Era." In *Judah and the Judeans in the Fourth Century B.C.E.*. Edited by Oded Lipschits, Gary N. Knoppers and Rainer Albertz, 95-124. Winona Lake: Eisenbrauns, 2007.

Kratz, Reinhard G. "Israel als Staat und als Volk." *ZTK* 97 (2000): 1-17.

Kraus, Hans-Joachim. *Psalms 1-59: A Commentary.* Translated by Hilton C. Oswald. Minneapolis: Augsburg, 1988.

Kruger, Paul A. "The Hem of Garment in Marriage: The Meaning of the Symbolic Gesture in Ruth 3:9 and Ezek 16:8." *JNSL* 12 (1984): 79-86.

Kühne, Hartmut. "The Urbanization of Assyrian Provinces." In *Nuove fondazioni nel Vicino Oriente Antico: Realtà e ideologia.* Edited by Stefania Mazzoni, 55–84. Pisa: Giardini, 1994.

Kutsko, John F. *Between Heaven and Earth: Divine Presence and Absence in the Book of Ezekiel.* Biblical and Judaic Studies 7. Winona Lake: Eisenbrauns, 2000.

LaBianca, Øystein. "Salient Features of Iron Age Tribal Kingdoms." In *Ancient Ammon.* Edited by Burton MacDonald and Randall W. Younker, 19-23. Studies in the History and Culture of the Ancient Near East 42. Leiden: Brill, 1999.

LaBianca, Øystein S., and Randall W. Younker. "The Kingdoms of Ammon, Moab and Edom: The Archaeology of Society in Late Bronze/Iron Age Transjordan (ca. 1400-500 BCE)." In *The Archaeology of Society in the Holy Land.* Edited by Thomas E. Levy, 399-415. London: Facts on File, 1995.

LaCocque, André. *Ruth*. Translated by K. C. Hanson. CC. Minneapolis: Fortress, 2004.
Lalleman, Hetty. *Celebrating Law? Rethinking Old Testament Ethics*. Carlisle: Paternoster, 2004.
Lamarque, Peter. "On Not Expecting Too Much from Narrative." *Mind & Language* 19 (2004): 393-408.
Lapsley, Jacqueline E. *Whispering the Word: Hearing Women's Stories in the Old Testament*. Louisville: Westminster John Knox, 2005.
Lau, Peter H. W. "Gentile Incorporation into Israel in Ezra–Nehemiah?" *Bib* 90 (2009).
———. "Review of Hetty Lalleman, *Celebrating Law? Rethinking Old Testament Ethics*." *RTR* 65 (2006): 177-78.
Leach, Edmund R. *Culture and Communication*. Cambridge: Cambridge University Press, 1976.
Leeb, Carolyn S. "The Widow: Homeless and Post-Menopausal." *BTB* 32 (2002): 160-62.
Leggett, Donald A. *The Levirate and Goel Institutions in the Old Testament*. Cherry Hill: Mack, 1974.
Lemche, Niels P. *Early Israel: Anthropological and Historical Studies on the Israelite Society before the Monarchy*. Leiden: Brill, 1985.
Levering, Matthew. *Ezra and Nehemiah*. Grand Rapids: Brazos Press, 2007.
Levin, Yigal. "Who Was the Chronicler's Audience? A Hint from His Genealogies." *JBL* 122 (2003): 229-45.
Levine, Amy-Jill. "Ruth." In *The Women's Bible Commentary*. Edited by Carol A. Newsom and Sharon H. Ringe, 78-84. London: SPCK, 1992.
Levine, Baruch A. "In Praise of the Israelite *Mišpaḥâ*: Legal Themes in the Book of Ruth." In *The Quest for the Kingdom of God: Studies in Honor of George E. Mendenhall*. Edited by Herbert B. Huffmon, Frank A. Spina and Alberto R. W. Green, 95-106. Winona Lake: Eisenbrauns, 1983.
———. *Numbers 21-36*. AB 4A. New York: Doubleday, 2000.
LeVine, Robert A., and Donald T. Campbell. *Ethnocentrism: Theories of Conflict, Ethnic Attitudes, and Group Behavior*. New York: Wiley, 1971.
Levinson, Bernard M. "The Reconceptualization of Kingship in Deuteronomy and the Deuteronomistic History's Transformation of Torah." *VT* 51 (2001): 511-34.
Linafelt, Tod, and Timothy K. Beal. *Ruth & Esther*. Berit Olam. Collegeville: Liturgical Press, 1999.
Lipiński, E. "Le mariage de Ruth." *VT* 26 (1976): 124-27.
Lipschits, Oded. "Archaemenid Imperial Policy and the Status of Jerusalem." In *Judah and the Judeans in the Persian Period*. Edited by Oded Lipschits and Manfred Oeming, 19-52. Winona Lake: Eisenbrauns, 2006.
———. *The Fall and Rise of Jerusalem: Judah under Babylonian Rule*. Winona Lake: Eisenbrauns, 2005.

Lohfink, Norbert. "Poverty in the Laws of the Ancient Near East and of the Bible." *TS* 52 (1991): 34-50.
Longman, Tremper. *The Book of Ecclesiastes*. NICOT. Grand Rapids: Eerdmans, 1998.
———. *Fictional Akkadian Autobiography: A Generic and Comparative Study*. Winona Lake: Eisenbrauns, 1991.
Lowery, Richard H. *The Reforming Kings*. JSOTSup 120. Sheffield: JSOT Press, 1991.
Lys, Daniel. "Résidence ou repos? Notule sur Ruth ii 7." *VT* 21 (1971): 497-501.

Macalister, R. A. Stewart. *The Philistines: Their History and Civilization*. Oxford: Oxford University Press, 1914.
Maccoby, Eleanor E. *The Two Sexes: Growing Up Apart, Coming Together*. Cambridge, Mass.: Belknap Press, 1998.
MacIntyre, Alasdair. *After Virtue: A Study in Moral Theory*. 2d ed. Notre Dame: University of Notre Dame Press, 1984.
MacKinnon, Catharine A. *Feminism Unmodified: Discourses on Life and Law*. Cambridge, Mass.: Harvard University Press, 1987.
Malina, Bruce J. "Interpretation: Reading, Abduction, Metaphor." In *The Bible and the Politics of Exegesis: Essays in Honour of Norman K. Gottwald on His Sixty-fifth Birthday*. Edited by David Jobling, Peggy L. Day and Gerald T. Shepherd, 253-66. Cleveland: Pilgrim Press, 1991.
———. "The Social Sciences and Biblical Interpretation." In *The Bible and Liberation: Political and Social Hermeneutics*. Edited by Norman K. Gottwald, 11-25. Maryknoll: Orbis, 1983.
Malina, Bruce J., and Jerome H. Neyrey. "First-Century Personality." In *The Social World of Luke-Acts: Models for Interpretation*. Edited by Jerome H. Neyrey, 67-96. Peabody: Hendrickson, 1991.
———. "Honor and Shame in Luke-Acts: Pivotal Values of the Mediterranean World." In *The Social World of Luke-Acts: Models for Interpretation*. Edited by Jerome H. Neyrey, 25-65. Peabody: Hendrickson, 1991.
Malina, Bruce J., and Jerome H. Neyrey. *Portraits of Paul: An Archaeology of Ancient Personality*. Louisville: Westminster John Knox, 1996.
Mann, Thomas W. *The Book of the Torah: The Narrative Integrity of the Pentateuch*. Atlanta: John Knox Press, 1988.
Martin, Michael W. "Betrothal Journey Narratives." *CBQ* 70 (2008): 505-23.
Matthews, Victor H. "The Determination of Social Identity in the Story of Ruth." *BTB* 36 (2006): 49-54.
———. *Judges/Ruth*. NCBC. Cambridge: Cambridge University Press, 2004.
Matthews, Victor H., and Don C. Benjamin. *Social World of Ancient Israel, 1250-587 BCE*. Peabody: Hendrickson, 1993.
———, eds. *Honor and Shame in the World of the Bible*, Semeia 68. Atlanta: Scholars Press, 1994.

Mazar, Amihay. *Archaeology of the Land of the Bible: 10,000-586 B.C.E.* New York: Doubleday, 1992.
McBride, S. Dean. "Polity of the Covenant People: The Book of Deuteronomy." *Int* 41 (1987): 229-44.
McConville, J. G. *Exploring the Old Testament: The Prophets.* Vol. 4. London: SPCK, 2002.
———. "Ezra-Nehemiah and the Fulfilment of Prophecy." *VT* 36 (1986): 205-24.
McKeating, Henry. "Ezekiel the 'Prophet Like Moses'?" *JSOT* 61 (1994): 97-109.
McNutt, Paula M. *Reconstructing the Society of Ancient Israel.* Louisville: Westminster John Knox, 1999.
Meinhold, Arndt. "Theologische Schwerpunkte im Buch Ruth und ihr Gewicht für Datierung." *TZ* 32 (1976): 129-37.
Mendels, Doron. *The Rise and Fall of Jewish Nationalism: Jewish and Christian Ethnicity in Ancient Palestine.* Grand Rapids: Eerdmans, 1997.
Meyers, Carol L. *Discovering Eve: Ancient Israelite Women in Context.* Oxford: Oxford University Press, 1988.
———. "Everyday Life of Women in the Period of the Hebrew Bible." In *The Women's Bible Commentary.* Edited by Carol A. Newsom and Sharon H. Ringe, 251-59. Louisville: Westminster John Knox, 1998.
———. "The Family in Early Israel." In *Families in Ancient Israel.* Edited by Leo G. Perdue, Joseph Blenkinsopp, John J. Collins and Carol Meyers, 1-47. Louisville: Westminster John Knox, 1997.
———. "Returning Home: Ruth 1.8 and the Gendering of the Book of Ruth." In *A Feminist Companion to Ruth.* Edited by A. Brenner, 85-114. Sheffield: Sheffield Academic Press, 1993.
———. "'To Her Mother's House': Considering a Counterpart to the Israelite *bêt'ab*." In *The Bible and the Politics of Exegesis: Essays in Honour of Norman K. Gottwald on His Sixty-fifth Birthday.* Edited by David Jobling, Peggy L. Day and Gerald T. Shepherd, 39-51. Cleveland: Pilgrim Press, 1991.
———. "'Women of the Neighbourhood' (Ruth 4.17): Informal Female Networks in Ancient Israel." In *Ruth and Esther: A Feminist Companion to the Bible.* Edited by Athalya Brenner, 110-27. Sheffield: Sheffield Academic Press, 1999.
Meyers, Carol L., and Eric M. Meyers. *Haggai, Zechariah 1-8.* AB 25B. New York: Doubleday, 1987.
Milgrom, Jacob. *Leviticus 1-16.* AB 3. New York: Doubleday, 1992.
———. *Leviticus 23-27.* AB 3B. New York: Doubleday, 2000.
Millar, J. Gary. *Now Choose Life: Theology and Ethics in Deuteronomy.* New Studies in Biblical Theology 6. Leicester: Apollos, 1999.
Miller, J. Maxwell, and John H. Hayes. *A History of Ancient Israel and Judah.* 2d ed. Louisville: Westminster John Knox, 2006.
Miller, James C. "Ethnicity and the Hebrew Bible: Problems and Prospects." *CurBS* 6 (2008): 170-213.

Mills, Mary E. *Biblical Morality: Moral Perspectives in Old Testament Narratives*. Aldershot: Ashgate, 2001.

Moore, Michael S. "To King or Not to King: A Canonical-Historical Approach to Ruth." *BBR* 11 (2001): 27-41.

Morgenstern, Mira. "Ruth and the Sense of Self: Midrash and Difference." *Judaism* 48 (1999): 131-45.

Morris, Leon. *Ruth: An Introduction and Commentary*. TOTC. Downers Grove: InterVarsity, 1968.

Murdock, George P., and Caterina Provost. "Factors in the Division of Labor by Sex: A Cross-Cultural Analysis." *Ethnology* 12 (1973): 203-25.

Myers, Jacob M. *Ezra, Nehemiah*. AB 14. New York: Doubleday, 1965.

———. *The Linguistic and Literary Form of the Book of Ruth*. Leiden: Brill, 1955.

Na'aman, Nadav. "When and How Did Jerusalem Become a Great City? The Rise of Jerusalem as Judah's Premier City in the Eighth-Seventh Centuries B.C.E." *BASOR* 347 (2007): 21-56.

Nash, Peter T. "Ruth: An Exercise in Israelite Political Correctness or a Call to Proper Conversion?" In *The Pitcher is Broken: Memorial Essays for Gösta W. Ahlström*. Edited by Steven W. Holloway and Lowell K. Handy, 347-54. JSOT 190. Sheffield: Sheffield Academic Press, 1995.

Nelson, Richard D. *Raising Up a Faithful Priest: Community and Priesthood in Biblical Theology*. Louisville: Westminster John Knox, 1993.

Netzer, Ehud. "Domestic Architecture in the Iron Age." In *The Architecture of Ancient Israel from the Prehistoric to the Persian Periods*. Edited by Aharon Kempinski and Ronny Reich, 193-201. Jerusalem: Israel Exploration Society, 1992.

Newsome, James D., Jr. "Toward a New Understanding of the Chronicler and His Purposes." *JBL* 94 (1975): 201-17.

Neyrey, Jerome H. *Honor and Shame in the Gospel of Matthew*. Louisville: Westminster John Knox, 1998.

Nicholson, Ernest W. *Deuteronomy and Tradition*. Philadelphia: Fortress, 1967.

———. "'Do Not Dare to Set a Foreigner Over You': The King in Deuteronomy and 'The Great King'." *ZAW* 118 (2006): 46-61.

———. "The Meaning of the Expression עם הארץ in the Old Testament." *JSS* 10 (1965): 59-66.

Niditch, Susan. "Legends of Wise Heroes and Heroines." In *The Hebrew Bible and Its Modern Interpreters*. Edited by Douglas A. Knight and Gene M. Tucker, 445-63. Philadelphia: Fortress, 1985.

Niehoff, Maren. "Do Biblical Characters Talk to Themselves? Narrative Modes of Representing Inner Speech in Early Biblical Fiction." *JBL* 111 (1992): 577-95.

Nielsen, Kirsten. *Ruth: A Commentary*. Translated by Edward Broadbridge. OTL. Louisville: Westminster John Knox, 1997.

Noth, Martin. *Numbers*. OTL. London: SCM, 1968.

Noth, Martin. *The History of Israel*. Translated by Peter R. Ackroyd. 2d ed. London: A. C. Blace, 1960.
Novitz, David. *The Boundaries of Art*. Philadelphia: Temple University Press, 1992.
Nussbaum, Martha C. *Love's Knowledge: Essays on Philosophy and Literature*. New York: Oxford University Press, 1990.

Oakes, Penelope J. "The Salience of Social Categories." In *Rediscovering the Social Group: A Self-Categorization Theory*. Edited by John C. Turner, Michael A. Hogg, Penelope J. Oakes, S. D. Reicher and M. S. Wetherell, 117-41. Oxford: Basil Blackwell, 1987.
Oakes, Penelope J., S. Alexander Haslam, and John C. Turner. *Stereotyping and Social Reality*. Oxford: Basil Blackwell, 1994.
Oded, Bustenay. *Mass Deportations and Deportees in the Neo-Assyrian Empire*. Wiesbaden: Reichert, 1979.
———. "Where Is the 'Myth of the Empty Land' To Be Found? History versus Myth." In *Judah and the Judeans in the Neo-Babylonian Period*. Edited by Oded Lipschits and Joseph Blenkinsopp, 55-74. Winona Lake: Eisenbrauns, 2003.
Ogden, Graham S. "The Northern Extent of Josiah's Reform." *ABR* 26 (1978): 26-34.
Olyan, Saul M. "Honor, Shame, and Covenant Relations in Ancient Israel and Its Environment." *JBL* 115 (1996): 201-18.
———. "Purity Ideology in Ezra-Nehemiah as a Tool to Reconstitute the Community." *JSJ* 35 (2004): 1-16.
———. *Rites and Rank: Hierarchy in Biblical Representations of Cult*. Princeton: Princeton University Press, 2000.
———. "The Search for the Elusive Self in Texts of the Hebrew Bible." In *Religion and the Self in Antiquity*. Edited by David Brakke, Michael L. Satlow and Steven Weitzman, 40-50. Bloomington: Indiana University Press, 2005.
Otto, Eckart. "Review of John Barton, *Understanding Old Testament Ethics: Approaches and Explorations*." *Review of Biblical Literature* [http://www.bookreviews.org] (2003).
———. *Theologische Ethik des Alten Testaments*. Theologische Wissenschaft 3/2. Stuttgart: Kohlhammer, 1994.

Parry, Robin A. *Old Testament Story and Christian Ethics: The Rape of Dinah as a Case Study*. Paternoster Biblical Monographs. Bletchley: Paternoster, 2004.
Patrick, Dale, and Allen Scult. *Rhetoric and Biblical Interpretation*. JSOTSup 82. Sheffield: Almond, 1990.
Pedersen, Johannes. *Israel: Its Life and Culture*, Vol. I-II. London, Oxford University Press, 1926.

Peristiany, John G. "Introduction." In *Honor and Grace in Anthropology*. Edited by John G. Peristiany and Julian A. Pitt-Rivers, 1-17. Cambridge: Cambridge University Press, 1992.

Pettigrew, Thomas F. "Intergroup Contact Theory." *Annual Review of Psychology* 49 (1998): 65-85.

Pettigrew, Thomas F., Oliver Christ, Ulrich Wagner, and Jost Stellmacher. "Direct and Indirect Intergroup Contact Effects on Prejudice: A Normative Interpretation." *International Journal of Intercultural Relations* 31 (2007): 411-25.

Pfeiffer, Robert H. *Introduction to the Old Testament*. London: Adam & Charles Black, 1948.

Phillips, Anthony. "The Book of Ruth - Deception and Shame." *JJS* 37 (1986): 1-17.

Polkinghorne, Donald. *Narrative Knowing and the Human Sciences*. Albany: State University of New York Press, 1988.

Polzin, Robert. *Late Biblical Hebrew: Toward an Historical Typology of Biblical Hebrew Prose*. HSM 12. Missoula: Scholars Press, 1976.

Porten, Bezalel. "The Scroll of Ruth: A Rhetorical Study." *Gratz College Annual* 7 (1978): 23-49.

Pratto, Felicia. "Sexual Politics: The Gender Gap in the Bedroom, the Cupboard, and the Cabinet." In *Sex, Power, and Conflict: Evolutionary and Feminist Perspectives*. Edited by David M. Buss and Neil M. Malamuth, 179-230. New York: Oxford University Press, 1996.

Pressler, Carolyn. *Joshua, Judges, Ruth*. Westminster Bible Companion. Louisville: Westminster John Knox, 2002.

Prinsloo, W. S. "The Theology of the Book of Ruth." *VT* 30 (1980): 330-41.

Rad, Gerhard von. *Das Geschichtsbild des chronistischen Werkes*. BWANT 54. Stuttgart: Kohlhammer, 1930.

———. *Old Testament Theology*. Translated by D. M. G. Stalker. Edinburgh: Oliver & Boyd, 1965.

Rainey, Anson F. "Whence Came the Israelites and Their Language?" *IEJ* 57 (2007): 41-64.

Rauber, D. F. "Literary Values in the Bible: The Book of Ruth." *JBL* 89 (1970): 27-37.

Redfield, Robert, Ralph Linton, and Melville J. Herskovits. "Memorandum for the Study of Acculturation." *American Anthropologist* 38 (1936): 149-52.

Rendsburg, Gary A. "Eblaite *U-MA* and Hebrew *WM-*." In *Eblaitica: Essays on the Ebla Archives and Eblaite Language*. Edited by Cyrus H. Gordon, Gary A. Rendsburg and Nathan H. Winter, 33-41. Winona Lake: Eisenbrauns, 1987.

Renz, Thomas. *The Rhetorical Function of the Book of Ezekiel*. Leiden: Brill, 1999.

Reviv, Hanoch. *The Society in the Kingdoms of Israel and Judah*. Jerusalem: Bialik Institute, 1993.

Reynolds, Katherine J., John C. Turner, and S. Alexander Haslam. "When are We Better than Them and They Worse than Us? A Closer Look at Social Discrimination and Positive and Negative Domains." *Journal of Personality and Social Psychology* 78 (2000): 64-80.

Ricoeur, Paul. *Interpretation Theory: Discourse and the Surplus of Meaning.* Fort Worth: Texas Christian University Press, 1976.

———. "The Model of the Text: Meaningful Action Considered as a Text." In *Hermeneutics and the Human Sciences: Essays on Language, Action, and Interpretation.* Edited by John B. Thompson, 197-221. Cambridge: Cambridge University Press, 1981.

———. "Myth as the Bearer of Possible Worlds." In *A Ricoeur Reader: Reflection and Imagination.* Edited by Mario J. Valdés, 482-90. New York: Harvester Wheatsheaf, 1991.

———. "Reply to Peter Kemp." In *The Philosophy of Paul Ricoeur.* Edited by Lewis Edwin Hahn, 395-98. Chicago: Open Court, 1995.

———. *Time and Narrative.* Translated by Kathleen Blamey and David Pellauer. 3 vols. Chicago: Chicago University Press, 1984-1988.

Riley, William. *King and Cultus in Chronicles: Worship and the Reinterpretation of History.* Sheffield: JSOT Press, 1993.

Ringgren, Helmer. *Israelite Religion.* Translated by David Green. London: SPCK, 1966.

Robbins, Vernon K. "Social-Scientific Criticism and Literary Studies: Prospects for Cooperation in Biblical Interpretation." In *Modelling Early Christianity: Social-Scientific Studies of the New Testament in Its Context.* Edited by Philip F. Esler, 274-89. London: Routledge, 1995.

Robinson, H. Wheeler. "Hebrew Psychology." In *The People and the Book: Essays on the Old Testament.* Edited by Arthur S. Peake, 353-82. Oxford: Clarendon, 1925.

Rogerson, John W. "The Hebrew Conception of Corporate Personality: A Re-Examination." *JTS* 21 (1970): 1-16.

Rom-Shiloni, Dalit. "Socio-Ideological *Setting* or *Settings* for Penitential Prayers?" In *Seeking the Favor of God. Volume 1: The Origins of Penitential Prayer in Second Temple Judaism.* Edited by Mark J. Boda, Daniel K. Falk and Rodney A. Werline, 51-68. Atlanta: Society of Biblical Literature, 2006.

Rooker, Mark F. *Biblical Hebrew in Transition: The Language of the Book of Ezekiel.* JSOTSup 90. Sheffield: JSOT Press, 1990.

Roop, Eugene F. *Ruth, Jonah, Esther.* Believers Church Bible Commentary. Scottsdale: Herald, 2002.

Rosaldo, Michelle Z., and Louise Lamphere. "Introduction." In *Woman, Culture, and Society.* Edited by Michelle Z. Rosaldo and Louise Lamphere, 1-16. Stanford: Stanford University Press, 1974.

Rowley, H. H. "The Marriage of Ruth." In *The Servant of the Lord and Other Essays on the Old Testament*, 169-94. Oxford: Blackwell, 1965.

Rowton, M. B. "Dimorphic Structure and the Parasocial Element." *JNES* 36 (1977): 181-98.
Ruble, Diane N., and Carol L. Martin. "Gender Development." In *Handbook of Child Psychology*. Edited by William Damon, 933–1016. New York: J. Wiley, 1998.
Rudolph, Wilhelm. *Das Buch Ruth, das Hohe Lied, die Klagelider*. KAT 17. Gütersloh: Mohn, 1962.
Rust, Eric C. *Judges, Ruth, 1 & 2 Samuel*. The Layman's Bible Commentaries. London: SCM, 1961.

Sahlins, Marshall D. *Tribesmen*. Englewood Cliffs: Prentice-Hall, 1968.
Sakenfeld, Katharine D. *Just Wives?: Stories of Power and Survival in the Old Testament and Today*. Louisville: Westminster John Knox, 2003.
———. *The Meaning of Hesed in the Hebrew Bible: A New Enquiry*. HSM 17. Missoula: Scholars Press, 1978.
———. *Ruth*. Interpretation. Louisville: John Knox Press, 1999.
Sarna, Nahum M. *Genesis*. JPS Torah Commentary. Philadelphia: JPS, 1989.
Sasson, Jack M. "Ruth." In *The Literary Guide to the Bible*. Edited by R. Alter and F. Kermode, 320-28. London: Fontana, 1987.
———. *Ruth: A New Translation with a Philological Commentary and a Formalist-Folklorist Interpretation*. 2d ed. Sheffield: JSOT Press, 1989.
Satlow, Michael L. *Jewish Marriage in Antiquity*. Princeton: Princeton University Press, 2001.
Saxegaard, Kristin M. "'More than Seven Sons': Ruth as Example of the Good Son." *SJOT* 15 (2001): 257-75.
Schniedewind, William M. *How the Bible Became a Book: The Textualization of Ancient Israel*. Cambridge: Cambridge University Press, 2004.
Service, Elman R. *Primitive Social Organization: An Evolutionary Perspective*. New York: Random House, 1962.
Shepherd, David. "Violence in the Fields? Translating, Reading, and Revising in Ruth 2." *CBQ* 63 (2001): 444-63.
Sherif, Muzafer, and Carolyn W. Sherif. *Groups in Harmony and Tension: An Integration of Studies on Intergroup Relations*. New York: Harper, 1953.
Shiloh, Yigal. "The Population of Iron Age Palestine in the Light of a Sample Analysis of Urban Plans, Areas, and Population Density." *BASOR* 239 (1980): 25-35.
Shulman, Ahouva. "The Particle נָא in Biblical Hebrew Prose." *HS* 40 (1999): 57-82.
Smith, Daniel L. *The Religion of the Landless: The Social Context of the Babylonian Exile*. Bloomington: Meyer Stone Books, 1989.
Smith, Mark S. "'Your People Shall Be My People': Family and Covenant in Ruth 1:16-17." *CBQ* 69 (2007): 242-58.

Smith, Peter B., and Michael H. Bond. *Social Psychology Across Cultures: Analysis and Perspectives.* New York: Harvester Wheatsheaf, 1993.

Sonsino, Rifat. *Motive Clauses in Hebrew Law: Biblical Forms and Near Eastern Parallels.* SBLDS 45. Chico, Calif.: Scholars Press, 1980.

Sparks, Kenton L. *Ethnicity and Identity in Ancient Israel: Prolegomena to the Study of Ethnic Sentiments and Their Expression in the Hebrew Bible.* Winona Lake: Eisenbrauns, 1998.

Spina, Frank A. "Israelites as *gerim*, 'Sojourners,' in Social and Historical Context." In *The Word of the Lord Shall Go Forth: Essays in Honor of David Noel Freedman in Celebration of His Sixtieth Birthday.* Edited by Carol L. Meyers and Michael P. O'Connor, 321-35. Winona Lake: Eisenbrauns, 1983.

Stager, Lawrence E. "The Archaeology of the Family in Ancient Israel." *BASOR* 260 (1985): 1-35.

Stangor, Charles, Laure Lynch, Changming Duan, and Beth Glass. "Categorization of Individuals on the Basis of Multiple Social Features." *Journal of Personality & Social Psychology* 62 (1992): 207-18.

Stern, Ephraim. *Archaeology of the Land of the Bible: The Assyrian, Babylonian, and Persian Periods, 732-332 BCE.* New York: Doubleday, 2001.

Sternberg, Meir. *The Poetics of Biblical Narrative.* Bloomington: Indiana University Press, 1985.

Sussman, Nan M. "The Dynamic Nature of Cultural Identity Throughout Cultural Transitions: Why Home Is Not So Sweet." *Personality and Social Psychology Review* 4 (2000): 355-73.

Sweely, Tracy L. "Gender, Space, People, and Power at Cerén, El Salvador." In *Manifesting Power: Gender and the Interpretation of Power in Archaeology.* Edited by Tracy L. Sweely, 155-71. London: Routledge, 1999.

Tadmor, Hayim. "'The People' and the Kingship in Ancient Israel: The Role of the Political Institutions in the Biblical Period." *Journal of World History* 11 (1968): 46-68.

Tajfel, Henri. *Differentiation between Social Groups: Studies in the Social Psychology of Intergroup Relations.* London: Academic, 1978.

———. "La catégorisation sociale." In *Introduction à la Psychologie Sociale.* Edited by Serge Moscovici. Paris: Larousse, 1972.

———. "Social Stereotypes and Social Groups." In *Intergroup Behaviour.* Edited by John C. Turner and Howard Giles, 144-67. Oxford: Basil Blackwell, 1981.

Tajfel, Henri, and John C. Turner. "An Integrative Theory of Intergroup Conflict." In *The Social Psychology of Intergroup Relations.* Edited by William G. Austin and Stephen Worchel, 33-47. Monterey: Brooks/Cole, 1979.

Taylor, Charles. *Sources of the Self: The Making of the Modern Identity.* Cambridge: Cambridge University Press, 1989.

Terry, Deborah J., and Michael A. Hogg. "Group Norms and the Attitude-Behavior Relationship: A Role for Group Identification." *Personality and Social Psychology Bulletin* 22 (1996): 776-93.
Thompson, Thomas L. *The Mythic Past: Biblical Archaeology and the Myth of Israel.* New York: Basic Books, 1999.
Thompson, Thomas, and Dorothy Thompson. "Some Legal Problems in the Book of Ruth." *VT* 18 (1968): 79-99.
Throntveit, Mark A. *Ezra-Nehemiah.* Interpretation. Louisville: John Knox Press, 1992.
Tigay, Jeffrey H. *Deuteronomy.* JPS Torah Commentary. Philadelphia: The Jewish Publication Society, 1996.
Trafimow, David, Ellen S. Silverman, Ruth M. Fan, and Josephine S. F. Law. "The Effects of Language and Priming on the Relative Accessibility of the Private Self and the Collective Self." *Journal of Cross-Cultural Psychology* 28 (1997): 107-23.
Triandis, Harry C. "Collectivism and Individualism as Cultural Syndromes." *Cross-Cultural Research* 27 (1993): 155-80.
———. "Individualism and Collectivism." In *The Handbook of Culture and Psychology.* Edited by David R. Matsumoto, 35-50. Oxford: Oxford University Press, 2001.
Triandis, Harry C., Robert Bontempo, Marcelo J. Villareal, Masaaki Asai, and Nydia Lucca. "Individualism and Collectivism: Cross-Cultural Perspectives on Self-Group Relationships." *Journal of Personality and Social Psychology* 54 (1988): 323-38.
Triandis, Harry C., Christopher McCusker, Hector Betancourt, Sumiko Iwao, Kwok Leung, Jose Miguel Salazar, Bernadette Setiadi, Jai B. P. Sinha, Hubert Touzard, and Zbigniew Zaleski. "An Etic-Emic Analysis of Individualism and Collectivism." *Journal of Cross-Cultural Psychology* 24 (1993): 366-83.
Triandis, Harry C., and David Trafimow. "Cross-National Prevalence of Collectivism." In *Individual Self, Relational Self, Collective Self.* Edited by Marilynn B. Brewer and Constantine Sedikides, 259-76. Philadelphia: Psychology Press, 2001.
Trible, Phyllis. *God and the Rhetoric of Sexuality.* Philadelphia: Fortress, 1978.
———. "Ruth, Book of." In *ABD.* Edited by David N. Freedman, 5:842-47. New York: Doubleday, 1992.
Tropp, Linda R., and Thomas F. Pettigrew. "Differential Relationships between Intergroup Contact and Affective and Cognitive Dimensions of Prejudice." *Personality And Social Psychology Bulletin* 31 (2005): 1145-58.
Turner, John C. *Rediscovering the Social Group: A Self-Categorization Theory.* Oxford: Basil Blackwell, 1987.
———. "Social Categorization and the Self-Concept: A Social Cognitive Theory of Group Behaviour." In *Advances in Group Processes.* Edited by Edward J. Lawler, 77-122. Greenwich: JAI Press, 1985.

———. "Social Identification and Psychological Group Formation." In *The Social Dimension: European Developments in Social Psychology.* Edited by Henri Tajfel. Cambridge: Cambridge University Press, 1984.

———. "Towards a Cognitive Redefinition of the Social Group." In *Social Identity and Intergroup Relations.* Edited by Henri Tajfel, 15-40. Cambridge: Cambridge University Press, 1982.

Turner, John C., and Howard Giles. *Intergroup Behaviour.* Oxford: Basil Blackwell, 1981.

Turner, John C., and Rina S. Onorato. "Social Identity, Personality, and the Self-Concept: A Self-Categorization Perspective." In *The Psychology of the Social Self.* Edited by Tom R. Tyler, Roderick Moreland Kramer and Oliver P. John, 11-46. Mahwah, N.J.: Lawrence Erlbaum Associates, 1999.

Turner, Victor W. *The Ritual Process: Structure and Anti-Structure.* London: Routledge & Kegan Paul, 1969.

Ullendorff, Edward. "C'est de l'hebreu pour moi!" *JSS* 13 (1968): 125-35.

Vesco, Jean-Luc. "La date du livre de Ruth." *RB* 74 (1967): 235-47.

Voci, Alberto, and Miles Hewstone. "Intergroup Contact and Prejudice toward Immigrants in Italy: The Mediational Role of Anxiety and the Moderational Role of Group Salience." *Group Processes & Intergroup Relations* 6 (2003): 37-54.

Wallace, Constance. "*WM-* in Nehemiah 5:11." In *Eblaitica: Essays on the Ebla Archives and Eblaite Language.* Edited by Cyrus H. Gordon, Gary A. Rendsburg and Nathan H. Winter, 31. Winona Lake: Eisenbrauns, 1987.

Weeks, Stuart D. E. "Biblical Literature and the Emergence of Ancient Jewish Nationalism." *BibInt* 10 (2002): 144-57.

Weinberg, Joel P. *The Citizen-Temple Community.* Translated by Daniel L. Smith-Christopher. Sheffield: JSOT Press, 1992.

Weinfeld, Moshe. "Ruth, Book of." In *Encyclopaedia Judaica*, 518-22. Jerusalem: Keter Publishing House, 1996.

Welch, Adam C. "The Death of Josiah." *ZAW* 43 (1925): 255-60.

Wenham, Gordon J. "The Gap between Law and Ethics in the Bible." *JJS* 48 (1997): 17-29.

———. *Story as Torah: Reading the Old Testament Ethically.* Edinburgh: T&T Clark, 2000.

Westbrook, Raymond. *Property and Family in Biblical Laws.* JSOTSup 113. Sheffield: Sheffield Academic, 1991.

White, Hayden V. *The Content of the Form: Narrative Discourse and Historical Representation.* Baltimore: Johns Hopkins University Press, 1987.

Wilch, John R. *Ruth: A Theological Exposition of Sacred Scripture.* Concordia Commentary. St. Louis: Concordia Publishing House, 2006.

Willi-Plein, Ina. "Problems of Intermarriage in Postexilic Times." In *Shai: Studies in the Bible, Its Exegesis and Language Presented to Sara Japhet*. Edited by Moshe Bar-Asher, Dalit Rom-Shiloni, Emanuel Tov and Nili Wazana, 177-89. Jerusalem: The Bialik Institute, 2007.

Williams, Gareth. "The Genesis of Chronic Illness: Narrative Re-Construction." *Sociology of Health and Illness* 6 (1984): 175-200.

Williamson, H. G. M. *Ezra and Nehemiah*. OTG. Sheffield: JSOT Press, 1987.

———. *Ezra, Nehemiah*. Waco: Word, 1985.

———. "The Family in Persian Period Judah: Some Textual Reflections." In *Symbiosis, Symbolism, and the Power of the Past: Canaan, Ancient Israel, and Their Neighbors from the Late Bronze Age through Roman Palaestina: Proceedings of the Centennial Symposium W. F. Albright Institute of Archaeological Research and American Schools of Oriental Research Jerusalem, May 29-31, 2000*. Edited by William G. Dever and Seymour Gitin, 469-85. Winona Lake: Eisenbrauns, 2003.

———. "Judah and the Jew." In *Studies in Persian History: Essays in Memory of David M. Lewis*. Edited by Maria Brosius and Amelie Kuhrt, 145-63. Leiden: Nederlands Instituut voor het Nabije Oosten, 1998.

Willis, Timothy M. *The Elders of the City: A Study of the Elders-Laws in Deuteronomy*. Atlanta: SBL, 2001.

Wirth, Louis. "Urbanism as a Way of Life." *The American Journal of Sociology* 44 (1938): 1-24.

Wolde, Ellen van. *Ruth and Naomi*. London: SCM, 1997.

———. "Texts in Dialogue with Texts: Intertextuality in the Ruth and Tamar Narratives." *BibInt* 5 (1997): 1-28.

Wolf, C. Umhau. "Terminology of Israel's Tribal Organization." JBL 65 (1946).

Wood, Wendy, and Alice H. Eagly. "A Cross-Cultural Analysis of the Behavior of Women and Men: Implications for the Origins of Sex Differences." *Psychological Bulletin* 128 (2002): 699-727.

Wright, Christopher J. H. *Old Testament Ethics for the People of God*. Leicester: IVP, 2004.

Wright, Jacob L. "Writing the Restoration: Compositional Agenda and the Role of Ezra in Nehemiah 8." *Journal of Hebrew Scriptures* 7 (2007): 19-29.

Würthwein, Ernst. *Die fünf Megilloth: Ruth, Das hohelied, Esther*. HAT 18. Tübingen: Mohr, 1969.

Wyer, Robert S., and Thomas K. Srull. "Human Cognition in Its Social Context." *Psychological Review* 93 (1986): 322-59.

Yamasaki, Gary. *Watching a Biblical Narrative: Point of View in Biblical Exegesis*. New York: T&T Clark, 2008.

Yorburg, Betty. "The Nuclear and the Extended Family: An Area of Conceptual Confusion." *Journal of Comparative Family Studies* 6 (1975): 5-14.

Young, Ian. "Biblical Texts Cannot be Dated Linguistically." *HS* 46 (2005): 341-51.
———. "Evidence of Diversity in Pre-Exilic Hebrew." *HS* 38 (1997): 7-20.
———. "Late Biblical Hebrew and the Qumran Pesher Habakkuk." *Journal of Hebrew Scriptures* 8 (2008): 1-38.
Young, Ian, Robert Rezetko, and Martin Ehrensvärd. *Linguistic Dating of Biblical Texts*. London: Equinox, 2008.
Younger, K. Lawson. *Judges and Ruth*. NIV Application Commentary. Grand Rapids: Zondervan, 2002.
Yuki, Masaki. "Intergroup Comparison versus Intragroup Relationships: A Cross-Cultural Examination of Social Identity Theory in North American and East Asian Cultural Contexts." *Social Psychology Quarterly* 66 (2003): 166-83.

Zakovitch, Yair. *Das Buch Rut: Ein jüdischer Kommentar*. Translated by Andreas Lehnardt. SBS 177. Stuttgart: Katholisches Bibelwerk, 1999.
Zenger, Erich. *Das Buch Ruth*. ZBK 8. Zürich: Theologischer Verlag, 1986.
Zertal, Adam. "The Wedge-Shaped Decorated Bowl and the Origin of the Samaritans." *BASOR* 276 (1989): 77-84.
Zevit, Ziony. "Dating Ruth: Legal, Linguistic and Historical Observations." *ZAW* 117 (2005): 574-600.
Zlotnick-Sivan, H. "The Silent Women of Yehud: Notes on Ezra 9-10." *JJS* 51 (2000): 3-18.

Scripture Index

Hebrew Bible

Genesis

2:24	102
3:14-19	22
12:1-9	111
16	49
16:1-3	70
19	13, 49, 91, 131
19:30-38	62, 91, 111
21:21	128
24	63, 181
24:14	62
24:16	62
24:28	122
24:33-53	128
25:1-5	62
28:1-9	181
29	13, 63
29-30	111
30:1-6	70
30:3-13	142
30:9-13	70
34	5
34:3	102
35:18	35
38	13, 49, 71-72, 111, 131
38:6	128
38:11	122
38:26	72
38:28-30	139
38:29-30	80
46	168
48:6	69

Exodus

1-18	3
2	63
4:18-26	5
12:39	94
12:43-49	94
19-24	3
19:5	178
20:1-2	3
21-23	5
21:2-11	173
22:22-24	59
22:24-26	173
23:10-11	59
23:11	135
34:11-16	180

Leviticus

5:14-16	180
18-20	5
18:16	72
18:24	28
19	180, 183
19:9-10	59
19:19	180
20:9	22
20:11-12	22
20:16	22
20:21	72
20:27	22

21:7	181	2:8-9	91
21:14-15	181	4-30	3
22:13	122	4:3-4	91
23:22	59, 135	4:6-8	27
25	68, 72, 76, 173, 174	4:40	4
		5:1	178
25:1-7	59	5:1-6	3
25:8-22	173	5:14	158
25:24-25	58	5:15	3
25:25	72, 173	5:16	4
25:35	72	5:33	4
25:35-36	173	6	178
25:36	173	6:3	4
25:39	72, 173	6:18	4
25:43	173	6:24	4
25:46-48	173	7	180, 181
25:47	72	7:1-3	182
25:47-54	58	7:1-4	180, 181
25:49	72	7:1-5	183
		7:3	180
Numbers		7:3-6	180
5:5-8	58	7:13	4
13:1-14:38	22	8:1	4
22-24	91	8:6	179
25	91	9:11-14	181
25:1	91	10:18	59, 68
25:1-3	91	11:2-7	155
26	168	12-25	5
27:4	69	14:21	158
30:10	123	14:22-29	59
35:9-28	58	14:29	59, 135
36:6-9	121	15:1-18	173
		16:9-12	100
Deuteronomy		16:11	59, 94, 135
1-3	3	16:14	94, 135
1-4	3	17:8-18:22	155
1:16	158	17:14-20	156, 185, 186
1:27-30	156	17:15	156
2:1	156	17:16-17	156

17:16c	156	6:25	94
17:20	156	7:16-18	33
19:4-13	58	15	187
21:10-14	180	22:17	91
22-25	174		
22:15	62	*Judges*	
22:16	62	1:1	45, 138
23:1	100	3:12-30	91
23:3-4	28	3:29	91
23:3-6	91	4:17-22	13
23:4-9	181	5:2	187
23:20-21	173	6:15	33
24:10-13	173	10:6	91
24:14	158	11	138
24:16	22, 195	14:2-3	128
24:17	59, 135, 158	15	187
24:19-21	59, 68, 135, 158	15:6	138
25	69, 71	17:6	138, 185
25:5-10	69, 71	18:1	138, 185
25:6	77, 136	19	62, 138
25:8-10	78	19:1	138, 185
25:15	4	19-21	12
26:12-13	59, 68, 135, 158	21	138
26:12-15	59	21:25	138, 185
27:19	158		
27:20	100	*Ruth*	
28:15	179	1	98, 166
28:68	156	1:1	12, 45, 47, 138
29:11	94	1:1-5	53
29:13-14	155	1:1-6	150
29:16-21	195	1:3-5	97, 142
29:21-23	158	1:4	50, 90
30:16	178	1:4-5	77
31-34	3	1:6	90, 130
31:12	94	1:6-9	142
		1:7	90
Joshua		1:8	82, 90, 107, 113, 122, 140
2:19	22		
3-4	33, 156	1:8-9	108, 112, 130

1:8-13	78, 127	2:8-9	57, 60, 98, 102
1:8-15	96	2:9	56, 57, 62
1:9	104	2:10	60, 97, 103, 158
1:11	57, 90	2:10-11	61
1:11-13	71, 85	2:11	58, 65, 70, 96, 98, 103, 107
1:12	57, 90		
1:13	50, 57, 90, 125	2:12	61, 98, 100, 104
1:14	102	2:13	99, 100, 103
1:14-15	95	2:14	56, 60
1:15	93	2:14-16	57, 102, 103
1:16	132	2:15	99
1:16-17	92-93, 96, 102	2:15-16	56, 61, 98
1:17	93	2:16	62
1:19	70, 108, 121, 124	2:17	61, 127
		2:18	60, 96
1:19-21	123	2:18-19	127
1:20	125	2:19	96
1:21	97, 123, 124, 125, 128	2:20	50, 58, 71, 72, 82, 90, 105, 106, 122, 127, 128, 129
1:22	75, 90, 93, 113, 130		
2	55, 58, 60, 62, 63, 64, 83, 102, 105,	2:21	57, 75, 90, 113
		2:22	57, 62, 90, 96, 98, 127, 128, 129
2:1	55, 56, 57, 58, 62, 63, 65, 72, 82, 100, 105, 113, 122, 123		
		2:22-23	99
		2:23	56, 61, 96,
		3	13, 62, 64, 73, 104, 105
2:2	57, 59, 75, 90, 96, 127, 128, 129	3:1	57, 90, 104, 134, 136, 142
2:3	58, 63	3:1-4	106, 130
2:4	55	3:1-5	64
2:5	56, 57, 90, 105, 112	3:2	72, 99, 105, 128
		3:2-4	129
2:6	63, 75, 90, 97, 108, 113	3:3	99, 131
		3:4	139
2:7	102	3:5	104
2:8	57, 90	3:6	64, 104

Reference	Pages	Reference	Pages
3:7-8	131	4:9-10	68, 71, 83, 105, 141
3:7-13	64		
3:8	90, 112	4:10	74, 75, 81, 90, 100, 113, 123, 135, 136, 141
3:9	64, 99-100, 104, 105, 106, 111, 122, 139		
		4:11	90, 101, 111, 138, 142
3:9-13	71, 106		
3:10	57, 65, 78, 81, 82, 83, 90, 108, 133	4:11-12	71, 112, 141, 142
		4:12	80, 90, 111, 138
3:10-12	65	4:13	50, 81, 90, 100, 113, 132
3:11	57, 65, 66, 70, 82, 90, 100, 108, 109	4:14-15	97, 142
		4:14-17	126, 142
3:11-12	133	4:15	90, 97, 113, 170
3:11-13	109	4:15-17	97
3:12	66, 122	4:16-17	71
3:12-13	83, 84, 109	4:17	12, 43, 47, 85, 128, 134, 135
3:13	66, 132		
3:14	21, 66, 90, 112	4:17-22	13, 83, 97, 101, 138, 142
3:15	57		
3:16	57, 90	4:18-22	45, 47, 112, 141
3:18	57, 66, 90, 139	4:22	12, 43
4	69, 150		
4:1-12	105	*1 Samuel*	
4:2	57	2:5	97
4:3	21, 68, 72, 123	4-6	156
4:3-4a	86	9:1	36
4:4	75, 123	10:20-21	33, 36
4:4b	86	15:22	178
4:5	67, 69, 74, 75, 83, 86, 90, 105, 113, 123, 137, 141, 191	15:32	125
		22:3-4	91
		25:41	100
4:5-6	73, 76, 123	*2 Samuel*	
4:6	70, 75, 79, 87	7:11	48
4:7	45, 50, 141	8:16	163
4:7-8	71	8:17	163
4:9	74	11	138

11:3	94	23:15-20	153, 155
12:20	99	23:19-20	153
14:1-7	122	23:22	48, 155
14:7	69	23:28-35	154
13	138	24:7	154
15:19-23	94	24:14	160
15:21	93	25:12	160
20:24	163		
20:25	163	*1 Chronicles*	
22:45-46	98	2:3-15	45
		3:24	97
1 Kings		17:6	48
1:3	62	17:10	48
1:4	62	23:11	168
4:3	163		
4:7-19	147	*2 Chronicles*	
6	177	3	177
		3:17	56
7:21	56	15:3	164
8:41-43	158	29-31	177
8:66	131	34-35	177
9:10-10:29	151		
11:1-8	151, 181	*Ezra*	
22	52	1	177
22:1-36	46	1:1-2	186
		1:2-4	175
2 Kings		1:4-6	172
12:11	163	1:5	161, 162
17	175	1:6	161
17:24	153, 163	1:7	161
17:24-41	176	1:8	161
18	177	1:11	161
18:18	163	2	161, 175, 178
18:37	163	2:1	162
19:2	163	2:2-20	169
22-23	177	2:21-35	169
23:4-14	155	2:28-33	154
23:12-14	155	2:36-58	177
23:15	153	2:59	168

Reference	Pages
2:68-69	172
3	178
3:1-6	177
3:3-6	177
3:10-11	177
4:1	162
4:1-3	175
4:1-4	163
4:2	153, 163
4:8–6:18	162
4:9-10	153
4:10	163
6:15	177
6:18	177
6:19	162
6:19-20	177
6:20	162
6:21	169, 175, 179, 181, 183, 184, 195
7:1-5	164
7:6	163, 186
7:10	164
7:11-26	183
7:16	172
7:27-28	186
8:1	164
8:2	164
8:4	164
8:9	164
8:13	164
8:24-30	164
8:35	162, 177
9-10	162
9:1	91, 180, 181
9:2	180
9:4	162, 180
9:6-14	181
9:9	186
10	111, 182
10:2	162, 180, 182
10:3	180
10:6	162, 180
10:7	162
10:8	162
10:10	162, 180
10:10-11	182
10:14	182
10:16	162
10:17-18	182
10:19	180
10:44	182

Nehemiah

Reference	Pages
1:5-11	181
2:8	186
3:1	177
3:1-32	172
5	171, 173, 195
5:1	172, 173
5:2	168, 171
5:2-3	171
5:2-5	173
5:4	171
5:5	173
5:7	172, 173
5:8	173
5:9	173
5:10	173
5:11	68
5:11-13	173
5:15	173
7	162, 178
7:1	177
7:6	162
7:8-24	169
7:12	163
7:21	163

7:25-38	169	*Job*	
7:61	168	1:2	97
8	164, 178	3:20	125
8:1	177, 178	7:11	125
8:1-10:40	177	10:1	125
8:13-18	176	21:25	125
9	187, 188	24:3	59
9:2	98	27:2	125
9:6-37	181	42:13	97
9:35	187		
9:36-37	187	*Psalms*	
10:28-29	179, 181, 195	68:15	125
10:29	183	94:6	59
10:29-30	179	106	188
10:29-39	176	106:28	91
10:31-40	179	109:13	136
10:32-33	172	109:15	136
11	187	113:9	69
11:1	177		
11:2	187	*Proverbs*	
11:18	177	7:4	58, 122
11:25-35	187	15:15	131
12:24	176	31:10-31	65
12:27-30	177		
12:27-43	183	*Ecclesiastes*	
12:45-46	176	7:8	21
13	182	9:7	131
13:1	91		
13:1-3	184	*Song of Songs*	
13:4-9	184	3:4	122
13:10-14	176	5:7	131
13:22	177	8:2	122
13:23	183		
13:23-27	111, 184	*Isaiah*	
13:24	182	1:21-23	59
13:26	181	10:1-2	59
13:27	180	10-12	156
13:28-29	184	15-16	91
13:30	98		

29:24	21	33:23-29	163
38:17	125	34:1-16	184
60:10	158	34:23-24	184
61:5-6	158	36:24	161
		37:1-14	161
Jeremiah		37:21-22	161
2:1-7	156	37:22-25	164
7:1-20	178	44:22	181
7:21-26	178	45:8-9	184
15:19	97		
16:14-15	156	*Daniel*	
18:1-32	22	1-5	6
18:18	164		
23:1-8	156	*Hosea*	
24:1-10	163	6:6	178
31:29-30	22, 195	9:1	131
32:6-15	35	9:10	91
33:4	22		
35:6-10	35	*Joel*	
40:7	160	1-2	172
41:5	176		
48	91	*Amos*	
		2:1-3	91
Ezekiel		2:7	62
1:24	125	2:9-10	156
7:26	164	3:1-2	156
11:15-21	163	5:11-15	59
11:16	184	8:4-6	59
11:16-17	161		
11:19-20	21	*Micah*	
16:8	65, 100	3:1-3	59
17	184	3:9-10	152
18	195	6:1-5	156
18:1-32	22		
19	184	*Haggai*	
20:41-42	161	1:5-6	172
22:6	184	1:10-11	172
25:8-11	91	2:4	163
33:4	22	2:15-16	172

Zechariah
6:9-14   172
7:5   163

Malachi
2:7   164
2:16   100
3:8-10   172
3:9-12   172

New Testament

Matthew
1:1-16   142

John
1:46   190